Centering Ourselves

African American Feminist and Womanist Studies of Discourse

THE HAMPTON PRESS COMMUNICATION SERIES
Communication Alternatives
Brenda Dervin, supervisory editor

Liberating Alternatives: The Founding Convention of the Cultural
Environment Movement
Kate Duncan (ed.)

Hearing Many Voices
M. J. Hardman and Anita Taylor (eds.)

Theorizing Fandom: Fans, Subcultures, and Identity
Cheryl Harris and Alison Alexander (eds.)

Centering Ourselves: African American Feminist and Womanist
Studies of Discourse
Marsha Houston and Olga Idriss Davis (eds.)

Responsible Communication: Ethical Issues in Business, Industry,
and the Professions
James A. Jaksa and Michael S. Pritchard (eds.)

Value and Communication: Critical Humanistic Perspectives
Kevin F. Kersten, SJ, and William E. Biernatzki, SJ (eds.)

Communication and Trade: Essays in Honor of
Meheroo Jussawalla
Donald Lamberton (ed.)

Communication and Development: The Freirean Connection
Michael Richards, Pradip N. Thomas and Zaharom Nain (eds.)

Fissures in the Mediascape: An International Study of Citizens' Media
Clemencia Rodriguez

Nature Stories: Depictions of the Environment and Their Effects
James Shanahan and Katherine McComas

forthcoming

The Arsenal of Democracy
Claude-Jean Beltrand (ed.)

U.S. Glasnost: Missing Political Themes in U.S. Media Discourse
Johan Galtung and Richard Vincent

On Matters of Liberation (II): Introducing a New Understanding
of Diversity
Amardo Rodriguez

Centering Ourselves

African American Feminist and Womanist Studies of Discourse

edited by

Marsha Houston
University of Alabama

Olga Idriss Davis
Arizona State University

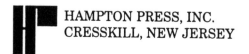
HAMPTON PRESS, INC.
CRESSKILL, NEW JERSEY

Printed in the United States of America

Library of Congress Cataloging-in-Publication Data

Centering ourselves : African American feminist and womanist studies of
    discourse / edited by Marsha Houston, Olga Idriss Davis.
       p. cm. -- (Hampton Press communication series. Communication
      alternatives)
    Includes bibliographic references and index.
    ISBN 1-57273-350-0 -- ISBN 1-57273-351-9
    1. African American women--Language. 2. English language--United
States--Discourse analysis. 3. English languge--United States--Sex
differences. 4. Feminists--United States--Languages. 5. Women--United
States--Languages. 6. African Americans--Languages. 7. Black English--
United States. 8. Americanisms. I. Houston, Marsha. II. Davis, Olga Idriss.
III. Series.

PE3102.N44C46 2001
306.44'.082'0973--dc21
                                      2001039131

Cover: Photograph © 1997 by Stephanie Newell
The unity doll is sculpted by workers at the Kumase Cultural Centre in Ghana.

Hampton Press, Inc.
23 Broadway
Cresskill, NJ 07626

For the women who first taught me to honor Black women's public
discourse and to cherish our private talk, especially sister "Jo,"
and in memory of

Lillian Tyson Houston (1904-1994)
and
Gloria Houston Oglesby (1927-1998)

—*Marsha Houston*

To the foremothers, othermothers, and sisterfriends who have
inspired me in my efforts to reveal the stories of Black women's
discursive contributions to American life and culture.

—*Olga Idriss Davis*

Contents

PART II: CASE STUDIES

Foreword

Geneva Smitherman
Michigan State University

> Jerene and Darlene come help me with the business. Plus, Darlene
> trying to teach me how to talk. . . . Every time I say something the
> way I say it, she correct me until I say it some other way. Pretty
> soon it feel like I can't think. My mind run up on a thought, git
> confuse, run back and sort of lay down. . . .Bring me a bunch of
> books. White folks all over them talking bout apples and dogs. What
> I care bout dogs? . . . But Darlene worry on. Sometimes I think bout
> the apples and the dogs, sometimes I don't. Look like to me only a
> fool would want you to talk in a way that feel peculiar to your mind.
> —Celie in Alice Walker's novel, *The Color Purple*

"Sistas" have always known that it is foolish–and self-destructive as
well–to speak in a dissonant tongue. That being the case, Black
women in this country have crafted a language, a style of speaking
reflective of harmony, balance, their lived experiences, and just plain
good sense. This pioneering collection is the first book to testify to the
existence and vitality of a language that has been largely ignored
within mainstream linguistics and communication studies. In an
overview of studies of African American speech (a.k.a. "Ebonics,"
"Black English," "African American Vernacular English," "Black
Talk"), published in 1988, I took scholars to task for the way in which
their descriptions of our language had been disseminated to the lay

public, reinforcing the worst stereotypes of Black men as clowns, low-lifes, and sex-crazed. As I reviewed the work that had come out of the 1960s and 1970s era of social transformation, I recall thinking that the voices of Black women were absent from this body of scholarship, but maybe that had been a blessing in disguise. To be ignored, or to be caricatured? Perhaps the former is the lesser of two evils.

From the vantage point of the one who has been on the language battlefield for more than two decades, *Centering Ourselves* is the balm of Gilead. What the editors call "a new angle of vision" in this book forces an expansion of the canonical world of language and rhetoric. Indeed, it calls into question the very notion of the canon itself. This book is looong overdue.

The Afrafeminist/womanist perspective in this volume allows for the meaningful examination of public discourse and private talk. We read about Black women's ordinary, everyday conversations as well as about speeches and other public discourse. The editors indicate that the book has been conceived with scholars and university students (graduate as well as undergraduate) in mind. I think *all* Americans can benefit from reading this book—if they plan to live in the 21st century. The studies and analyses presented here are about the language of African American women, to be sure, but on another level, they raise issues applicable to communication in all groups. For example, there is a lot to be said for all groups' constructing discourses grounded in the authority of experience. This volume is not only for the emancipation of Black women; simultaneously it prods the reader to reflect on the person in the mirror.

Acknowledgments

This project began in the summer of 1996 when we facilitated a seminar on Black women's Studies in Communication at the NCA Black Caucus/African American Communication and Culture Division Summer Conference. The ideas generated by the participants in that meeting, several of whom are contributors to this volume, and by those who took part in a subsequent seminar at the NCA national meeting the following November, shaped this volume. We are grateful to the participants in both seminars and to all our colleagues in the Black Caucus and AACC Division for their ongoing collegiality and support for scholarship on Black women.

We are also grateful to the following individuals:

> For their scholarship, dedication, and patience in seeing this project come to fruition, we thank each of our contributors. Without your commitment to uncover the significance of Black women's discourse in America, our vision of illuminating this space could not have become a reality.

> For immediately and enthusiastically embracing this project for her Communication Alternatives series at Hampton Press, we thank Prof. Brenda Dervin; and for

their thoughtful criticism and guidance in revising the original manuscript, we thank each of the readers that she selected.

For her unflagging support and wise counsel as we moved forward—sometimes haltingly—with this volume, we thank Hampton's Publisher Barbara Bernstein.

Special thanks for Olga: To my beloved family, thank you for your support and understanding in my endeavor to balance personal and professional obligations, and for loving me in spite of myself.

Finally, we are each grateful for the chance to collaborate on a project.

To my co-editor, mentor, and friend, Marsha Houston: Thank you for your grand dignity and inspiring persona. Your commitment and dedication to excellence permeates throughout this project. Thank you for the opportunity to work with you, learn from you, become inspired by you, and be honored to be called your colleague.

—Olga Davis

To Olga Davis, my colleague and co-editor: Thank you for being both brilliant and bold as a scholar and a sisterfriend, and for living the womanist adage: "She who learns teaches."

—Marsha Houston

Contributors

Brenda J. Allen is an associate professor in the Department of Communication at the University of Colorado at Denver. Her research area is organizational communication, with emphases on workplace diversity (specifically, race-ethnicity and gender) and computer-mediated communication. Her publications include "'Diversity' and Organizational Communication" in the *Journal of Applied Communication Research* (1995), "Feminist Standpoint Theory: A Black Woman's (Re)View of Organizational Socialization" in *Communication Studies* (1996), and "Black Womanhood and Feminist Standpoints" in *Management Communication Quarterly* (1998). She is currently working on a book entitled *Difference Matters in Organizational Communication*.

Sakile Kai Camara received her doctorate from the Department of Journalism and Communication at The Ohio State University and is a visiting professor at Otterbein College. She is currently exploring the production and reproduction of racism in intercultural and interracial interaction.

Patricia Hill Collins is Charles Phelps Taft professor of sociology in the Department of African American Studies at the University of Cincinnati.

Jessica Davis is a doctoral candidate at the Annenberg School for Communication in the University of Pennsylvania. She is interested in the intersection of race, gender, and communication, media coverage of Black life, images of Africa and peoples of the African Diaspora, audience practices, and international telecommunications policy. Her dissertation research explores the role of information in the everyday activities of individuals and organizations in West Africa, and the potential uses of the Internet therein. This project is part of her larger goal to understand the ways in which people, especially women of color, negotiate the nexus of identity, language, personal expression, community, consciousness, and activism.

Olga Idriss Davis is an assistant professor at The Hugh Downs School of Human Communication at Arizona State University where she teaches Performance Studies and is an affilitate member of Women's Studies. She earned MA and Ph.D degrees from the University of Nebraska, and is an alumna of The Juillard School. Awarded a Rockefeller Fellowship, she conducted research on the performative and liberatory nature of black female slave narratives. Her current scholarship extends the role of narrative in the lives of African American survivors of the Tulsa, Oklahoma Race Riot of 1921. Her research interests include identity construction, the body as text, the dialectics of power, and the discourse of activism. By examining performative pedagogy, riot survivor narratives, and the discursive nature of African American women's blues and quilt traditions, Davis blends together expressions of survival of black women throughout the African disaspora.

Catherine Dobris is an associate professor in the Department of Communication Studies, Indiana University, Indianapolis. She teaches and does research on contemporary rhetorical criticism with an emphasis on the interrelationships between gender and ethnicity. She is currently at work on a collaborative project on the gendered narratives of older women.

Darlene K. Drummond is an assistant professor of communication theory in the Department of Communication Studies at the University of North Carolina at Charlotte. Her research interests address the development, maintenance, and transformation of ethnic, social, and gender identities in interaction. She is currently exploring the impact of social support on the health of African American women with chronic illnesses.

Marsha Houston is professor and chair of the Communication Studies Department at the University of Alabama. Her scholarship on intercultural communication, feminist communication theories, and the communication of African American women has appeared in numerous journals and anthologies. With Alberto Gonzalez and Victoria Chen, she co-edited *Our Voices: Essays in Culture, Ethnicity, and Communication* (now in its third edition with Roxbury Press). She has chaired both the African American Culture and Communication and Feminist and Women Studies Divisions of the National Communication Association. Currently she is at work on a book on Black women's everyday talk.

Joni Lee Jones is associate professor of performance studies in the Department of Speech Communication and Associate Director of the Center for African and African American Studies at the University of Texas at Austin. She is an artist/scholar who is currently engaged in performance ethnography and videography around the Yoruba deity Oshun. In Austin, Texas and Washington, DC, she received acting awards for her work in professional theatre. Her articles on performance and identity have appeared in *Text and Performance Quarterly, The Drama Review, Theatre Insight* and *Black Theatre News*. While on a Fulbright Fellowship in Nigeria (1997-1998), Jones taught at Obafemi Awolowo University and contributed Theatre for Social Change workshops for the Forum on Governance and Democracy in Ife-Ife. Her dramaturgical work includes *Clay Angels* for the New WORLD Theatre in Amherst, Massachusetts, and *Shakin' the Mess Outa Misery* and *Phil Hill* for First Stage Productions in Austin, Texas.

Mark P. Orbe is an associate professor of communication and women's studies at Western Michigan University. His teaching and research interests center on the inextricable relation between culture and communication.

Karla D. Scott is an associate professor in the Department of Communication and Director of the African American Studies Program at Saint Louis University where she teaches courses in intercultural communication and gender. Her research on the relation of cultural identity and language includes two foci: Black women as a speech community and the role of culture in HIV prevention education programs in communities of color.

Geneva Smitherman is university distinguished professor of English and director of the African American Language and Literacy

Program at Michigan State University. She is also director of My Brother's Keeper Program in Detroit.

Denise Troutman is associate professor of American thought and language and linguistics at Michigan State University, where she teaches undergraduate courses in writing and undergraduate and graduate courses in linguistics. Troutman publishes work on both writing and linguistics with an emphasis on discourse analysis. Her publications include, "Tongue and Sword: Which is Master?" in *African American Women Speak Out on Anita Hill-Clarence Thomas* (1995), "Culturally Toned Diminutives within the Speech Community of African American Women" in *Journal of Commonwealth and Postcolonial Studies* (1996), and "Black Women's Language" (co-authored) in *Reader's Companion to U.S. Women's History* (1998). Forthcoming work includes "African American Women: Talking that Talk" to appear in *Sociocultural and Historical Contexts for African American Vernacular English* and "Ain't I a Woman?: African American Women and Language" to appear in *Discourse and Society*.

Teri Lynn Varner is a doctoral candidate in performance studies at the University of Texas at Austin. Her dissertation is titled, "Performing Cultural Identity Through Natural Hairstyles: The Case of African-American Females."

Eric King Watts is assistant professor of communication studies at Wake Forest University. Trained in rhetorical theory and criticism, his doctoral dissertation on hip-hop culture an outstanding dissertation award. Watts has published and presented several papers related to rap music and African American culture and rhetoric.

Cindy L. White is associate professor of communication and coordinator of the Women's Studies Program at Central Connecticut State University. She is particularly interested in the intersection between feminist studies and rhetorical studies. Her current research includes work on the broad range of 19th-century African American women's rhetorical activities on issues of racism, social justice, and gender.

Introduction:
A Black Women's Angle of Vision on Communication Studies

Marsha Houston
University of Alabama

Olga Idriss Davis
Arizona State University

> *Placing the ideas of ordinary African American women as well as those of better-known Black women intellectuals at the center of analysis produces a new angle of vision . . . one infused with Afrocentric feminist sensibility.*
> —Collins (1990, p. 16)

The last three decades of the 20th century witnessed an unprecedented flourishing of literature and scholarship by and about African American women.[1] Scholars throughout the humanities and

---

[1]We respect the differing meanings of Black as an identity label outside the United States (e.g., see Kanneh, 1998); however, for the purposes of this book, we use the term as it is commonly understood by readers in the United

1

social sciences engaged in recovering African American women's history, enlarging our[2] intellectual tradition, and articulating our unique social standpoints, our angles of vision on the social world.[3] As a result of this burgeoning body of scholarship, and a host of novels and other popular books, Black women's words and wisdom are now read and discussed in high school and university classrooms where Black women themselves were not admitted as students or professors during the first half of the century.

When we look across disciplines, however, we cannot help but notice that contributions to this explosion of knowledge about African American women are uneven. Some disciplines seem to have embraced and nurtured research in African American women's studies, while others appear to have ignored or silenced it. When Marsha Houston wrote her dissertation on Black women's conversations in the early 1980s, she found an appalling dearth of literature on the rhetorical and interpersonal communication styles of Black women. More than a decade and a half later, when Olga Davis analyzed the rhetoric of narratives by Black women slaves for her dissertation study, the situation had not appreciably improved. The unfortunate fact is that communication scholars have yet to develop a substantial body of

---

States our primary audience. Thus, we use *Black* as synonymous with *African American* and intend it to signify the varied and historically situated identities claimed by people of African descent in the United States.

[2]As Black women who are also feminist/womanist scholars, we have chosen to use first-person references to African American women in an effort to avoid objectifying ourselves and artificially separating ourselves from the women about whom we write.

[3]Pathbreaking works in what has come to be known as African American women's studies include: Toni Cade's anthology, *The Black Woman* (1970); Joyce Ladner's (1971) analysis of African American women's conceptions of womanhood, *Tomorrow's Tomorrow*; the literary theory and analysis offered by contributors to Roseann Bell, Bettye Parker and Beverly Guy-Sheftall's (1979) *Sturdy Black Bridges*; the social criticism offered by contributors to Gloria T. Hull, Patricia Bell Scott, and Barbara Smith's (1982) wide-ranging collection, *All the women are white; all the blacks are men: But some of us are brave;* bell hooks' (1984) critique of second wave feminism, *Feminist Theory: From Margin to Center*; Paula Giddings' (1984) documentary history, *When and Where I Enter*; Alice Walker's (1983) articulation of womanism, *In Search of Our Mother's Gardens*; and Patricia Hill Collins' (1990) theoretical triumph, *Black Feminist Thought*. Beverly Guy-Sheftall's (1995) collection, *Words of Fire: An Anthology of African American Feminist Thought*, captures the history, breadth, continuity, and diversity of African American feminist and womanist intellectual and political traditions.

scholarship that explores the lived communicative experiences of African American women. The paucity of literature on Black women's public discourse and private talk is one incentive for this collection, but merely increasing the *quantity* of communication scholarship about African American women is not its primary goal. Because black women as a social group are still marginalized and oppressed in the United States, research *about* us is not necessarily empowering or emancipatory *for* us. For example, "us too" or "add Black women and stir" studies that uncritically apply masculinist or whitecentric concepts and methods to Black women's communicative lives may actually have the effect of maintaining or deepening gendered racism[4] and other oppressive communication practices. Producing *more* research without careful attention to the conceptual frameworks underlying that research places Black women in jeopardy.

As African American women as well as feminist communication scholars, we would be disingenuous if we pretended to a disinterested stance in editing this collection. In the years since completing our dissertations, we have become aware of disjunctures between the theories and research questions that preoccupy our field and occupy the pages of our journals and issues that are central to our communicative lives as African American women and to the lives of the women whom we study. In addition, we see theoretical perspectives that illumine African American women's communication, particularly those that acknowledge black women as voices of authority on our own rhetorical history and contemporary communication encounters, marginalized, ignored, or devalued.[5] In this volume, we suggest an approach to the study of Black women as communicators that centers the knowledge and wisdom conveyed throughout the 19th and 20th centuries both in the public rhetoric of notable Black women and in ordinary women's everyday conversations. Our goal is to present what is not found in other communication books and journals, an angle of vision on Black

---

[4]Essed (1991) introduced this concept in order to capture the interrelatedness of sexism and racism in the communicative lives of Black women (see also St. Jean & Feagin, 1998).

[5]Marsha has served on the editorial boards of four communication journals, some more than once (*Quarterly Journal of Speech, Southern Communication Journal, Women's Studies in Communication, Howard Journal of Communications* [*HJC*]) and has served as an occasional reviewer for several others (most recently *Central States Communication Journal* and *Communication Theory*). With the exception of the *HJC*, she has always found herself to be a lone advocate for work that analyzes black women on our own terms.

women's rhetoric and everyday talk that both takes account of the material circumstances and ideological contexts of Black women's communication and honors Black women's interpretations of our discourse. For this reason, although the authors in this collection employ a variety of contemporary communication concepts and theories, all make the traditions of African American feminist and womanist thought central to their analyses. Because the labels *African American* (or Black) *feminist* and *womanist* represent interrelated traditions of thought and action in pursuit of social justice and human equality, yet resonate with different groups of contemporary Black women thinkers, we have chosen to embrace both labels. Following, we discuss the ways in which the concepts signified by these labels intersect and diverge.

AFRICAN AMERICAN FEMINIST/WOMANIST INTELLECTUAL TRADITIONS

The beginnings of African American feminist and womanist thought can be traced to the words of enslaved Black women in the South and the free women in the North who were their contemporaries. Because it began with ordinary women sharing the experiences of their everyday lives, Black women's intellectual tradition never has been merely the province of the academy. Throughout history, African American women have recognized many paths to wisdom.

Narratives of enslaved Black women graphically recount their horrendous suffering and steadfast resistance: "They resisted beatings, involuntary breeding, sexual exploitation by white masters, family separation, debilitating work schedules, bad living conditions, and . . . bringing into the world children who would be slaves" (Guy-Sheftall, 1995, p. 2). In the 1830s, a small group of free Black women in the North began to make their voices heard in the abolitionist movement. Among these Black feminist-abolitionists were the distinguished orators Maria Stewart, Sojourner Truth, and Frances E.W. Watkins Harper (Guy-Sheftall, 1995; Lerner, 1972). From their inception to the present, the traditions of thought and activism established by Black feminists have remained a vital part of the struggles for social justice by African American women *and* men and have been catalysts for every movement for the liberation of marginalized groups in U.S. history. As Guy-Sheftall pointed out, however, "Black feminism is not a monolithic, static ideology" (p. 2). Its diversity is suggested by our choice to label Black women's liberatory intellectual tradition as both "feminist" *and* "womanist." In addition, as James (1999) noted, like the lives of the African American women who have developed them, "Black feminisms" have intersected with other social movements and borrowed from other political ideologies, from abolitionism to socialism. Before we explore some of the ways that Black feminist and womanist ideologies diverge, it is important to understand the premises they share.

The central premise of African American feminist/womanist thought is "multiple jeopardy" (Beale, 1970; King, 1989). This concept entails both multiple, interlocking identities (e.g., Black, female, and working class) and multiple, interdependent oppressions (such as racism, sexism, and classism). In her 1861 autobiography, *Incidents in the Life of a Slave Girl: Written by Herself*, Harriet Jacobs (Yellin, 1987) concluded: "slavery is terrible for men; but it is far more terrible for women. Superadded to the burden common to all, *they* have wrongs, sufferings, and mortifications peculiarly their own" (p. 77). Every major Black woman thinker has acknowledged that African American women confront both a "woman question and a race question" (Cooper, 1892) most often complicated by our limited access to economic resources. Speaking to the class status of the masses of Black women, both free and enslaved in the early 19th century, political activist Maria Miller Stewart, the first woman in the United States to speak in public and leave a record of her speeches, asked:

> How long shall the fair daughters of Africa be compelled to bury their minds and talents beneath a load of iron pots and kettles? . . . Few white persons of either sex are willing to spend their lives and bury their talents in performing mean, servile labor. And such is the horrible idea that I entertain respecting a life of servitude that if I conceived there being no possibility of my rising above the condition of servant I would gladly hail death as a welcome messenger. (Stewart, 1832, cited in Guy-Sheftall, 1995, pp. 29, 31)

African American women's multiple identities and burdens, lead us to develop what Patricia Hill Collins (1990) called a "both/and conceptual orientation" (p. 207). Viewing the world holistically, rather than in opposites or dichotomies, Black women negotiate the contradictions of being simultaneously similar to and different from other groups (e.g., Black men, other women of color), "simultaneously a member of a group and yet standing outside it" (Collins, 1990, p. 207).

A second common premise of Black feminist and womanist thought is that African American women accord primacy to concrete lived experience as a criterion of knowledge and meaning (Collins, 1990). "I might not know how to use thirty-four words where three will do," said Ruth Shays, one of anthropologist John Gwaltney's

(1980) "ordinary" African American women, "but I know what I'm talking about . . . because I'm talking about myself. I'm talking about what I've lived" (pp. 27-33). James (1999) argued:

> Collectively, black women's experiences encompass historical, cultural worldviews that privilege ancestors and community. Such experiences grapple with the legacy of a genocidal diaspora in the Americas and centuries of antiblack racism from a motley assortment of ethnic groups, state institutions, and policing agencies. (p. 184)

African American feminist and womanist epistemologies are profoundly rooted in lived experience. This experiential knowledge base is the genesis of our commitment to the liberation of Blacks and women. In this sense, African American feminist and womanist thought coincide with other traditions of feminist theory that prioritize women's lived experiences as ways of knowing and understanding the world (e.g., Belenky, Clinchy, Goldberger, & Tarule, 1982; Gilligan, 1982).

Third, both Black feminism and womanism share a "culture of resistance" (Collins, 1990). African American women's tradition of personal and collective struggle against racism, patriarchy, and other forms of human oppression has been well documented (Hine, 1990; see also White & Dobris, chap. 8, and J. Davis, chap. 10, this volume). In her analysis of radical Black women's participation in anti-racist, anti-capitalist feminism, James (1999) noted that "[r]esistance has historically challenged and shaped Black female conduct across a broad ideological spectrum" (p. 189), ranging from the "moderate to the militant" (p. 1). Our legacy of resistance and struggle also reflects our conceptual orientation:

> Black women must struggle for black liberation and gender equality simultaneously; . . . [for black women], there is no inherent contradiction in the struggle to eradicate sexism and racism as well as the other "isms" which plague the human community, such as classism, and heterosexism. (Guy-Sheftall, 1995, p. 2)

Out of our specific situations of multiple oppression, African American women have developed traditions of thought, discourse, and activism intended to create not simply our own liberation, but a truly humane social order (O. Davis, 1998; chap. 2, this volume).

Although each of these premises has been identified, theorized, and incorporated into the scholarship on African American women in other academic disciplines, communication scholars, particularly those in rhetorical, interpersonal and language studies, have yet to sufficiently explore their significance for Black women's public and private discourse. As the epigraph for this chapter suggests, placing the intellectual traditions of African American women *at the center* of our analyses, as the authors in this volume have done, produces an angle of vision on Black women's communication that is rare, if not wholly new, in communication studies.

African American Feminism(s). So far, we have suggested that Black feminist and womanist ideologies are not monolithic, essentialist views of African American womanhood, but are derived from African American women's varied, historically rooted patterns of experience, including our lived experiences of multiple, interdependent identities and our traditions of resistance to multiple, interlocking oppressions. As previously suggested, the ideological diversity of Black feminist thought and activism encompasses, for example, the bourgeois feminism of 19th and early 20th-century club women, such as Mary Church Terrell (see White & Dobris, chap. 8, this volume) as well as the radicalism of Black Panther women of the 1960s and 1970s, such as Assata Shakur (James, 1999). African American feminisms are genres of the global struggles for the emancipation of women, which of course includes the work of academic feminists worldwide. To claim the label *African American* or *Black feminist* is to position oneself and one's scholarship within those global struggles, examining how the global feminist agenda, which includes multiple issues related to women's economic status, political rights, health, and marital and family status and rights, affect Black women in the United States. Moreover, to call oneself an "African American feminist" disrupts and challenges the recalcitrant racism within the feminist movement in the United States, "reminding white feminists that they are neither the only nor the normative feminists" (Collins, 1996, p. 13).

Despite its ideological pluralism, and its connection to our intellectual and political history, most African American women do not consider themselves feminists. Collins (1996) suggested that there are at least four reasons why. First, few African American women are exposed to the meanings for feminism that we have discussed here, or even to such culture-specific terms as *Black feminism, Afrocentric feminism*, or *African American feminism*.[6] Both

---

[6]Throughout this book, readers will encounter a number of different terms by which authors choose to identify African American feminist and womanist thought. "African American feminism," "Black feminism," "Afrocentric feminism," "Afrafeminism," and so on represent the same body of thought and action. "Womanism" or "Afrowomanism" are also synonyms that

school curricula and the media portray feminism as a narrowly focused, "for-Whites-only movement," and White women's general acceptance of this portrayal has led both Black and White women to view feminism as the "cultural property of white women" (Collins, 1996, p. 13). Some who are familiar with the culture-specific terms just cited nevertheless perceive Black feminism as "a handmaiden to Euro-American [White] feminism," and therefore, "not Black enough" (James, 1999, p. 184). In this situation, Black women often recode those "sisters" who identify with feminism as "race traitors" (p. 182) who are "less authentically Black" (Collins, 1996, p. 13). Some Black women communication scholars can attest to being overlooked during the formation of feminist bodies within national communication associations, of feeling unwelcome when, as late as the 1980s, we attempted to join, and of being labeled "difficult," and "hostile" when we challenged the Whitecentric research agendas then dominating feminist communication scholarship. Some of us also can attest to being treated with suspicion and subtle ostracism by some of our African American women (and men) colleagues when we called ourselves "Black feminists."

A second reason many Black women reject the "African American feminist" label is that by counseling Black women not to remain silent in the face of symbolic or physical domination, violence, and abuse, no matter who perpetrates it, "Black feminism" disrupts the longstanding and unquestioned reliance on Black racial solidarity. As Guy-Sheftall pointed out, "if you inject gender and suggest there's a problem with men wanting to dominate or control . . . you're automatically 'talking white.' Dividing the race. Hating the brothers" (Milloy, 1997, p. 118). If the Clarence Thomas-Anita Hill affair taught us nothing else, it is that Black men more often accrue greater personal and political benefits than Black women from our cultural propensity to prioritize race over gender, racial over sexual oppression.

Third, Collins (1996) argued that some Black women suspect the motives of Black feminism because it appears to be so well-received by White women. Black women political activists have grown weary of nearly two decades of "supporting white women in their efforts to foster an anti-racist feminism," diverting their

---

indicate another, related way of conceiving African American women's experiences. Unless authors note that the term they choose represents an ideological departure from the contrasts between African American feminism and womanism offered in this introduction, the reader may consider terminological differences to be the result of the author's preference for a particular label.

energies away from addressing social issues facing African American communities (p. 14). Black women scholars have come to realize that Black women's texts are much more welcomed in higher education classrooms than Black women themselves. For example, White feminist communication professors may require their students to read a speech by Barbara Jordan or they may publish analyses of the rhetoric of Sojourner Truth or Audre Lorde, but some African American feminists question whether such symbolic inclusion (some might even argue appropriation) of Black feminist texts merely "masks how the everyday institutional policies that suppress and exclude African Americans as a collectivity remain virtually untouched" and unchallenged in our field, as often occurs in the larger social order (p. 9).

Fourth, because "Black feminism" respects and accepts Black lesbians, it conflicts with the religious traditions followed by many Black women in which an article of faith is that homosexuality is a sin. Although lesbian women, such as Audre Lorde and Barbara Smith, have made invaluable contributions to African American political and intellectual life, religious arguments often erroneously reduce lesbians to their sexuality, conceived as one that chooses women over men. Such arguments also reconfigure lesbian women as enemies of Black men. Reminding us that Black lesbians have fathers, brothers, and sons of their own whom they love, Collins asked: "Who ultimately benefits when the presence of Black lesbians in any Black social movement leads to its rejection by African Americans" (p. 14)?

Womanism. Some who reject the label *Black feminist* claim the label *womanist.* Many see this as a way for African American women to claim the power to name their activist traditions in a way that distinguishes it from those of white women. Collins (1996) summarized the five, interdependent definitions of womanism offered by Alice Walker (1983) in "In Search of Our Mother's Gardens," the book in which Walker introduced this label.

1. A womanist is "a black feminist or feminist of color" (Walker, 1983, p. xi).
2. Womanists are "womanish" (Walker, 1983, p. xi), signifying that, from girlhood on, Black women respond to our concrete history of racial and gender oppression by acting in "outrageous, courageous, and willful ways . . . that [free us] from the conventions long limiting white women." As womanish girls we were "responsible, in charge, and serious." Implicit in this definition is the

    idea that Black women not only are different from but
are superior to white women because of our history of
multiple oppression: "black women are 'womanist' while
white women are merely 'feminist' (i.e., "frivolous,
irresponsible, . . . girlish") (Collins, 1996, p. 10).

3. Womanists are "committed to survival and wholeness of
   an entire people, male and female" (Walker, 1983, p. xi),
   a definition that seemingly supplies a way to "address
   gender oppression without attacking black men," in fact
   to foster stronger relationships between black women
   and black men (Collins, 1996, p. 11).
4. Womanism entails a pluralist or social group version of
   racial integration in which "women and men of all colors
   coexist like flowers in a garden yet retain their cultural
   distinctiveness" (Collins, 1996, p. 11).
5. And finally, the definition often neglected by theological
   womanists: A womanist is "a woman who loves other
   women, sexually and/or nonsexually" (Walker, 1983, p.
   xi).

Collins (1996) argued that those who have claimed the womanist
label have treated it in the same way many people treat the Bible,
"carefully selecting the parts that agree with their worldview and
rejecting the rest" (p. 12).

    The first group of scholars to embrace "womanism," and those
who have done the most to enlarge and theorize its meanings, are
Black women theologians (e.g., Canon, 1996; Hudson-Weems, 1998;
Sanders, 1995). Hayes (1995) argued that women theologians'
"appropriation" of Walker's term "sacralizes" it, bringing to bear
African American women's "rich, dense, and diverse spiritual
tradition" (p. 50). In a lecture at St. Mary's College, Hayes drew on
the work of 19th century Black women activists, and such
contemporary scholars as Collins, Audre Lorde, and bell hooks[7] to
describe a "womanist way of being in the world":

> one which draws out the contradictions within the Black community
> and its most significant institution, the Black church, exposing them to
> the harsh light of a new day, and calling for constructive changes which
> are, in the truest sense, subversive as they shake the very foundations
> of the Black world, leading to a reappraisal and concomitant renewal of
> its relationship with and ties to the Black community and the white

---

[7]In their own works, these contemporary scholars have most often labeled
themselves African American feminists.

dominant society. . . . To be a womanist is . . . to be the continuation of
the Black past and builders of the Black future. It encompasses the
theological, yes, but also the political, cultural, social and economic
traditions of Black being in the world. (pp. 52, 54)

As Hayes' description suggests, the central focus of
womanism is *intra*racial. Thus, some African American women are
attracted to womanism because at least *some* of its definitions are
compatible with the ideology of Black nationalism. It promises a way
to address feminist issues, such as the empowerment of individual
women or the creation of gender equity within Black families and
institutions, *inside* African American communities (Collins, 1996),
freeing Black women scholars and activists from acting as Euro-
American feminism's "handmaidens" (James, 1999, p. 184).

Beyond Labels. Some Black women, for example Alice
Walker's daughter Rebecca, suggest avoiding labels altogether:
"Many in my generation don't want to be defined by one word,
because they experience themselves as many different things . . . but
you do need to be mindful of how gender functions in our society"
(Milloy, 1997, p. 162). Collins (1996) also suggested that we move
"beyond naming" and develop analytical frameworks that account for
the heterogeneity of Black communities in terms of class, nationality,
sexuality, and age, as well as gender. She pointed out that, like many
of the issues that preoccupy feminist academics, the womanist/Black
feminist debate occurs among relatively privileged women and is but
one symptom of:

the increasing mismatch between what privileged women, especially
those in the academy, identify as important themes and what [might
be deemed] worthy of attention . . . [by] the masses of black women
doing the dry cleaning, cooking the fast food, and dusting the
computer of the sister who has just written the newest theoretical
treatise on black women. (pp. 15-16)

Other Black feminist and womanist scholars also have begun
seriously to question the emphasis on theorizing in contemporary
feminist scholarship. Holloway noted "how off-putting and stifling
the language and theory of feminism . . . are for a lot of [Black]
women outside the academy." Holloway suggested that "many of us
in the academy have let the language get ahead of the illustrations"
(Milloy, 1997, p. 164). To reconnect our scholarship with the concerns
of ordinary Black folk, Collins (1996) argued for inquiring into "how
institutionalized racism operates in gender-specific ways" so that we

may "provide a clearer perspective on how gender oppression works in tandem with racial oppression for both black women *and* men" (p. 15, italics added).

Despite the tensions between African American feminism and womanism, they remain interrelated ideologies. For this reason, and because each resonates with somewhat different groups of African American women, we have chosen to use both terms to encompass the essays in this volume. Like Holloway and Collins, we consider ideological labels to be less important than the questions authors raise and the methods by which they pursue their answers. We have encouraged authors to eschew abstractions and to produce contributions that illumine how African American women use communication to negotiate gendered cultural identities, affirm sisterhood, build community, and confront, demystify, and overcome oppression. Such an experientially grounded approach to research is not only consistent with the traditions of Black feminist *and* womanist thought, but also with the tradition of "practical wisdom" in the discipline of communication.

LIBERATORY RESEARCH: AN OVERVIEW OF THIS COLLECTION

In a 1988 article in *Women's Studies in Communication*, Marsha Houston called for communication research on African American women to "employ theoretical perspectives and methods of inquiry that are developed for and thus uniquely suited to exploring" Black women's experiences (p. 30). Minimally, explanatory frameworks should "account for black women's place in the social order, illumine the central social experiences of our lives, and assume the need for change" in the material circumstances and cultural representations of the masses of Black women (p. 28). Such frameworks facilitate *liberatory scholarship* (Houston 1988; Allen, chap. 1, this volume). Conceived as research that connects with the situations and concerns of the masses of ordinary African American women, liberatory scholarship celebrates our communication competencies, empowers us to enlarge our range of communication skills, and encourages more humane discourse environments for Black women speakers. As epistemic traditions, African American feminism and womanism afford the critical edge necessary for liberatory scholarship.

These gender- and culture-specific traditions of thought promote research that illumines the strengths and pleasures of Black women's communicative lives without erasing its difficulties and struggles. In addition, they demand that scholars conceive African

American women in the manner that they conceive all other speakers, as active agents who create and interpret their own and others' discourse within specific political, sociocultural, and historical contexts; thus they connect the study of African American women to a primary goal of human communication research, understanding how all individuals negotiate the social world through public and private talk. The authors in this collection draw on a variety of African American feminist and womanist perspectives in their efforts to produce liberatory research.

In Part I, we propose a framework for liberatory research. Brenda Allen (chap. 1) delineates the purposes and outcomes of African American feminist/womanist studies in communication and proposes research objectives that center Black women's intellectual tradition. Olga Davis (chap. 2) and Karla Scott (chap. 3) explore African American feminist/womanist approaches to scholarship on Black women's language and discourse. Scott argues that African American women's multiple, interlocking social identities are central to explorations of the language of our everyday talk. Drawing on her own studies of Black women's linguistic style-switching, Scott discusses "the ways in which talk is used to negotiate identity across . . . cultural borders." Davis argues the need for advancing communication theory by embracing a discourse of experience that centers the public and private spheres of women's lives. She explores how locating African American women in theorizing conceptions of publicness and privateness broadens our notions of human communication practices.

Each author in Part II endeavors to provide concrete, socially useful description and critique of African American women's discourse. Three of the major themes that interweave in these chapters are multiple consciousness, the value of sisterhood and community, and the culture of resistance.

In the first three case studies, the authors identify, describe, and analyze repertoires of discourse strategies that Black women use to create, sustain, and reproduce fluid, dynamic, gendered ethnic identities and to negotiate diverse interpersonal relationships. Marsha Houston (chap. 4) analyzes a conversational narrative genre she calls "triumph stories." She explores how Black women friends collaboratively produce narratives that simultaneously validate the individual as a "voice of authority" on her own experiences and reproduce a gendered cultural vision of Black women as active agents who create and sustain positive changes in their lives. Denise Troutman (chap. 5) explores her own subject position as a womanist scholar, and suggests the value of womanist theory for explicating the discourse of "strong" Black women speakers. Finally, Mark Orbe, Darlene Drummond, and Sakile Kai Camara (chap. 6) examine the extent to which a demographically diverse group of African American women express Black feminist ideology in their everyday talk. They identify multiple consciousness and sisterhood, two central themes in Collins' (1990) analysis of Black feminist thought, as central to their participants' communication.

The next chapter emphasizes the role of sisterhood and community in Black women's communicative lives. Every Black woman, including those who have gained great fame as orators and political leaders, honed their skills within a community of speakers where common norms for women's speech were shared and nurtured. African American women celebrate the uniqueness of the individual within the communal embrace. Through an examination of plays and essays by African American feminist writer Pearl Cleage, Joni Jones and Teri Varner (chap. 7) center Black women's ethic of caring, which highlights the importance we give to "personal expressiveness, emotions, and empathy [in] the knowledge validation process" (Collins, 1990, p. 215). By exploring Black women's sense of community and "sisterhood," Jones and Varner attempt to determine precisely what this writer means by the admonition, "Take care of your sisters."

The authors of the last three chapters undertake the task of identifying rhetorical strategies through which Black women have resisted silencing and exclusion and transformed situations of inequality and disadvantage into opportunities for speech and other forms of action. Emphasizing the primacy of identity in Black women's intellectual tradition, Cindy White and Catherine Dobris (chap. 8) examine how Black women active in the 19th-century club movement rhetorically constructed a version of womanhood that enabled and mobilized collective resistance to anti-Black racism and sexism. Eric Watts (chap. 9) situates Audre Lorde's notion of the Erotic within an exploration of female rap narratives and images, revealing what they suggest about the character, status, and importance of eroticism in the lives of Black women. He argues that although they are constrained by a patriarchal capitalist industry, a few women rappers manage to construct alternative, feminist definitions of the Black woman's erotic self. Finally, Jessica Davis (chap. 10) frames the a capella group "Sweet Honey in the Rock" as a Black feminist woman whose music is a rhetoric of resistance that articulates the struggles of African American women, calls for political change, and sustains culture.

CONCLUSION

In her landmark essay "Talking Back," African American feminist cultural critic bell hooks (1989) reminds us that:

> Moving from silence into speech is for the oppressed, the colonized, the exploited . . . a gesture of defiance that heals, that makes new life and new growth possible. It is the act of speech, of "talking back," that is no mere gesture of empty words, that is the expression of our movement from object to subject—the liberated voice. (p. 9)

This collection is an effort to break two long and suffocating silences: to make the voices of communication scholars heard in the ongoing conversation within African American women's studies and the voices of African American feminist and womanist scholars heard in the ongoing conversation within communication. Without critical communication scholarship on Black women's public and private discourse, African American women's studies presents only a partial understanding of our history and contemporary social life. Similarly, scholarship in communication presents only the most narrow vision of the power and potential of human interaction without attention to the ways speakers differently negotiate exigencies of gender, race, class, sexual orientation, and other socially significant aspects of identity. In her vision of the field in the 21st century, Turner (1998) prioritized consistently considering race, class, and gender, "not as simple variables but constituent, interactive parts of [rhetorical] processes" (p. 331). African American feminist and womanist scholarship accomplishes that vision in ways that respect the lived experiences of Black women.

In addition, African American feminist/womanist studies in communication is scholarship that speaks to the needs not only of African American women, but of all members of African American communities and of the larger human community of which they are a part. As hooks (1981) argued:

> feminism is not simply a struggle to end male chauvanism or a movement to ensure that women have equal rights with men; it is a commitment to eradicating the ideology of domination that permeates Western culture on various levels—sex, race, class, to name a few. (p. 194)

And Collins (1990) concluded:

> Taken together, the ideas of Anna Julia Cooper, Pauli Murray, bell
> hooks, Alice Walker, Fannie Lou Hamer, and other Black women
> intellectuals too numerous to mention suggest a powerful answer to
> the question, What is Black feminism? Inherent in their words and
> deeds is a definition of Black feminism as a process of self-conscious
> struggle that empowers women and men to actualize a humanist
> vision of community. (p. 39)

Bringing the concepts, theories, and practical wisdom of
communication together with Black women's intellectual traditions
illumines the complexity and heterogeneity of Black women's
communication. Whether the scholar is an African American woman
or not, this liberatory approach to scholarship accords Black women a
voice of authority on our own experiences and further empowers us
as speakers in the myriad communication contexts of our social lives.
The scholars whose work appears in this collection are women and
men, Black, white, and mixed race; each of them offers an angle of
vision on African American women and communication that centers
Black feminist and womanist intellectual traditions. We invite our
readers to share and enlarge our visions.

REFERENCES

Beale, F. (1970). Double jeopardy: To be black and female. In T. Cade
    (Ed.), *The black woman* (pp. 90-100). New York: Signet.
Belenky, M. F., Clinchy, B. M., Goldberger, N. R., & Tarule, J. M.
    (1986). *Women's ways of knowing*. New York: Basic Books.
Bell, R., Parker, B., & Guy-Sheftall, B. (1979). *Sturdy black bridges:
    Visions of black women in literature*. Garden City, NY: Anchor.
Canon, K. (1996). *Womanism and the soul of the black church*. New
    York: Contiuum.
Collins, P. H. (1990). *Black feminist thought: Knowledge,
    consciousness, and the politics of empowerment*. New York:
    HarperCollins.
Collins, P. H. (1996). What's in a name? Womanism, black feminism,
    and beyond. *The Black Scholar, 26*(1), 9-17.
Cooper, A. J. (1892). *A voice from the South: By a black woman of the
    South*. Xenia, OH: Aldine.
Davis, O. I. (1998). A black woman as rhetorical critic: Validating self
    and violating the space of otherness. *Women's Studies in
    Communication, 21*(1), 77-89.

Essed, P. (1991). *Understanding everyday racism: An interdisciplinary theory.* Newbury Park, CA: Sage.

Giddings, P. (1984). *When and where I enter: The impact of black women on race and sex in America.* New York: Bantam.

Gilligan, C. (1982). *In a different voice.* Cambridge, MA: Harvard University Press.

Guy-Sheftall, B. (Ed.). (1995). *Words of fire: An anthology of African-American feminist thought.* New York: New Press.

Gwaltney, J. L. (1980). *Drylongso: A self-portrait of black America.* New York: Vintage.

Hayes, D. L. (1995). *Hagar's daughters: Womanist ways of being in the world.* New York: Paulist Press.

Hine, D. C. (1990). *Black women in U.S. history* (8 vols.). Brooklyn, NY: Carlson.

hooks, b. (1981). *Ain't I a woman?: Black women and feminism.* Boston: South End Press.

hooks, b. (1984). *Feminist theory: From margin to center.* Boston: South End Press.

hooks, b. (1989). *Talking back: Thinking feminist, thinking black.* Boston: South End Press.

Houston (Stanback), M. (1988). What makes scholarship about black women and communication feminist communication scholarship? *Women's Studies in Communication, 11,* 28-31.

Hudson-Weems, C. (1998). *Africana womanism: Reclaiming ourselves.* Troy, MI: Bedford.

Hull, G. T., Scott, P. B., & Smith, B. (Eds.). (1982). *All the women are white, all the blacks are men, but some of us are brave.* Old Westbury, CT: The Feminist Press.

James, J. (1999). *Shadowboxing: Representations of black feminist politics.* New York: St. Martin's Press.

Kanneh, K. (1998). Black feminisms. In S. Jackson & J. Jones (Eds.), *Contemporary feminist theories* (pp. 86-97). New York: New York University Press.

King, D. (1989). Multiple jeopardy, multiple consciousness: The context of a black feminist ideology. *Signs, 14,* 42-72.

Ladner, J. (1971). *Tomorrow's tomorrow: The black woman.* Garden City, NY: Doubleday-Anchor.

Lerner, G. (1972). *Black women in white America: A documentary history.* New York: Vintage.

Milloy, M. (1997, September). The new feminism. *Essence,* 117-118, 120, 162, 164.

Sanders, C. (Ed.). (1995). *Living the intersection: Womanism and afrocentrism in theology.* Minneapolis, MN: Fortress Press.

St. Jean, Y., & Feagin, J. R. (1998). *Double burden: Black women and everyday racism.* Armonk, NY: M.E. Sharpe.

Turner, K. (1998). Rhetorical studies in the twenty-first century: Envisioning the possibilities. *Southern Communication Journal, 63,* 330-336.

Walker, A. (1983). *In search of our mothers' gardens: Womanist prose.* New York: Harcourt, Brace, Jovanovich

Yellin, J.F. (Ed.). (1987). *Incidents in the life of a slave girl written by herself.* Cambridge, MA: Harvard University Press.

PART I

CONCEPTUAL FRAMEWORK

ONE

Goals for Emancipatory Communication Research on Black Women

Brenda J. Allen
University of Colorado-Denver

As this volume demonstrates, communication scholars have begun to add our voices to the chorus of academicians in other disciplines who study the unique perspectives and experiences of African American women.[1] We hope to provide distinctive contributions to research on Black women by viewing them from the field of communication. We believe that Black women's social identities preclude[2] us to enact communicative lives that, in many ways, differ from those of other members of U.S. society. This book illuminates some of these differences by providing a pioneer, full-length treatment of the topic.

From a new angle of vision, we view Black women not as marginal, but as the center of our research. To correct the persistent exclusion and misrepresentation in communication studies of a group of persons who embody a significant segment of Western society, we

---

[1] I use African American and Black interchangeably.
[2] I use first-person plural pronouns because I am a Black woman.

need to specify the goals that guide our efforts. Therefore, in this chapter, I offer an agenda for research on African American women's communication. First, I list and discuss seven goals that can help us to center our research on Black women's communicative lives. Then, I describe challenges to meeting these goals. I conclude by exploring potential outcomes of our endeavors.

RESEARCH GOALS

A research project encompasses several stages. A scholar usually needs to specify a theoretical viewpoint, develop research question(s), choose method(s), locate participants or other sources of study (e.g., texts), gather data, and analyze findings. A researcher also must write and/or talk about the project, often drawing conclusions, making recommendations for future study, and discussing practical and theoretical implications. As a communication researcher engages in the radical act of placing Black women at the center, she[3] must be especially conscientious of her choices and actions. She may have to challenge traditional, mainstream knowledge, ideas, and approaches. She also may need to rely on and even create alternatives. Consequently, in the following discussion about goals, I frequently address issues related to various aspects of the research process. I intend this discussion to be neither exhaustive nor definitive. I offer the following goals to provide preliminary direction. Often, I cite sources that delve more deeply into issues that I raise. Although I present the goals in a linear fashion, they do not exist independently of one another. Rather, they often overlap.

GOAL 1: TO EMANCIPATE BLACK WOMEN

Although several interdependent goals guide our mission, our primary purpose is to emancipate African American women. We want our work to improve Black women's lives. This goal is the touchstone and the focal point of our research. It motivates our efforts and it grounds the remaining goals. It also informs every aspect of the research process. Our research strives to illuminate and to fight effects of gendered racism. We hope to release Black women from stereotypical, pejorative notions about us, to liberate Black women

---

[3]To refer to researchers, I use the generic "she" or "he."

from imposed meanings that members of society have set on us and our ways of communicating, and to free us from the chains of negative labels such as *marginalized* or *stigmatized.*

Thus, our research focuses on Black women, for Black women. We aim to describe, celebrate, and enhance African American women's communicative lives. Moreover, in the tradition of African American feminist and womanist (see Collins, 1991; and Introduction, this volume) thought, we hope that our work also will help to promote social change for *all* disenfranchised persons.

GOAL 2: TO CHALLENGE ESSENTIALIST NOTIONS OF BLACK WOMANHOOD

Studies about African American women and communication frequently clump us under general categories, as if we all naturally are alike. As Houston (1996) observed, "one of the most persistent and egregious tendencies in both speech and language studies of African Americans is defining our speech and speakers monolithically" (p. 1; also see Smitherman-Donaldson, 1988). For instance, researchers may presume that the communication behaviors of one group of Black women represent those of all Black women. Or, they may classify Black women with Black men, with White women, or with women of color. This bias neglects to consider the unique position of being both Black *and* woman. Thus, it renders Black women invisible rather than as distinct persons who experience and resist multiple jeopardy or interlocking oppressions based on their race, their gender, and intersections of these and other aspects of their identity. Moreover, it neglects to recognize differences among Black women.

Therefore, our research should refute essentialist ideas about Black women and communication. The next goal provides guidance for how we might design, conduct, and report research that counteracts views of Black women as indistinguishable from one another.

GOAL 3: TO STUDY A VARIETY OF BLACK WOMEN

We should conduct research that honors and represents Black women's diversity. Contrary to how the media and studies often characterize us, we embody a variety of aspects of identity (e.g., age, sexual orientation, socioeconomic status, educational background, religion, physical ability, and ethnicity). We also enact a wide variety of roles, within numerous public and private contexts. In addition, we engage in myriad types of interactions, with numerous types of individuals. Furthermore, we employ various communication behaviors to survive or to thrive in many different situations. Thus, a central goal of our research is to reveal the complexity and heterogeneity of Black women's communicative lives, even as we seek commonalties of experience.

To reach this goal, we might study contemporary Black women (and girls!) across the multiplicity of contexts and roles that we grace. We could study everyday interactions and Black women's attitudes toward those interactions. Although we should research exceptional African American women (e.g., individuals who have made inroads in professions that traditionally have not welcomed us), we also should consider Black women in roles that we traditionally have enacted. For example, the rare studies of Black women and organizational communication usually focus on Black women managers (Allen, 1995). We might extend this body of work by researching Black women in numerous roles (e.g., secretary, janitor, receptionist, data processor, and cafeteria worker) within an organization.

We also should study African American women from the past. We should recover and accurately represent the expanse and influences of Black women's communication throughout the history of the United States. This connects with the goal of emancipation, because learning our history can help us to understand our strengths and to refute negative representations of Black women.

Researchers may need to revise what counts as valid sources of data, as feminist scholars Cirksena and Cuklanz (1992) explained:

> It is necessary to redefine "legitimate" texts, "significant" events, and "important" ideas. Because women have been excluded either formally (legally) or informally (ideologically) from areas such as politics, public speaking, military participation, and even higher education and scholarship, scholars interested in studying women have had to search elsewhere for evidence of women's experiences of life. (p. 39)

Scholars may need to study "less public forms of communication such as the diaries, letters, and gossip of ordinary women, because they constitute the record of women's lives throughout most of recorded history" (Cirksena & Cuklanz, 1992, p. 39). In addition to studying ordinary women from the past, we might investigate renowned Black women leaders and pioneers. Researchers can analyze narratives, biographies, or autobiographies of Black women. For example, James (1993) provided a compelling discussion about studying autobiographies of revolutionary Black women activists, and Etter-Lewis (1993) analyzed oral narratives of Black professional women. Other potential objects of study include film, art, and artifacts and objects such as quilts.

Similar to the research projects reported in this book, we should study from within various areas of the discipline, including rhetoric, interpersonal, organizational communication, mass media, health communication, and intercultural studies. Moreover, we should observe various modes of communication (e.g., face-to-face, written, small group, public address, and computer-mediated).

To help demonstrate our heterogeneity and complexity, we should contextualize our findings. For instance, we should not report findings as if they could have occurred anywhere, at any time, to any Black woman. Basically, we should acknowledge and assess the situatedness of our research and those whom we have studied. We should recognize and acknowledge sociohistorical factors (e.g., the Black women's club movement or the Civil Rights Movement) as well as local contextual variables (e.g., an organization's history of [not] hiring Black women). We should link findings and the context in which they occurred. In essence, we should offer "sufficiently rich, nuanced, and context-sensitive analyses" (Houston, 1996, p. 2).

GOAL 4: TO STUDY DOMINATION AND OPPRESSION

Our research needs to meet an important principle of African American feminist and womanist thought: to study domination and oppression. This represents a necessary step toward consciousness raising and emancipation. To emancipate, one first must acknowledge the interlocking oppressions of gendered racism. These oppressions often are compounded by other variables such as class, ability, age, and sexual orientation. Together, they comprise a "matrix of domination" that affects Black women's lives (Collins, 1991). However, our work should conscientiously reject the notion of a Black woman as "victim," and "stigmatized other," even as we illuminate oppression (see Moraga & Anzaldua, 1983).

We must identify or develop theoretical frameworks that authorize us to look for domination and oppression. For instance, scholars might refer to Africana Womanism (Hudson-Weems, 1993), womanist theology (see Thomas, 1996), or critical feminism (see

Hawkesworth, 1989). I endorse feminist standpoint theory (see Allen, 1996). This perspective uses women's lives as a foundation for constructing knowledge (Longino, 1993). It asks women to speak from and about their views of reality. Moreover, feminist standpoint studies women's everyday lives to expose domination and oppression, and to criticize claims based on the lives of men from dominant cultures. Notably, feminist standpoint theory moves beyond early feminist work that concentrated on White women's lives by encouraging us to listen to voices of many women. It also stresses the importance of the multiplicity of contexts that women encounter (Buzzanell, 1995).

In addition, researchers who take this approach assess women's historically shared, group experiences, and they emphasize social conditions that construct oppressed groups (Allen, 2000; Collins, 1991; Harding, 1991; Hennesey, 1993). This corresponds with African American feminist and womanist thought because its roots lie in lived experience rather than abstractions. Thus, feminist standpoint situates women's lived, concrete experiences in local contexts, while also connecting them to broader social and institutional issues. Feminist standpoint theory also directs researchers to highlight acts of resistance, an important element of the next goal.

GOAL 5: TO DISCOVER BLACK WOMEN'S SKILLS AND STRATEGIES

To facilitate emancipation, researchers should identify Black women's communicative skills and strategies, including acts of resistance. We should discover how Black women presently and previously use(d) communication not only to cope, but also to flourish. In addition, we might illuminate positive effects of Black women's communication (on Black women as well as those with whom they interact). As we accentuate the positive, we will continue to free ourselves from effects of gendered racism because we will have concrete examples to emulate. Furthermore, information about skills and strategies will help us to generate practical wisdom, as I discuss next.

GOAL 6: TO GENERATE PRACTICAL WISDOM

Consistent with African American feminist epistemology (see Collins, 1991), our research should generate practical wisdom that can help to emancipate Black women in our various public and private roles. We should analyze and interpret data for insight, information, and resources. We can use our findings to develop positive models that Black women can emulate and embellish. These models can address pressing social issues and promote social change. They also can help Black women to successfully negotiate everyday interactions.

GOAL 7: TO USE PROCEDURES AND METHODS THAT HONOR OUR PRIMARY PURPOSE

During the various stages of designing and conducting a study, a researcher should make choices and behave in ways that honor the purposes of emancipatory research. She may have to assume nontraditional attitudes, or employ innovative, creative, and even radical strategies that contradict academic training that socializes us to be authoritative, detached, and disinterested (see Cirksena & Cuklanz, 1992). For instance, a researcher should resist the urge toward thinking that she knows the answers to research questions. This tendency might be especially pronounced for Black women researchers who identify with those whom they are studying.

In addition, a researcher should take a receptive, cooperation-oriented attitude toward research participants (see Orbe, 1998, who referred to participants as "co-researchers"). She might invite participants to help conceptualize her research project. Where appropriate and feasible, she should ask participants to review and critique her analyses, to see if her interpretations reflect their reality.

She also could use principles of co-inquiry that Denton (1990) used in a study on bonding and supportive relationships among professional Black women. Denton based this approach on a research philosophy (Argyris, 1970) that studies participants and their needs, and allows researchers and participants to engage in dialogue and exchange with one another. The following conditions framed Denton's method of co-inquiry:

> (1) Mutuality of relationship between researcher and participant; . . .
> (2) Serious attention to participants' phenomenal experience and modes of construing themselves and their world; (3) Exploration of experiences in stressful situations with a problem-solving orientation;
> (4) Responsiveness to participants' needs for self-understanding and for skills in coping and self-enhancement; (5) a safe environment and enabling structures for sharing data that can be used by participants; . . . (6) A commitment to sharing with participants

both individual and generalized results in ways that can support
their learning and development. (p. 450)

This model seems conducive to achieving our goal of emancipation.

We should recognize that the research process itself can be
emancipatory, for researchers as well as participants. Moreover, we
should self-consciously reflect on our roles within the research
process (see Olivas, 1997). Our efforts should take a proactive
approach that encourages Black women to find their voice. For
instance, as we interact with participants, we can help them to
empower themselves by altering negative self-conceptions and
reinforcing positive ones. As they talk about the oppressions that
have faced and resisted, participants may experience "consciousness
raising" (D. Smith, 1987). This sharing process might encourage
women to engage in acts of resistance (Collins, 1991).

As researchers design projects, they must make decisions
about sampling—whom or what to study. Traditional social science
research methods call for scientific approaches that permit the
researcher to make claims about an entire group based on
observations about a percentage of that group (see Babbie, 1992).
This type of sampling often will not be feasible because a researcher
needs to know how many members comprise the primary group that
she intends to study. Such figures may not be available about Black
women. Furthermore, this type of sampling may not be appropriate
for certain projects. Rather than randomly choosing participants, a
researcher might base sampling on her judgment and/or the purpose
of the study. Babbie (1992) explained: "it may be appropriate for you
to select your sample on the basis of your own knowledge of the
population, its elements, and the nature of your research aims" (p.
230). A researcher also might use self-selected, or convenience,
samples based on soliciting volunteers to participate in the project
(see M. J. Smith, 1988).

For research that requires participants, we should be prepared
to work harder and differently than usual to identify research
participants and to enlist their cooperation. Reporting a comparative
study of Black and White women, Cannon, Higginbotham, and Leung
(1988) observed, "researchers who are committed to incorporating
subjects of different races and classes in their qualitative research
designs must be prepared to allow more time and money for subject
recruitment and data collection" (p. 450). These authors report using
labor-intensive recruitment strategies, such as "personal presentations
to women's organizations' meetings, snowball techniques of calling
individuals to recommend others . . . and identifying special
newsletters to receive advertisements" (p. 454).

To place African American women at the center of research, we must move beyond work that looks at race and gender as independent variables. Rather, we need to address race, gender, and other aspects of identity as socially constructed, analytic categories. Therefore, qualitative methods such as narratives, oral histories, interviews, focus groups, participant observation, and ethnographies seem particularly appropriate. However some research questions will elicit quantitative methods, such as experiments and surveys, which also might be fruitful. Moreover, researchers might use multiple methods or multiple sources of evidence.

Basically, we should employ methods that show respect for the persons whom we study. We should design, conduct, and report research that adheres to the idea that Black women's lives and values often are different than other persons' lives, not negatively deviant or inferior. In addition, as we collect "data," we should be mindful of time constraints that many Black women face, even as we provide time and a safe space for participants to express themselves freely. Cannon et al. (1988) described psychological and structural factors that constrained Black women's cooperative participation in their comparative study. Some of the Black women were skeptical about the purpose of the project. Many of them had less free time than White participants. Many of the Black women asked for additional assurance or guarantees about anonymity.

Therefore, when we report our research, we must be careful to ensure participants' confidentiality and anonymity. This may be a challenge in situations where Black women are easy to identify, due to their limited numbers. We also must make informed, sensitive decisions about what to divulge to whom. We need to avoid sharing findings that do not provide positive insight or information.

Where possible, we should conduct face-to-face interviews with individual women or women in groups. This procedure might facilitate emancipatory interactions between co-researchers. It allows researchers to revise questions, to clarify, to probe, and to respond to nonverbal cues. However, to allow for time and/or distance constraints, we also could use telephone interviews or computer-mediated communication (e.g., e-mail or videoconferencing). We also might collaborate with other researchers.

Longitudinal projects could follow a cohort of Black women to study developmental issues. Comparative studies could reveal similarities and differences among and between groups of Black women. Studies that compare teens and elders might not only provide insight, but also create a forum for emancipation as Black women from different generations interact with one another.

These seven goals frame an ambitious agenda that will help us view Black women from a new angle of vision. Although the previous discussion implies or explicitly cites challenges that might confront us, here I highlight a few that seem particularly noteworthy.

CHALLENGES

The discipline of communication seems slowly to be accepting the idea that socially constructed aspects of identity (e.g., gender and race) influence ways that human beings interact. However, scholars can anticipate numerous challenges from various sources as they conduct research on Black women. For instance, Black men, other women of color, or White women who conduct work on race or gender may view our work as divisive, as counterproductive to scholarship on traditionally disenfranchised persons. Consider forming alliances with some of these scholars. Initiate collaborative research and teaching projects that will allow you and them to concentrate on your specific areas of interest, and to address areas of overlap.

An enduring challenge stems from others' sense of the centrality and importance of our work. Colleagues who evaluate us for tenure and promotion, reviewers of journal articles, students, and convention planners (to name a few specific sources) may view our work and our intellectual capabilities as marginal. Mainstream communication journals seem to publish articles about Black women or other traditionally disenfranchised persons only in special issues. Consequently, communication scholars often submit their work to publications in other disciplines (e.g., Black studies, ethnic studies, or women's studies). Unfortunately, personnel committee members may penalize persons whose work has not been published in mainstream journals.

To positively affect how others evaluate your scholarship, inform your colleagues early and often that your work may not always be published in mainstream journals, and explain why. During hiring and performance review discussions, clarify your research agenda, and specify outlets that typically publish your type of scholarship. As you approach the tenure review process, provide the personnel committee with names of well-reputed scholars whose work aligns with yours, and request that the committee invite them to assess your case. To establish yourself as a communication scholar, explicitly address communication issues (theory and/or practice) in your publications and presentations. That way, reviewers should clearly see the relevance of your work to the discipline of communication, even if it is not published or presented in mainstream communication venues. Finally, ask established scholars who study African American women and communication for additional advice about how to successfully navigate the tenure track.

As we confront these and other challenges, each scholar will have to weigh her options and proceed thoughtfully. However, we can develop effective methods for supporting one another, as I explain in the following discussion on potential outcomes of our research efforts.

OUTCOMES

We seek to emancipate Black women, and we aim our work toward all Black women. To achieve this primary goal, we hope to build as well as critique theories about Black women's communication. We can draw from the relatively few studies about Black women and communication, but we also will have to rely on other disciplines to establish foundations for our projects. Fortunately, rich resources exist in history, sociology, education, literary criticism, religious studies, psychology, women's studies, African American studies, ethnic studies, organizational behavior, anthropology, and other areas of study. We should mine these for insight and ideas for developing and conducting emancipatory communication research.

Thus, our research can contribute to the burgeoning body of literature on the intellectual tradition of African American women. It can respond to the critical need to ascertain common themes that thread through African American women's lives and histories. Also, we can enhance feminist/women's studies as well as African American/ethnic studies. And, we can advance the general study of human communication. Furthermore, our findings can inform pedagogy within those and other disciplines. For instance, Omolade (1994) outlined a Black feminist pedagogy that a researcher might use to assess African American women teachers' interactions with students.

To disseminate our work, we should seek diverse audiences, and accordingly tailor our reports and presentations. For instance, we can target traditional, mainstream outlets (e.g., publications or conferences) within and outside of the discipline of communication. We also can submit our work to special issues of journals. In addition, we can create opportunities to publish and present our work. For example, we could commission a special edition of a journal, or develop conference panels. This volume evolved from the

editors' vision, and steps toward its completion included a session at
a summer conference of the Black caucus of the Speech
Communication Association, as well as a National Communication
Association panel.

We also can accomplish our goals by broadening our markets
to include nonacademic audiences. We could offer insight and
guidance for educators (at all levels), service providers, managers,
administrators, and health care professionals. I would love to see
communication scholars respond to current issues related to or about
Black women (e.g., Betty Currie, President Clinton's secretary). We
should speak out in forums such as government hearings or
television news and talk shows (e.g., *Nightline, Larry King Live*).

Finally, we could develop an active, dynamic community of
scholars who routinely collaborate on projects (including
interdisciplinary studies), synthesize findings from unrelated
projects, provide constructive criticism for each other's work,
celebrate successes, and develop strategies for achieving our goals.
We should mentor graduate students interested in our cause. These
types of groups can provide a haven for support and consciousness-
raising among academics. We also might forge alliances with
community activists as well as professionals engaged in work that
can inform our endeavors and vice versa (e.g., diversity trainers,
human resources personnel, social workers, and public school
teachers).

In conclusion, as we enter the new millennium, we must form
more accurate and holistic depictions of Black women's
communication, for the purpose of emancipating Black women.
Although the task seems formidable, I believe that we can succeed,
especially if we ponder the backbreaking and soul-depleting
experiences of African American women who preceded us.

While writing a draft of this chapter, I felt frustrated because
I could not figure out how to express a thought. Unexpectedly, a
picture flashed in my mind of my mother, Thelma L. Allen, leaving
home on cold, icy nights to work the 11 p.m. to 7 a.m. shift at the post
office (in a windowless building under the watchful eye of a ruthless
supervisor). I recalled also several times when she resisted authority,
often in defense of her children, whom she raised by herself. I
thought also of Ella Josephine Baker, a Black woman whose
autobiography I recently read (Grant, 1998). Miss Baker was a quiet,
dignified, yet determined activist who played a crucial but
unheralded role in the Civil Rights Movement. Her story fascinated,
moved, and inspired me.

I paused a few moments to reflect on these two Black
women's lives. Although tears blurred my sight, in my mind I saw

clearly what to write. I wiped my eyes and picked up my pen. From my renewed angle of vision, I continued to record my ideas. I hope that my words inspire and guide any researcher whose emancipatory research centers on African American women's communication.

REFERENCES

Allen, B. J. (1995). "Diversity" and organizational communication. *Journal of Applied Communication Research, 23,* 143-155.

Allen, B. J. (1996). Feminist standpoint theory: A black woman's (re)view of organizational socialization. *Communication Studies, 47,* 257-271..

Allen, B. J. (2000). "Learning the ropes": A Black feminist critique. In P. Buzzanell (Ed.), *Rethinking organizational and managerial communication from feminist perspectives* (pp. 177-208). Thousands Oaks, CA: Sage.

Argyris, C. (1970). *Intervention theory and method: Behavioral science view.* Reading, MA: Adison-Wesley.

Babbie, E. (1992). *Practicing social research* (6th ed.). Belmont, CA: Wadsworth.

Buzzanell, P. (1995). Reframing the glass ceiling as a socially constructed process: Implications for understanding and change. *Communication Monographs, 62,* 327-354.

Cannon, L. W., Higginbotham, E., & Leung, M. L. A. (1988). Race and class bias in qualitative research on women. *Gender and Society, 2,* 449-462.

Cirksena, K., & Cuklanz, L. (1992). Male is to female as ——— is to ———: A guided tour of five feminist frameworks for communication studies. In L. F. Rakow (Ed.), *Women making meaning* (pp. 18-44). New York: Routledge.

Collins, P. H. (1991). *Black feminist thought: Knowledge, consciousness, and the politics of empowerment.* New York: Routledge.

Denton, T. C. (1990). Bonding and supportive relationships among Black professional women: Rituals of restoration. *Journal of Organizational Behavior, 11,* 447-457.

Etter-Lewis, G. (1993). *My soul is my own: Oral narratives of African American women in the professions.* New York: Routledge.

Grant, J. (1998). *Ella Baker: Freedom bound.* New York: Wiley.

Harding, S. (1991). *Whose science? Whose knowledge?* Ithaca, NY: Cornell University Press.

Hawkesworth, M. E. (1989). Knowers, knowing, known: Feminist theory and claims of truth. *Signs, 14,* 533-557.

Hennesey, R. (1993). Women's lives/feminist knowledge: Feminist standpoint as ideology critique. *Hypatia, 8,* 14-34.

Houston, M. (1996, November). *Position paper for "a new angle of vision: Black feminist thought and communication scholarship."* Paper presented at annual meeting of the Speech Communication Association, San Diego, CA.

Hudson-Weems, C. (1993). *Africana womanism: Reclaiming ourselves.* Troy, NY: Bedford Press.

James, J. (1993). African philosophy, theory, and "living thinkers." In J. James & R. Farmer (Eds.), *Spirit, space, and survival: African American women in (white) academe* (pp. 31-46). New York: Routledge.

Longino, H. E. (1993). Feminist standpoint theory and the problems of knowledge. *Signs, 19,* 201-212.

Moraga, C., & Anzaldua, G. (Eds.). (1983). *This bridge called my back: Writings by radical women of color.* New York: Kitchen Table, Women of Color Press.

Olivas, M. R. (1997, February). *Two peas in a pod: A dialogue toward understanding the intersection of race, class, and gender.* Paper presented at the convention of the Western States Communication Association, Monterey, CA.

Omolade, B. (1994). *The rising song of African American women.* New York: Routledge.

Orbe, M. P. (1998). *Constructing co-cultural theory: An explication of culture, power, and communication.* Thousand Oaks, CA: Sage.

Smith, D. (1987). *The everyday world as problematic: A feminist sociology.* Boston, MA: Northeastern University Press.

Smith, M. J. (1988). *Contemporary communication research methods.* Belmont, CA: Wadsworth.

Smitherman-Donaldson, G. (1988). Discriminatory discourse on Afro-American speech. In G. Smitherman-Donaldson & T. A. van Dijk (Eds.), *Discourse and discrimination* (pp. 144-175). Detroit, MI: Wayne State University Press.

Thomas, L. E. (1996). Womanist theology, epistemology, and a new anthropological paradigm. *Journal of Constructive Theology, 2,* 19-31.

TWO

Theorizing African American Women's Discourse: The Public and Private Spheres of Experience

Olga Idriss Davis
Arizona State University

> *Our children did not know us*
> *They were bought and sold.*
> *Our children did not know us*
> *For our stories were erased or twisted*
> *When the truth could not be hidden.*
> *A people with no history, no stories to tell,*
> *No rituals to pass along*
> *Will die unknown.*
> *But we have never forgotten . . .*
> —Farmer (1993a, p. 221)

Since the enslavement of Africans in North America, African American women have been determined to maintain a culture of survival. Although history attempted to obfuscate our stories, and thus our experiences, the supreme perseverance and heroic resistance of Black women became thoroughly intertwined as themes of survival in the fabric of daily existence. That discourse served to center the stories of Black women brings to the fore the relation between discourse and resistance. Our survival was a response to the extreme subjugation and oppression by which discourse provided a vehicle for resistance and change. Discourse then, became the grounds on which to challenge power and exploitation while expanding new vistas of meaning and experience. Similarly, Black women's slave narratives chronicle the sexual realm of struggle, the rhetorical act of claiming self, and the liberatory nature of symbolic language. Discourse provides not only a space for experiencing and remembering, but also repudiating the myths and stereotypes of Black women's existence while recording our historical contributions on the contours of American life.

Centering ourselves in human discourse reveals a distinct position in the rhetorical nature of discourse. Framed within the exigencies of each period of history, Black women's discourse is a *story* of "rhetorical strategies of women who transformed the 'ordinariness of daily life' into a rhetoric of survival not only for themselves but for generations beyond" (O. Davis, 1998, p. 81). More to the point, the public and private spheres of discourse of Black women's lives inform our struggle for self-definition and personal respect in relation to the complexities of American life and culture. Our experience of struggle and survival by way of telling our story in our own discourse continues to illuminate the dynamics between the public and private spheres of social reality. Rhetoric and history then, are redefined in terms that reveal how the unassuming, unpretentious, underrepresented, and the unthought-of resist discourses of power. The rhetorical tradition of Black women informs a continuum of struggle of crafting liberating discourses while centering experience as a theoretical framework for human discourse.

The purpose of this chapter is to explore the theoretical notions of African American women's discourse that are illuminated by the public and private spheres of experience. I contend that when centering human communication from a standpoint of African American women's lives, the public and private spheres work in concert to shape a conceptual framework for the role experience plays in the creation of thought and meaning. In so doing, I examine how experience shapes discourse and illuminates the struggles of Black women. First, a new angle of vision on theory is posited. Second, I explore African American women's discourse in the manifestations of slave narratives, Black women's oratory and public address, the discourse of blues women, and the discourse of Black women in the academy. Each discourse reveals the resistance to power within Black women's experience and demonstrates that African American women maintain a tradition of crafting liberating discourses in particular ways distinct to our negotiating race, gender, and class in America. Finally, I offer future directions of exploration on the discourse of experience in African American women's public and private spheres of reality.

THEORIZING EXPERIENCE: A NEW ANGLE OF VISION ON THEORY

The exclusion of African American women's ideas from mainstream academic discourse has spurred Black feminist scholars in a variety of disciplines to confront the domain of traditional theory by redefining the definitions of intellectual discourse (Christian, 1985; Collins, 1991; McDowell, 1990; Spillers, 1988; Stanback, 1985). Most traditional rhetorical theories reflect a patriarchal bias by defining rhetoric as persuasion (Foss & Griffin, 1995). From the incipience of our Western discipline, rhetoric has been that human activity that celebrates the conscious effort to dominate and gain power over others in a competitive milieu. Implicit in this conception of rhetorical theory is the assumption that humans are on earth to alter the environment and to influence the social affairs of others.

Rhetorical scholars believe that it is a proper and even necessary human function to attempt to change others (Gearhart, 1979). Gearhart contended that the reward gained from such efforts is a rush of power. This suggests a feeling of self-worth and authority that comes from controlling others. Foss and Griffin (1995) furthered the argument by noting that in this rhetorical system:

> The value of the self comes from the rhetor's ability to demonstrate superior knowledge, skills, and qualifications, in order to dominate the perspectives and knowledge of those in their audiences. The value of the self derives not from a recognition of uniqueness and inherent value of each living being but from gaining control over others. (p. 3)

The act of changing others not only establishes the power of the rhetor over others, but devalues the lives and perspectives of others. In short, a rhetoric of patriarchy reflects the values of competition, control, and domination. It also suggests that others' belief systems and experiences are inadequate or insignificant and thus, need to be changed. In the paradigm of traditional rhetoric, the public and private spheres are separate entities. That is, the public sphere is defined by the rhetor's power and control over the audience or *opponent,* whereas the privateness of discourse is the distancing of self from other, characterized by creating the rhetor at the center of discourse and the audience as *other.*

It seems to me, this model of rhetoric poses problems when discussing African American women's lives. Such a model narrowly defines the breadth of rhetoric and its public and private spheres of experience. Moreover, it embraces the values of domination and control, both of which are antithetical to African American women's cultural, intellectual, and rhetorical traditions (Foster, 1993). As Foss and Griffin (1995) noted, these are not the only values on which a rhetorical system can be constructed. Some may argue that our values of contemporary rhetorical theories embrace African American women's culture. I am cautious of that notion. Postmodernism, for example, argues for the death of the author and a negation of the subject (Foucault, 1991; Lyotard, 1979). This becomes quite problematic when the subject is the historically voiceless other. To theorize the rhetoric of African American women from the perspective of our traditional and contemporary theories is what Lorde (1983) called "using the Master's tools to dismantle the Master's house" (p. 99). That is, the tools of a racist patriarchy cannot nor will not adequately reveal its strategies of domination nor offer ways to change and eradicate itself. I propose values more intrinsic to the celebration of community—an alternative way of knowing, a discourse of experience that illuminates rhetoric as narrative in both the private and public spheres of discourse while broadening our traditionally held assumptions of epistemology and ontology.

A discourse of experience celebrates the construction of knowledge and meaning of African American women and situates rhetoric as a site of struggle for inclusion and survival. It emphasizes the ongoing interplay between Black women's oppression and Black women's activism within the matrix of domination as a response to human agency (Collins, 1991). Wrage (1947) argued in the late 1940s that oratory is a repository of ideas. It seems to me Wrage's argument supports a discourse of experience by illuminating how the power of ideas influences the liberatory dimension of human discourse. Offering a space to engage in the values of self-definition, change, and empowerment, a discourse of experience then, centers African American women's ethnic culture as the central organizing concept for theory and research (Houston, 1991). Unlike the traditional rhetorical model, a discourse of experience celebrates a racial and gendered consciousness of self that comes from knowing and locating multiple strategies of resistance in order to create a progressive means for change in the context of community. Thus, to conceive a new angle of vision on rhetorical theory informs the role of community and self-definition in African American women's experience and recognizes ethnic culture of experience as an organizing concept.

THEORIZING EXPERIENCE IN PUBLIC AND PRIVATE SPHERES OF THE 19TH CENTURY

The 19th century saw the birth of African American women's rhetorical tradition with discourse ranging from female slave narratives to the antilynching rhetoric of Ida B. Wells. The slave narrative genre arose out of a need to define and create Black identities. The discourse by Black women in their own words informed a nation, the world, of the experiences of Black women struggling with racial and sexual exploitation while on the journey toward self-definition. Washington (1987), in the introduction to her book *Invented Lives*, observed the "distinguishing feature" of Black women's writing as being about Black women. She noted that such writing "takes the trouble to record the thoughts, words, feelings, and deeds of black women" (p. xxi). Slave narratives reveal how African American women invented a way to respond to the complexities of the times within a specific intellectual and social context (Ehninger, 1968). They chose discourse as a means to declare their existence and when declaring it, they rose to find their voice. On the voicelessness of the female slave, Nobel Laureate Toni Morrison (cited in Giddings, 1984) stated that "she had nothing to fall back on; not maleness, not whiteness, not anything. And out of the profound desolation of her reality the Black female may well have invented herself" (p. 15). At the same time, slave narrative discourse shaped Black women's experience of oppression into a public discourse and redefined the prevailing ideologies of the period.

However, distinct to the rhetorical significance of African American women's slave narratives is that discourse was a response to multiple public-political impulses (O. Davis, 1999b). Slave narratives were protest literature that responded to the nature of the slave system. Narrative discourse afforded slaves the avenue to make statements about the system as well as to relate events that occurred in their private lives (Smith, 1974). Situating language at the center of their experience underscores narrative as a rhetorical act of survival and a discursive struggle for change. The slave narrative then, became an outgrowth of the experience to survive, redefine a meaning of self, and abolish the institution of slavery. O. Davis noted that

the narrative genre afforded black women, for the first time in
American history, a chance to declare their presence by rhetorically
stating, "I am here." This symbolic expression of claiming self . . .
begins the momentum for creating an oppositional discourse that
identified black women as thinkers, creators, and namers of
themselves in attempts to confront dominant discourses that
mythologized their existence as breeding sows. (p. 154)

Female slave narratives are unique to Western rhetorical theory by
revealing how humans under extreme subjugation locate their
personal and political identities by inventing and engaging in
persuasive discourse. Most importantly, the slave narrative genre
demonstrates how African American female slave narrators
understood the dynamics of rhetorical discourse and constructed
images that would both appeal to the virtues esteemed by the White
culture and that would create self-identity to serve as a means of
survival, control, and empowerment.

Although African American women's slave narratives reveal
the struggle for definitions of self in the private realm of the slave
system, the public sphere of 19th-century oratory and public address
presented challenges for which Black women under extreme pressure
ascended to the speaker's platform. Their appeals were centered in
the struggles of African American communities, often admonishing
the ideals of race pride, economic empowerment, and educational
advancement (Nero, 1995). Rhetoric defined an ethnic context in
which co-gendered and racial sites of struggle were transformed.
Recreating self within the purview of the gender-race dialectic
presents rhetoric as a solution in resisting, redefining, and
performing social reality.

Nineteenth-century African American women who rose and
found their voices on the oratorical stage of public address included
noted trailblazers as Maria W. Stewart, Fannie Barrier Williams,
Anna Julia Cooper, and Ida B. Wells. These women are among many
who maintained an African American women's rhetorical tradition of
survival and personified the struggle of experience in which discourse
helped to define their private and political identities within the
public sphere.

An African American woman was the first woman to speak
before a "promiscuous audience" (Nero, 1995, p. 263) and leave
extant copies of her text in September of 1832 (O. Davis, 1986).
Maria W. Stewart, a Black woman abolitionist, donned the Boston
speaker's platform and for 3 years invented a public persona that
challenged the widely held assumptions of Black female inferiority
and worked unceasingly toward the dismantling of American slavery.

Stewart crafted a rhetorical discourse that framed antislavery arguments in feminist terms (Logan, 1999). She addressed the gender-race dialectic of being both Black and a woman, and remained diligent to the call to Black women to "develop their highest intellectual capacities, to enter into all spheres of the life of the mind, and to participate in all activities within their communities" (p. 8). Stewart's rhetoric encouraged Black women to redefine and transform self-image through involvement in community, from religion and education, to politics and business, without the notion of female subserviency (Richardson, 1987). She exemplified a discourse of experience in the public sphere by creating a rhetoric of community among Black and White women. Stewart's contribution to African American women's rhetorical tradition offers a view of discourse as women's struggle for communalism to enable a liberatory rhetoric of social action (Logan, 1999).

The discourse of both Fannie Barrier Williams and Anna Julia Cooper can be characterized as rhetoric for the purpose of engaging in identification and coalition building among Black and White women. As the 19th century progressed, Black women became increasingly aware of the necessity to build coalitions with White women in order to garner advocacy for the needs of Black women. The purpose of coalition building was to unify women in the movement for racial uplift of young Black women. However, in order to gain the support of White women, Williams and Cooper faced the rhetorical challenge of crafting models of "true womanhood." Placing Black women in the universal category of "woman," offered Williams and Cooper the delicate rhetorical strategies necessary for the palatability of their message to White women auditors (Logan, 1999). Their rhetoric was a discourse of struggle for the purpose of claiming gendered rights, racial equality, and universal humanity of Black women.

Ida B. Wells is best known for her anti-lynching discourse of the 19th century. Trained as a journalist and educator, Wells sought to redefine the image of Black men as rapists by refuting the standard lynching-for-rape connection, and associating it instead with slavery and racial hatred (Logan, 1999). Wells' rhetoric spoke out forcefully against conditions of brutality and as a discourse of experience Logan noted, "her descriptive choices were shaped by the experiences of her own life, a life providing a model for resistance" (p. 95). Wells' anti-lynching rhetoric helped to launch the modern Civil Rights Movement and centered Black women in the discourse of struggle for Black and women's rights.

As with the slave narratives, Stewart, Williams, Cooper, and Wells embrace discourse as a means for resistance to oppressive systems. They reconstructed the public domain of oratory by claiming their voice for the struggle and survival of their community. Moreover, theirs was a rhetoric of resistance to dominant discourses of race and gender supremacy. Their rhetoric offers a provocative look at the unique strategies employed by Black women as they crafted and shaped the public sphere of discourse through lived experience as African American women.

Although these and many other African American women are stalwarts of American oratory, they are seldom found in our courses on public address or in our anthologies of landmark orations by great leaders. The model of great leaders established by White men often relegates African American women to an either/or dichotomy, placing their discourse in the category of "great African American leaders" or "great women leaders" (Nero, 1995, p. 267). A new theorizing embraces a both/and dichotomy and recognizes differences as strengths in the public and private spheres of experience. Lorde suggested the following:

> Difference must not be merely tolerated, but seen as a fund of necessary polarities between which our creativity can spark like a dialectic. Only then does the necessity for interdependency become unthreatening. (pp. 104-105)

Discourse that unites, builds coalitions, and makes connections among people in order to define a world in which we all flourish seems evident in the tradition of African American women's public and private discourse. The struggle for inclusion and recognition of our foremothers' contributions to rhetorical theory remains a discursive challenge in the 21st century.

NAVIGATING THE SPHERES OF EXPERIENCE: THE DIALECTIC OF OPPRESSION AND ACTIVISM

To conceptualize the notion of theorizing of African American women's discourse is to first acknowledge that people of color have always theorized, but in forms quite different from the Western form of abstract logic (Christian, 1985). Narrative forms such as the stories in riddles and proverbs, in blues and in quilts, in spirituals and in slave autobiographies, all point to the ways in which symbolic language redefines, renames, reinvents, and transcends the dominant formations of social reality. Narrative forms are symbolic representations of resistance that provide ways for oppressed and marginalized people to navigate, circumvent, and transcend the dynamics of dominance and change.

When I speak of the public and private spheres of experience to illuminate African American women's discourse, I am referring to the ongoing interplay between African American women's oppression (privateness) and activism (publicness). Feminist and activist Aida Hurtado (1989) observed:

> the public/private distinction is relevant only for the white middle and upper classes since historically the American state has intervened constantly in the private lives and domestic arrangements of the working class. Women of Color have not had the benefit of the economic conditions that underlie the public/private distinction. Instead the political consciousness of women of Color stems from an awareness that the public is *personally* political. (p. 14)

Hurtado's notion points to Abena Busia's (1988) observation of Black women's reality within a dialogical discourse of both/and:

> Our reality is not that we are *"neither* white nor male,"* our reality is that we are *both* black and female; and it is in the belief that our narratives can be transformational that we begin. (p. 23)

Out of this dynamic of the both/and dialectic and the fluidity of Black women's experiences within the public and private spheres, emerges a discourse of African American women's transformation of silence into language as action in knowing the world and making meaning of that world. African American women's epistemology constructs the world as a dynamic place where the goal is not merely to survive, to fit in, or to cope. Rather, the world becomes a place of ownership, citizenship, and accountability (Collins, 1991). Language provides the space to make choices about freedom. Within that space we confront history and situate our stories in their rightful place. Language as action is the freedom to confront contradictions of race, gender, class, and encourages change in ideologies. Freedom is the empowering of self through language to create safe spaces for resisting the objectification as the other. Rising to find one's voice means freedom to name ourselves, not as images of mammy, breeding sow, Jezebel, Aunt Jemima, whore, or bitch, but as community builders, lovers of the everyday folk, intellectuals, othermothers, and·phenomenal women.

The dialectical nature of oppression and activism reveals multiple dimensions of the rhetorical manifestations of African

American women's lives. Several of these dimensions include African American women's blues tradition, the quilt tradition and its metaphoric significance, and Black women in the critical classroom of the Academy.

THE SPHERES OF DISCOURSE: AFRICAN AMERICAN WOMEN'S BLUES AND QUILT TRADITIONS

Resistance to oppressive forces in American society was the birth child of the blues and quilt traditions. Through artistic expression, African American women located symbols that would point to the legacy of struggle. According to A. Davis (1998), "Art is special because of its ability to influence feelings as well as knowledge" (p. xiii). Art influences knowledge by providing new ways of understanding race and ethnicity through the cultural artifacts of music and fabric. For African American women, the blues tradition is a significant space for examining how feminist attitudes emerged from a discourse of music to challenge and resist patriarchal discourses. The theoretical notions of African American women's discourse point to the blues tradition as a space for Black women of the poor and working-class communities to locate their voice in the public sphere while illuminating the private sphere of love and sexuality as everyday experience.

Heretofore, the blues tradition of African American women has not been fully explored in the realm of rhetorical discourse and its implications on Black feminist studies of communication. This is in part because, as A. Davis (1998) pointed out, Black feminist traditions tend to exclude ideas produced by and within the poor and working-class communities of Black women. In addition, as discussed earlier, our theories of rhetoric and human communication fail to recognize the theoretical implications of everyday folk wisdom and experience. However, African American women's blues tradition has great implications to rhetorical theory, for it demonstrates discourse as a site in which Black women redefined the notions of domesticity and "women's place" to assert themselves publicly as sexual beings. According to Carby (1986):

> the women's blues . . . is a discourse that articulates a cultural and political struggle over sexual relations: a struggle that is directed against the objectification of female sexuality within a patriarchal order but which also tries to reclaim women's bodies as the sexual and sensuous subjects of song. (p. 12)

African American women employed the blues as a space to construct an ongoing independent womanhood that affirmed their subjectivity of love and sexuality in the private sphere of experience, and at the same time offered a liberating discourse from sexist models of women's conduct. As a public discourse for the poor and working-class women, the blues provided a site in which Black women challenged bourgeois notions of sexual purity and "true womanhood" and claimed their voices in defense of their class and gender. The blues, according to A. Davis, "also demonstrates that working-class women's names could be defended not only in the face of the dominant white culture but in the face of male assertions of dominance in black communities as well" (p. 65). It is evident that a discourse of experience illuminates the theoretical notions of African American women's discourse and the ways in which Black women transformed stereotypes of class distinction and crafted new discourses of the body, identity, love and sexuality. Moreover, the blues served as a site for coalition building among working-class Black women and served to maintain a political consciousness that the public sphere is personally political (Hurtado, 1989).

For African American women, the blues became a means of resisting political forms of degradation. In 1939, Billie Holiday recorded *Strange Fruit* during a decade of racial unrest. The lyrics were a direct connection to the anti-lynching discourse of Wells and other Black feminists of the era. Linking the tradition of a discourse of struggle, both public address and music worked in concert toward activism and change. In short, the blues tradition of African American women shaped a discourse of experience and liberation for many Black women writers, actors, artists, and rhetorical critics throughout America. On a historical continuum, the African American women's singing group *Sweet Honey in the Rock* demonstrates their ancestral connection to this rich musical tradition. *Sweet Honey*'s music provides a political site for social commentary on the public and private spheres of African American women's lived experience (see J. Davis, chap. 10, this volume).

In African American women's quilt tradition, discourse becomes the legacy of a people struggling for symbols of expression through pieces of cloth and a myriad of colors. A rhetorical focus on the quilt uncovers the choice of symbols Black women used as a way of creating a shared, common meaning of self and the world with their community. Thus, the quilt serves as a vehicle for reinventing the symbolic expression of identity and freedom. Moreover, the quilt employs metaphoric purposes by revealing relationships of power and contested meanings. For example, in the antebellum period, African American women's quilts served as codes for mapping escapes to freedom (Hopkinson, 1993). By viewing the quilt as a discursive site for liberation reveals the rhetorical nature of Black women's ability to transcend adversity. Woven within the quilt tradition are motifs of struggle, survival, and family relationships. The quilt is symbolic of the historical process within which African people have been engaged, a process that is an intertwining of tradition, enslavement, and the struggle for their people's freedom (Christian, 1985). The quilt tradition is also expressed in the metaphoric language of *weaving* life experiences together; forming identity through the tapestry of lives, and the oral tradition of meaning-making transforms lives through the strands of everyday experience. Baker and Pierce-Baker (1985) underscore the symbolism and transformative role of the quilt by pointing out that:

> The patchwork quilt . . . opens a fascinating interpretive window on vernacular dimensions of lived, creative experience in the United States. Quilts, their patched and many-colored glory offer not a counter to tradition, but in fact, an instance of the only legitimate tradition of "the people" that exists. (p. 714)

Like the quilt, African American women's discourse weaves stories of the public and private spheres to shape a theoretical framework for enhancing the study, methodology, and advancement of human communication. Both the blues and quilt traditions uncover the interplay between oppression and activism—the privateness and publicness of discourse—and celebrates an aesthetic community of resistance that in turn encourages and nurtures a political community of active and ongoing struggle for freedom and liberation.

THE NEW MILLENNIUM: A DISCOURSE OF EXPERIENCE IN THE ACADEMY

The discourse of African American women in the critical classroom of the Academy offers a space to craft the classroom as a site of resistance and liberation. African American women scholars have our place among the professorate and are transforming the Academy through strategies of resistance (O. Davis, 1999a). As with our foremothers of the 19th and 20th centuries, we embark on the new millennium with a discourse traditional of the struggle for survival, inclusion, and importance in our professional communities of the Academy. As Farmer (1993b) pointed out

It is difficult to talk about being Black in a White space, even
though in the United States such is usually the case. The difficulty
is to speak, to name, without appearing to whine, a near
impossibility, since African-American women are not expected to
speak at all. It is particularly difficult to be heard, since despite the
reality, the myth still prevails that African-American women are
making great strides. (p. 205)

Discourse by African American women in the Academy interrogates
the ways in which Black women scholars are activists in the struggle
to claim our presence, redefine, and transform the traditionally
White male-dominated space of the Academy. In a recent article by
Collison (1999a) on Black women in the Academy, several African
American women scholars from various disciplines spoke concerning
the dilemmas of negotiating the public and private spheres of
experience in the Academy. Hazel Carby (cited in Collison, 1999a),
chair of African American and African Studies at Yale University,
offered a provocative and insightful observation of the dilemma:

In the late 1990s, the work of Black women intellectuals is still
considered peripheral. . . . The intellectual work of Black women . . .
is not thought to be of enough significance to be engaged with,
argued with, agreed or disagreed with. Thus, terms like women,
gender, and sexuality have a decorative function only. (pp. 27, 32)

On the margins in the Academy, Black women scholars create
scholarship, engage the classroom, and forge community activism as
strategies of empowerment. Guy-Sheftall, professor of Women's
Studies at Spelman College, noted that "without looking at black
women, you don't get a complete picture of African American life"
(cited in Collison, 1999b, p. 27). Similarly, Professor Mobley
McKenzie observed that "many men . . . overlook or devalue the
extent to which women's voices are required to give scholarship a
complete view" (cited in Collison, 1999, p. 32). The struggle for
survival that has shaped our discourse from slave narratives of the
19th century to the present day milieu of the Academy maintains a
dialectic between power, resistance, and self-definition as tenets of a
discourse of experience. Challenging the White male-dominated
space of the Academy through scholarship and the critical classroom
environment encourages the tradition of Black women's discursive
strategies of empowerment.

I encourage African American women scholars to employ
scholarship as rhetorical acts of resistance and activism. As the
foremothers of oratory and public address demonstrated, discourse is

a space in which Black female political consciousness and political solidarity are maintained. It seems to me, the challenges of the academic community underscore the importance of African American women's histories in our collective understanding of the world. Moreover, our stories, our discourses of experience suggest the opportunity for transforming theory. Of the challenge to transform the Academy James (1993) observed:

> Playing by its *house* rules, academia can set standards which no African American woman can meet *as an African American woman*. It is assumed that we only speak as "Black women"—not as *women*—or "Black people"—not as *human beings*—our stories and theorizing are considered irrelevant or not applicable to women or people in general; they are reduced to descriptions of a part rather than analyses of a whole (humanity). (p. 121)

Drawing on African American women's rhetorical tradition, scholarship as activism engages the public and private spheres of experience by highlighting "the significance of examining women and culture and informing our discipline of innovations for theory and praxis" (O. Davis, 1999a, p. 377). As African American women scholars continue to shape the future of the academy with our scholarship, let us be ever cognizant of the significance of theorizing with a tradition of struggle and liberation that has been the hallmark of our historical and transforming discourse.

FUTURE DIRECTIONS TOWARD A DISCOURSE OF EXPERIENCE

The future appears challenging yet undaunting for directives on theorizing discourse of African American women's experience. As communication scholars, it seems to me that we have particularly exciting opportunities to use Black feminist and womanist perspectives to explore coalition building within and beyond the university. Providing scholarship that illuminates the liberatory function of African American women's oppression and activism points to the relevance of the public and private spheres as sites of exploration of a variety of discourses beyond our traditional forms of rhetorical discourse. Finally, I see theorizing a discourse of experience as an opportunity to collapse the glass ceiling of class hegemony to include scholarship on all classes of Black women, thus avoiding essentialism and providing explorations into new vistas of African American women's epistemology and ontology.

We have stories to tell and to teach. Those stories are our experience. That experience is our knowing. That knowing is our struggle. That struggle is our survival. That survival is our strength. That strength is our center.

REFERENCES

Baker, H. A., Jr., & Pierce-Baker, C. (1985). Patches: Quilts and community in Alice Walker's everyday use. *Southern Review, 21,* 706-720.

Busia, A. (1988). Words whipped over voids: A context for black women's rebellious voices in the novel of the African diaspora. In J. Weixlmann & H. Baker (Eds.), *Studies in black American literature* (pp. 1-41). Greenwood, CT: Penkeville.

Carby, H. (1986). It just be's dat way sometime: The sexual politics of women's blues. *Radical America, 20*(4), 12.

Christian, B. (1985). *Black feminist criticism.* New York: Pergamon Press.

Collins, P. H. (1991). *Black feminist thought.* New York: Routledge.

Collison, M. N-K. (1999a). Earning and demanding respect. *Black Issues in Higher Education, 16*(7), 30-32.

Collison, M. N-K. (1999). Race women stepping forward. *Black Issues in Higher Education, 16*(7), 24-27.

Davis, A. Y. (1998). *Blues legacies and black feminism: Gertrude "Ma" Rainey, Bessie Smith, and Billie Holiday.* New York: Pantheon Books.

Davis, O. I. (1986, November). *Maria W. Stewart: A stalwart figure of black American oratory.* Paper presented at the meeting of the Speech Communication Association, Chicago, IL.

Davis, O. I. (1998). A black woman as rhetorical critic: Validating self and violating the space of otherness. *Women's Studies in Communication, 21*(1), 77-89.

Davis, O. I. (1999a). In the kitchen: Transforming the academy through safe spaces of resistance. *Western Journal of Communication, 63*(3), 364-381.

Davis, O. I. (1999b). Life ain't been no crystal stair: The rhetoric of autobiography in black female slave narratives. In J. L. Conyers, Jr. (Ed.), *Black lives: Essays in African American biography* (pp. 151-159). Armonk, NY: M.E. Sharpe.

Ehninger, D. (1968). On systems of rhetoric. *Philosophy and Rhetoric, 1,* 131-144.

Farmer, R. (1993a). Conclusion. In R. Farmer & J. James (Eds.), *Spirit, space, & survival: African American women in (white) academe* (pp. 218-223). New York: Routledge.

Farmer, R. (1993b). Place but not importance: The race for inclusion in academe. In R. Farmer & J. James (Eds.), *Spirit, space, & survival: African American women in (white) academe* (pp. 196-217). New York: Routledge.

Foucault, M. (1991). What is an author? In C. Mukerji & M. Schudson (Eds.), *Rethinking popular culture: Contemporary perspectives in cultural studies* (pp. 446-464). Berkeley: University of California Press.

Foss, S., & Griffin, C. (1995). Beyond persuasion: A proposal for an invitational rhetoric. *Communication Monographs, 62*, 2-17.

Foster, F. S. (1993). *Written by herself: Literary production by African American women, 1746-1892*. Bloomington: Indiana University Press.

Gearhart, S. M. (1979). The womanization of rhetoric. *Women's Studies International Quarterly, 2*, 195-201.

Giddings, P. (1984). *When and where I enter: The impact of black women on race and sex in America*. New York: Bantam Books.

Hopkinson, D. (1993). *Sweet Clara and the freedom quilt*. New York: Knopf.

Houston, M. (1991). *Follow us into our world: Feminist scholarship on the communication of women of color*. (ERIC Document Reproduction Service No. ED 337 816/CS 507 510 [April], 10).

Hurtado, A. (1989). Relating to privilege: Seduction and rejection in the subordination of white women and women of color. *Signs: A Journal of Women and Culture in Society, 14*(4), 20-32.

James, J. (1993). Teaching theory, talking community. In J. James & R. Farmer (Eds.), *Spirit, space & survival: African American women in (white) academe* (pp. 118-135). New York: Routledge.

Logan, S. W. (1999). *We are coming: The persuasive discourse of nineteenth-century black women*. Carbondale: Southern Illinois University Press.

Lorde, A. (1983). The master's tools will never dismantle the master's house. In C. Moraga & G. Anzaldua (Eds.), *This bridge called my back: Writings by radical women of color* (pp. 98-107). New York: Kitchen Table, Women of Color Press.

Lyotard, J. F. (1979). *La condition postmoderne: Rapport sur le Savoir* [The postmodern condition: A report on knowledge]. Paris: Editions de Minuit.

McDowell, D. (1990). The changing same: Generational connections and black women novelists. In H. L. Gates, Jr. (Ed.), *Reading black, reading feminist* (pp. 91-115). New York: Meridian Book.

Nero, C. I. (1995). Oh, what I think I must tell this world! Oratory and public address of African-American women. In K. M. Vaz (Ed.), *Black women in America* (pp. 261-275). London: Sage.

Richardson, M. (1987). Introduction. In M. Richardson (Ed.), *Maria W. Stewart, America's first black woman political writer: Essays and speeches* (pp. i-xi). Bloomington: Indiana University Press.

Smith, S. (1974). *Where I'm bound; patterns of slavery and freedom in black American autobiography*. Westport, CT: Greenwood Press.

Spillers, H. (1988). Foreword. In H. L. Gates, Jr. (Ed.), *Six women's slave narratives* (p. xi). New York: Oxford University Press.

Stanback, M. H. (1985). Language and black women's place: Evidence from the black middle class. In P. A. Treichler, C. Kramarae, & B. Stafford (Eds.), *For Alma Mater: Theory and practice of feminist scholarship* (pp. 177-193). Urbana: University of Illinois Press.

Washington, M. H. (1987). Introduction. In M. H. Washington (Ed.), *Invented lives: Narratives of black women, 1860-1960* (pp. xv-xxxi). Garden City, NY: Anchor Press.

Wrage, E. J. (1947). Public address: A study in social and intellectual history. *Quarterly Journal of Speech, 33,* 451-457.

THREE

Conceiving the Language of Black Women's Everyday Talk

Karla D. Scott
Saint Louis University

> *And I am inclined to say that our theorizing (and I intentionally use the verb rather than the noun) is often in narrative forms, in the stories we create, in riddles and proverbs, in the play with language, since dynamic rather than fixed ideas seem more to our liking. . . . And women, at least the women I grew up around continuously speculated about the nature of life through pithy language that unmasked the power relations of their world. . . .*
> —Christian (1990, p. 336)

Ignoring Black women in communication studies is consistent with most areas of social scientific research. That a group made invisible by both race and gender would be overlooked is hardly surprising given that until recently both groups have been relegated to the margins of society. However, as the demand for, and interest in, the inclusion of marginalized groups continues (unfortunately in an often misguided quest for "diversity") it is important that the desire to bring Black women into the literature does not result in a flurry of studies that will only reinforce long-held stereotypes, negative interpretations and distorted views of this particular group.

As communication scholars, our challenge should be to remain conscious of the history and overarching assumptions that are attached to Black women as individuals, and as a community, and to assure that studies do not serve to reinforce existing inaccurate representations. Our job should be to examine this speech community in a way that takes into account the influence of that history and how it has shaped Black women's experiences in general and communication in particular.

For those who choose to pursue this study there is also cause for caution and consideration for the approach used. Because so little is known about Black women's communication, scholars run the risk of compounding a problem in the quest to right a wrong. When we choose to open up this area of study we have to be adamant in our efforts to emphasize and reemphasize that in no way does any one study attempt to define the way *all* Black women communicate. Although all studies qualify results by making claims that are limited to the particular study, research on groups that have been ignored run a particular risk of becoming *the* authority—particularly if the results are interpreted in a way consistent with dominant beliefs about the group.

In the case of Black women, where stereotypes have persisted, scholars need to be especially conscious of how they approach inquiry and interpret results because there is no vast body of knowledge to which another study can be added for a more complete picture. Without this larger view any study, any piece of information or insight offered, runs the risk of essentializing an entire community. And even if attempts are made by authors to discourage essentializing we all know that once in publication we cannot control how our work is used when making academic arguments.

It is therefore imperative that those who choose to pursue this area of study do so armed with a perspective and approach that results in a more accurate interpretation of Black women's communicative experiences and subsequently enriches the study of human communication. In this chapter I discuss both perspective and approach by advocating an Afrocentric feminist (Collins, 1989, and Introduction, this volume) study of Black women's everyday talk as a site where communication scholars can learn more about the complex communicative lives of Black women.

I begin this chapter with a more comprehensive look at the role of multiple identities in the lives of Black women and how those identities influence language use. Of particular interest in this discussion are findings of scholarly studies of Black women's communication that illustrate the ways in which language is used to negotiate identity. I conclude by suggesting that an Afrocentric feminist approach to the study of the language of everyday talk provides further understanding of the negotiation of an identity as Black and female while living at the intersection of larger social issues.

THE STRUGGLE OF MULTIPLE IDENTITIES

As many Black feminist theorists (Collins, 1989; hooks, 1981, 1989) argue, an identity in the United States as Black and female compounds the difficulties a woman encounters as she lives, moves, and experiences being in a world that is predominantly White and male. The plight of being both Black and female, described as "double jeopardy" by Beale (1970) and many others, has evolved into a recognition of multiple oppression that results from multiple interlocking identities of race, gender, class and sexual preference (Collins, 1989; Combahee, 1983; hooks, 1989). A critical point in these discussions is the realization that identity cannot be compartmentalized. An identity as Black woman is a result of being *both* Black and woman—one cannot be a genderless Black person or a woman stripped of racial identity. As Dill (1987) noted:

> For Black women and other women of color an examination of the ways in which racial oppression, class exploitation, and patriarchy intersect in their lives must be studied in relation to their perceptions of the impact these structures have upon them. Through studying the lives of particular women and searching for patterns in the ways in which they describe themselves and their relationship to society, we will gain important insights into the differences and similarities between Black and White women. (p. 165)

Examining the impact of social structures on various aspects of the lives of Black women aids in understanding the "legacy of struggle" that Collins (1989) identified as one of the core themes of Black feminist thought. Part of that struggle involves living in multiple worlds as described by Cannon (1985): "[T]hroughout the history of the United States, the interrelationship of White supremacy and male superiority has characterized the Black woman's reality as a situation of struggle—a struggle to survive in two contradictory worlds simultaneously, one White, privileged and oppressive, the other Black, exploited and oppressed" (p. 30).

Of particular interest to communication research is how that struggle to survive in contradictory worlds and multiple identities involves Black women's communicative behavior. As pointed out by feminist communication scholars (Carter & Spitzack, 1989; Ganguly, 1992; Houston, 1992; Rakow, 1992) issues of race and class have been virtually ignored in studies of women's communication. In a discussion of the need to include race in the study of women's communication, Houston (1992) noted:

> Making women's ethnic culture the central organizing concept for feminist theory and research means thinking of women as enculturated to a gendered communication ideal *within* specific ethnic groups, that is learning how they should communicate as women in the context of a particular ethnic experience. (p. 53)

Tejana feminist Gloria Anzuldua (1987) argued that people who inhabit multiple realities are forced to live in the interface between worlds and identifies the spaces, places, and positions in between categories (and identities) as the borderlands. Anzuldua said the result is *la mestiza*, the consciousness and identity of the borderlands:

> *La mestiza* [an Aztec word meaning torn between ways] is a product of the transfer of the cultural and spiritual values of one group to another. Cradled in one culture, sandwiched between two cultures, straddling all three cultures and their value systems, *la mestiza* undergoes a struggle of flesh, a struggle of borders, an inner war. (p. 78)

Like *la mestiza*, Black women must also straddle lives in multiple worlds and cultures. It is this process of cultural border crossing and how it involves Black women's language that can provide a focus for communication study. Of specific interest is a more thorough understanding of the language of everyday talk in Black women's cultural border crossings.

Unfortunately, little research has been done in the area of Black women's communication practices so it is difficult to even begin to conceptualize or discuss the ways in which Black women use language given that in everyday life they often cross the cultural borders of race, gender, and (for many, if not most Black women) class. Because life in the borderlands requires a negotiation of identity across cultures and with Black women there is no first language to abandon, or second language to learn in order to cross those borders, there must be some other way of marking identity in the different cultural worlds they inhabit.

EVERYDAY TALK AND CULTURAL BORDER CROSSINGS

Influenced by Anzuldua's theory of linguistic cultural border crossing, my interest in Black women's everyday talk grew out of my own experiences as a Black woman who, when moving from one cultural world to another as a part of normal everyday life, constantly had to use various language styles to mark who I was in each of those different worlds. Many instances of language use across cultural border crossings are found in the narratives and personal accounts of women who do not speak English as a first language (Anzuldua, 1987, 1990; Moraga & Anzuldua, 1983; Zook, 1990). Although compelled to learn English in order to assimilate and have better lives than their parents, they retain their native way of speaking for use when they are with their own, with those who share their identity and ways of looking at the world. For Black women, however, changes in language codes may not be as easily identifiable as are the language changes of Asian women, Latinas, or others who have a distinctly different language with words and grammatical structures that must be translated before one can speak English.

The influence of both race and gender as contexts for social interaction is the focus of Marsha Houston's research on Black middle-class women's communication that illustrates how moving between two cultures requires proficiency in both Black English, the language of their culture and Standard English, the language of the dominant culture (Houston, 1983). This movement across cultures "heightens ones awareness of communicative differences" between races or cultures (Houston, 1985, p. 185) resulting in a "double consciousness." In the context of gender she challenges traditional theories of male-female communication differences, noting that the historical division of labor is not as salient in the Black community where Black women traditionally worked outside the home and assumed a strong role in the family. The result of this history is a notable difference in Black and White women's language and places in various cultural worlds.

To further situate this conceptualization of Black women's everyday talk across cultural worlds, brief attention needs to be given to the area of language use in the Black community. An appropriate starting point for this discussion is the use of Black English, also known as Black English Vernacular, African American English, and Ebonics, which (thanks to the 1996 controversy in the Oakland School District) has become a term often used when referring to language in/and Black America.[1]

---

[1]Because I perceive a negative connotation of the term *Ebonics* I prefer not to use it in this chapter. I do, however, want to acknowledge that other

The relationship of language to the social lives of its speakers, the focus of sociolinguistics, answers many questions about how language functions in society and serves to mark identity and membership (Romaine, 1994). Historically, characterizations of language use in the Black community focused on the inability of a group of people to speak or use language correctly. Quite often, differences in language use were attributed to the inherent inferiority of Africans and their descendants (Smitherman & Cunningham, 1997). This unfair characterization removes the history of the speakers from the language being spoken and allows speakers to continually be evaluated by standards of a more dominant culture that possesses the power to determine "correct" and act on those judgments.

In her work on the language of Black America, Smitherman (1977) contended that Black English is a legitimate form of speech with a distinct history and origins; a position that forms the basis for perceiving language use in the Black community as indeed different (as is the case with many racial and ethnic groups) but not deficient or deviant—as Black English has often been perceived. In her early 1970s groundbreaking work, she identified uniqueness of the language as evident in three areas: grammar and pronunciation, continued importance of the oral tradition and specialized vocabulary or lexicon (Smitherman, 1977).[2]

It is important to note that proficiency in Standard English has long been considered an important mark of credibility as often demonstrated during slavery when freed Blacks offered linguistic competency as proof of status. Such markers still exist today and as discussed later in this chapter, a switch in language style or code does not presume a Black woman is incompetent in Standard English but rather, in the course of everyday talk, may choose not to speak Standard English as a means of marking and asserting identity across cultural worlds.

As noted previously, the ability to move back and forth between cultural worlds often requires competence in both languages

---

scholarly discussions and debates on the topic of Ebonics demonstrate the inaccuracy of the mainstream depiction while further explaining the validity of the concept (Smitherman & Cunningham, 1997; Williams, 1997). For the purposes of this chapter, when referring to the language used in many Black communities I use *Black English*. When referring to the language most often spoken and accepted as "correct" I use the term *Standard English*.

[2]For a more thorough discussion of each area and a better understanding of the history and present use of language in the Black community, see Smitherman (1977, 1994).

in order to negotiate identity across cultures. Code-switching is defined as "the juxtaposition of passages of speech belonging to two grammatical systems" (Gumperz, 1982, p. 59). For many speakers in Black communities code-switching is the selective use of Black English and Standard English depending on the situation (Giles, Bourhis, & Taylor, 1977). Style-switching, although it may include grammatical features of Black English and Standard English, is more general and involves more than just language choices. Features of communication that may be altered in style-switching include changes in prosody, paralanguage, narrative structure, and interaction strategies (Hecht, Collier, & Ribeau, 1994).

The literature on Black language reveals that the use of Black English Vernacular (Smitherman, 1977); code-switching (Garner & Rubin, 1986; Giles et al., 1977), and verbal performance (Garner, 1983; Hecht et. al., 1994; Kochman, 1981; Stanback & Pearce, 1981) exist as cultural identity markers in the Black community. However, as is the case with most scholarly inquiry, the studies fail to include the communicative experiences of Black women, do not view Black women as a distinct speech community or focus on the larger social forces impacting the lives of Black women. But as the next section demonstrates, Black women scholars are making valuable contributions to what we know about Black women's communicative lives and more specifically the language of everyday talk.

NEGOTIATING IDENTITY THROUGH EVERYDAY TALK

Nelson's (1990) study of code-switching in Black women's narratives was motivated in part by her

> [P]leasure in listening to the meandering rhythms, the hyperbole and the novel metaphors of the causal kitchen table discourse of my women friends and family members . . . much of the meaning lay in such performance strategies as Black stylistic intonational contours, in apparent approximations of the standard to Black dialect . . . as well as in cultural maxims. (p. 142)

Nelson's narratives were generated during her interviews with 30 Black women all over age 30 and described by Nelson as representative across socio-economic stratification lines. She noted that during the interviews speakers often began narratives in what one could identify as their approximation of Standard English and later switched to Black English depending on the speaker's perception of the relationship between the two women. The following exchange illustrates this cultural border crossing.

In response to the question "How would you describe who you are?" the interviewee stated: "I am a Black female, a Black woman who is married, a Black woman who is married, who is a mother, a Black woman who is married, who is a mother and who has a good idea of who she is and feels good about it." Nelson then asked: "What does it mean to be a Black female, a woman who is married, etc?" Nelson reported that the informant hesitated then said, "I was going to answer in the context of being Black in America, but . . ." at which point Nelson interjected: "Girl, go with your first mind!"

Nelson suggested that such encouragement not only made it possible for the respondent to continue but the use of "girl" also marked Nelson as a member of the Black dialectical speech community. Nelson reported that the respondent continues by almost preaching a response "in the repetitive, parallel clause structure so commonly used for emphasis in the Black church tradition." A portion of that response illustrates the power of the word in the oral tradition:

> An identity that says I am speaking to you out of my experience and if it sounds rough, please don't judge me because it sounds rough. Try to look at me and judge me for what I have come through. . . . I am a Black woman struggling for that identity, finding that identity, liking that identity and being proud of where it comes from. (p. 147)

The two women later engage in a call-and-response pattern, a feature of Black women's language also found in Houston's (1983) study of Black women's code-switching where Black women engage in this verbal interaction with other Black women but not in with White women. The inclusion of certain features of language when with one of the same race illustrates the negotiation of identity through everyday talk. The shared experience makes it possible to use a shared language.

Making the connection of language and cultural identity even more explicit Nelson referred to one of her participants who pointed out "that in order to talk about Black cultural experience" she needs the language created out of that experience, as opposed to the power code." Nelson (1990) also suggested that switches from Standard English to Black English are reported to mark an utterance with "profundity or authority or to indicate the narrator's solidarity with the elicitor." She further argues that we should hear such style switches as a "challenge to hegemony" (p. 152).

In Foster's (1995) study of Black women teachers, similar linguistic forms and discourse features were used to express and invoke solidarity, power, and community. She identified the following as stylistic devices employed by the women in their classroom: manipulation of grammatical structures, repetition, use of symbolism and figurative language, intonational contours, vowel elongation, and changes in meter, tempo, and cadence. In addition, she found code-switching among a group of women occurred despite Foster's deliberate intention not to initiate such switches. The most common switch was the use of multiple negation used to report the speech of others as illustrated in italics the following portion of talk:

> And do you know we have only one white teacher that will teach Black history. Only one, only one, She doesn't mind teaching the Black history, but the rest of them say, *"I don't know nothing about it!.* You see I don't know enough about it to teach it. I leave that with Miss Ruthie." (Foster, 1995, pp. 342-343)

Of particular note in this portion of talk is that Black English is used to report the speech of one who is not Black. Whether the speaker actually used the multiple negation or not is unknown but as Foster noted, that the Black women reporting the speech "immediately rephrased the statement in Standard English suggests that she is calling attention to the comment by setting it off using the African American English variant" (p. 343). It is worth reemphasizing that these women were teachers fluent in both Standard and Black English so the use of Black English was not a reflection of incompetency but rather an indication of competence.

Like Nelson, Foster also maintained that such switches index social identity and communicate a particular stance or point of view that cannot be expressed in Standard English. The behavior is an expression of solidarity and shared identity through which they "express their power and challenge the hegemony of public discourse" (p. 347).

Consistent with those findings is my own work on Black women's language use and cultural border crossings (Scott, 1995, 2000), which I briefly discuss to further illustrate how everyday talk (and the choices inherent in its use) can provide insight into Black women's communicative lives.[3] This study, which included an

---

[3]Individual and group interviews were conducted with nine young Black women attending a large midwestern university. Semi-structured interviews were used to guide discussions about the use of talk and the connection to an identity as a Black woman. All interviews were audiotaped and comparative

exploration of young Black women's everyday talk, demonstrates that the choice of language style of is not just a way to mark identity but can also be used to mark solidarity and an ideological stance about identity.

One of the questions presented to the women in the interview was designed to elicit descriptions of talking or ways of using language that they considered characteristic of a Black woman. This question and the subsequent discussions and narratives it produced provided the types of descriptions used for analysis. As shown in the following discussion, the words "girl" and "look" are used consistently by the women prior to a switch in language style. This switch includes rhythmical stress placement and marked intonation patterns. This type of switch involves a culturally specific contextualization cue, which allows the one who switches to embed an in-group message and signal ethnic identity.

The instances of the use of "girl" and "look" are included in larger portions of conversational interaction or in the women's responses in order to provide a context for the utterances. The context of the utterances is included in order to demonstrate that the switch in style occurs when issues of identity and ideology are discussed. The following portion of talk between two participants illustrates how the issues of identity, ideology, and solidarity are connected to Black women's language choices in their everyday lives.

(1)

Mary: It's uhm, comforting when you sit down and talk to someone who knows exactly where you're coming from. It's like, "yeah somebody understands me." It feels good to have somebody understand you and where you're coming from and when you're talking to them you don't have to explain everything you're saying and they're like, "But I don't understand." You can say, ((sucks teeth)) "*Gi: rl I had a rough day" "gi: rl I know exactly what you mean, " gi: rl my boyfriend* and she's like, "*girl I know, I know exactly*" you're like, "*Mama know girl, Mama know.*"

---

analysis used on taped talk to identify changes in vowel elongation, meter rhythm, cadence, and repetition reported by the women as "Talking like a Black woman." In addition, comparative analysis of the content of responses was employed to assess similarities in women's definition and understanding of "Talking like a Black woman." Transcript notations are a modified version of Heritage (1984) with italics indicating words spoken after a switch takes place. Elongated vowels are indicated by colons; capital letters are used to signal emphasis.

Although the use of "girl" was used most often in instances of the women's reported and reconstructed speech it also occurred in actual talk among interview participants. In the following instance, "girl" occurs in one of the small group interviews as the three women are struggling to find words to describe what they consider a primary difference in the way Whites and Blacks use language:

(2)
Janice: There's a vibe you get,
Laura: A, a Black
Janice: that vibe you get
Laura: yes, yes, ((laughter and hand slapping)) *GIRL, GIRL I'm not sure what.*
Janice: But it's that vibe
Laura: *YOU KNOW what I'm talking about.*

In the next instance Mary uses girl as she talks with two other interviewees and describes an incident in class where a White student was confronted by another Black woman in the class about his perception of Blacks:

(3)
Mary: [the Black woman said] Do you want to be poor? You think you wake up in the morning, "Oh let's have eight kids and let's be poor?" He was like, "I guess so." And she [the other Black woman in class] was like- you know, *Gi: : rl, she was about to get up and just smack him cause it was so stupid* ((laughter)).

Instances of the word "look" also occurred frequently in the women's responses. A recurring context for the use of look was in talk the young women reported they used when interacting with Whites.

(4)
Alison: But a true sister will be able to correlate and put it all together, "*Look, you know I'm Black too, and maybe if I changed my language then you'll understand where I'm coming from.*"

(5)
Kim: Like if I'm talking like this and someone's gonna say, "Well you people" and "I don't understand" then I have to come closer to them, be demonstrative and explain to them,

"Look, you don't understand. In the Black community," you know. You raise your voice tone and you have to be very firm with them especially when you're talking about something you know about and it's a very touchy subject. Anything dealing with Black people to me is a touchy subject so whenever White people say anything like, I'm always up ((snaps fingers)).

(6)
Alison: When you have to break it down, *"Look I'm Black"...sometimes I want to break it down to TA's* [teaching assistants] *"Look" you know, in a sisterly way.*

Results of this study indicate that in one world, the world shared with other Black women who are identified as "my girls," they reported "talking like a Black woman" to mark solidarity with other Black women who they perceive as sharing that same identity *and* an understanding of that identity. It is in this world they feel recognized and understood and here their ideology about that position is confirmed and validated by those who share it.

However, in another world, the world of predominantly White classrooms and meetings, the women perceive a need to mark identity in a different way. Their responses suggest it is when they are in this other world they feel invisible and raceless and a need to often assert identity in a world where it is not recognized. In this study, it appears that the women not only call attention to themselves by "talking like a Black woman" in such settings, they also use that time as an opportunity to assert their ideological position about that identity, often pointing out or correcting what they perceive as erroneous information their White classmates may have of Blacks and their experiences as a group of people.

The findings of my study suggest that for these women, the language of everyday talk functions as a way to mark both identity and ideology when crossing cultural borders. It is their belief that such a change in footing (Goffman 1981), or changing of hats, is needed in such instances where their in-group style may not be understood or accepted as serious.

Of course this study, like those conducted by Houston, Nelson, Foster, and others in this volume, makes no claims of generalizability, nor are they intended to explain the language use of *all* Black women. They do, however, attempt to promote an awareness of, and a preliminary understanding of, the role of everyday talk in the lives of Black women. Empirical studies in this area are lacking and studies such as these are a first step toward understanding the motivations and implications of such language code changes.

Of primary importance to a study such as this is the recognition that for these young Black women in predominantly White worlds, the language of everyday talk is a way of being recognized through an assertion of identity. For these women, the need to "talk back" is an ever present part of their life where they feel a need to demand respect for both their identity and ideology as Black women. It is an attitude of defiance to the silencing, it is an act of standing up and speaking out as described by hooks (1989):

> Moving from silence into speech is for the oppressed, the colonized, the exploited, and those who stand and struggle side by side, a gesture of defiance that heals, that makes new life and new growth possible. It is that act of speech, of "talking back" that is no mere gesture of empty words, that is the expression of our movement from object to subject—the liberated voice. (p. 9)

In this study, the women's responses indicate they see a need to speak out about their experiences even though they risk being labeled as an obstreperous "Sapphire," a nagging, verbose, emasculating woman. This deliberate act of talking back is counter to many of the expectations of a woman's place and language use that has been described as powerless and polite. Regardless of the risk of being negatively perceived, the young Black women in this study indicate they choose to speak and speak in their native language, reflecting their particular experience and the Black woman's tradition of resistance, of trying to be heard through silencing.

Another important aspect of the research conducted by Houston, Nelson, Foster, and myself is how it contributes to an understanding of the role of language in the cultural border crossings of the Black women. Studies of this type follow Phillipsen's (1975) suggestion that the deficit of information on how groups view speech be remedied by descriptive and comparative studies of American speech. These studies go beyond that suggestion and try to examine the role of everyday speech in the lives of those who live in multiple worlds, where the rules for speaking are often contradictory.

Chen (1994) captured this sense of living between cultures: "Living on the fault line between cultures and trying to hold them together is like oscillating between choices in a double bind" (p. 10). This same concept of life in two cultures was described by Black scholar W. E. B. DuBois (1918) as "double consciousness" and by Black writer Ralph Ellison as double vision.

An example of this type of contradiction comes from hooks in a discussion of the limits and problems of language. Citing Adrienne Rich's poem, "The Burning of Paper Instead of Children," hooks (1994) referred to the "oppressor's language":

> Standard English is not the speech of exile. It is the language of conquest and domination; in the United States, it is the mask which hides the loss of many tongues, all those sounds of diverse, native communities we will never hear, the speech of the Gullah, Yiddish, and so many other unremembered tongues. Reflecting on Adrienne Rich's words, I know that it is not the English language that hurts me, but what the oppressors do with it, how they shape it to become a territory that limits and defines, how they make it a weapon that can shame. humiliate, colonize. (p. 168)

Inherent in cultural border crossings is the double bind that comes from having to use a language that is not one's own but, at certain times, it must be used. The double bind is illustrated by hooks' use of the line from Rich's poem: "This is the oppressor's language yet I need it to talk to you" (hooks, 1994, p. 168). However, as the studies discussed in this chapter demonstrate, there are times when Black women choose not to use the "oppressor's language" and resist by using a native way of speaking that historically has been devalued and marginalized.

Studies where we attempt to identify not only changes in talk and language use or style, but more importantly the implications of such switches, will help us understand what life is like in the borderlands and how the (often) competing and conflicting voices are used in everyday living. As O'Connor (1991) noted in her discussion of subject, women, and voice: "The more voices that are ferreted out, the more discourses that a woman can find herself an intersection of, the freer she is from one dominating voice, from one stereotypical and sexist position" (p. 202).

Approaching Everyday Talk

How to ferret out the voices is the challenge for scholars who want to bring Black women's communicative lives into the study of human communication. As I argued in this chapter, one context for inquiry would be the talk that takes place in the everyday lives of the women, but just as important as the focus of inquiry is the scholar's approach to it. As noted previously in this chapter and in others in this volume, an approach grounded in an Afrocentric feminist theory could provide the knowledge needed to bring Black women's communication into the larger body of literature.

To ask women to talk about their language use across cultural borders requires a respect for and sensitivity to the implications of the process and the tensions that result from choosing to talk in one way versus another. Asking for reflections on self and one's place in multiple worlds requires a sense of trust and rapport on the part of both speaker and listeners in order to provide the caring environment needed for disclosures of such a sensitive nature. This has important implications for Afrocentric feminist communication scholarship.

To demonstrate the ways in which feminist methodology could be incorporated into such inquiry (and provide the more accurate interpretations we in this volume argue for), I briefly describe ways in which I sought to incorporate principles of feminist research into my study of Black women's talk.

Recognizing the sensitive nature of such a project and committed to a methodology that would allow the participants to define and interpret *their* experiences, I designed and conducted this study in accordance with the principles of both naturalistic and feminist methodologies with the objective being the search for meanings and patterns rather than locating evidence to be used for prediction and control (Lather, 1991). A naturalistic methodology (Denzin, 1971; Lincoln & Guba, 1985) incorporates the following principles: reality is multiple, constructed, and holistic; knower and known are interactive; researchers cannot produce generalizations, only time and context-bound working hypotheses; causes and effects are indistinguishable; and research is not value-free but value-bound (Lincoln & Guba, 1985). This naturalistic paradigm provides a way for me as a Black woman to research the language of Black women.

The study also incorporates a feminist method (Klein, 1983; Reinharz, 1983). Through the questions that feminism poses and the absences it locates, feminism argues the centrality of gender in the shaping of our consciousness, skills and institutions as well as in the distribution of power and privilege (Lather, 1991). Feminist research places the social construction of gender at the center of analysis and is often characterized as using already given situations both as the focus of investigation and as a means of collecting data (Fonow & Cook, 1991). My reasons for selecting a study of Black women's talk about their language use in cultural border crossings is consistent with Fonow and Cook's (1991) explanation of why opportunistic situations are often chosen: "Once a researcher finds herself in a particular situation and recognizes the research potential in her surroundings, she may decide to make a study of it" (p. 12).

In this study, a particular challenge as a communication scholar was to find a way to study what I saw myself doing with my own language of everyday talk. My challenge as a feminist was to find a way to allow other Black women to be a part of the knowledge production process of this study. I wanted more than just my words to be used in the generation of this knowledge. To this end, the study included a feminist approach to the interviewing process utilizing semi-structured, open-ended interviews favored by feminist ethicist Janice Raymond who noted that it "maximizes discovery and description" (Raymond, 1979). Open-ended interview research allows for the exploration of people's views of reality and offers researchers "access to people's ideas, thoughts, and memories in their own words rather than in the words of the researcher" (Reinharz, 1983, p. 19).

As noted by Graham (1984): "[T]he use of semi structured interviews has become the principal means by which feminists have sought to achieve active involvement of the respondents in the construction of data about their lives" (p. 12). Recognizing the dilemma of the superior-subordinate hierarchy inherent in these interviews, I also took extra efforts to minimize the power dynamics of the interview and foster trust, taking time to explain that one of my goals was to have other Black women's words be a part of this study and that I wanted them to ask me questions and/or make comments about the study. During interviews as I talked about my study and what I hoped to accomplish, I described myself as more of a listener interested in learning from and with the young women rather than as a researcher studying them. During the actual interviews and conversations, I shared my own stories of language use and experiences at the university and about being Black and female in general. This type of researcher self-disclosure encourages "a true dialogue rather than an interrogation" (Bristow & Esper, 1988) and was consistent with my goal of establishing a nonhierarchical relationship (Oakley, 1981) during the interview process.

Employing these aspects of feminist research allowed me to more accurately investigate and interpret the ways in which an identity as Black and female is negotiated in everyday talk. Although increasing knowledge of Black women's communication was a goal of my study, ensuring the accuracy of that knowledge was a primary objective in order to increase the understanding of Black women as a distinct speech community—a designation that has been overlooked and understudied.

CONCLUSION

In this chapter, I attempted to demonstrate a connection of language and identity with a specific focus on how roles as both Black and woman influence the language of everyday talk. Because of the paucity of research in the area of Black women's communication, multiple sites are ripe for study. However, as I argued here, everyday talk could prove to be an especially important area of inquiry because it is in the everyday world of Black women that the larger issues of race and gender are confronted. The findings of studies of conducted by Houston, Nelson, Foster, and myself suggest that it is through language that we mark our identity and solidarity as Black women in the course of everyday living. As our findings demonstrate, the talk we choose to engage in during that process of crossing cultural borders is how we mark membership with or distance ourselves from others in those various cultural worlds.

Another goal of this chapter is to illustrate how an Afrocentric feminist approach to the study of the language of everyday talk provides further understanding of the negotiation of an identity as Black woman while living at the intersection of larger social issues. Before concluding, I reemphasize the importance of this approach by noting that the conception of Black women's talk as a site of inquiry must include some attention to these larger issues if communication scholars want to make contributions that are no longer bound by historical stereotypes and inaccurate representations of Black women.

As communication scholars committed to bringing Black women's experiences into the literature, we are in the unique position to redefine what it means for a Black woman to live, move, and have her communicative being in this world and the various worlds in which she finds herself. Inherent in each of those worlds is the language of everyday talk that can provide a starting point to understanding how everyday talk helps negotiate various identities in those various worlds. Without attention to the influence of race and gender as frameworks much of the research on Black women has resulted in depictions as objectified other or as Harris (1982) stated:

Called Matriarch, Emasculator, and Hot Mama. Sometimes Sister, Pretty Baby, Auntie, Mammy and Girl. Called Unwed Mother, Welfare recipient and InnerCity consumer. The Black American woman as had to admit that while nobody saw the trouble she saw, everybody, his brother and his dog, felt qualified to explain her, even to herself. (p. 4)

With the knowledge produced through Afrocentric feminist scholarship, communication scholars can begin to close a glaring knowledge gap and begin the task of making visible the communicative worlds of Black women. More importantly we can not only put Black women into the literature but replace what is already there with more accurate representations

REFERENCES

Anzuldua, G. (1987). *Borderlands/La Frontera: The new mestiza.* San Francisco: Aunt Lute Books.

Anzuldua, G. (Ed.). (1990). *Making face, making soul, haciendo caras: Creative and critical perspectives by women of color.* San Francisco: Aunt Lute Books.

Beale, F. (1970). Double jeopardy: To be Black and female. In T. Cade (Ed.), *The black woman: An anthology* (pp. 90-100). New York: Signet.

Bristow, A. R., & Esper, J. (1988). A feminist research ethos. In The Nebraska Sociological Feminist Collective (Ed.), *A feminist ethic for social science research.* Lewiston, NY: The Edwin Mellen Press.

Cannon, K. G. (1985). The emergence of a Black feminist consciousness. In L. M. Russell (Ed.), *Feminist interpretations of the Bible* (pp. 30-40). Philadelphia: Westminister Press.

Carter, K., & Spitzack, C. (Eds.). (1989) *Doing research on women's communication.* Norwood, NJ: Ablex.

Chen, V. (1994). (De)hyphenated identity: The double voice in The Woman Warrior. In A. Gonzales, M. Houston, & V. Chen (Eds.), *Our voices: Essays in culture, ethnicity and communication* (pp. 3-11). Los Angeles: Roxbury Press.

Christian, B. (1990). The race for theory. In G. Anzuldua (Ed.), *Making face, making soul, hacienda caras: Creative and critical perspectives by women of color* (pp. 335-345). San Francisco: Aunt Lute Books.

Collins, P. H. (1989). *Black feminist thought: Knowledge, consciousness and the politics of empowerment.* New York: Routledge.

Combahee River Collective. (1983). A Black feminist statement. In C. Moraga & G. Anzuldua (Eds.), *This bridge called my back: Writings by radical women of color.* New York: Kitchen Table Women of Color Press.

Denzin, N. K. (1971). The logic of naturalistic inquiry. *Social Forces, 50,* 166-182.

Dill, B. T. (1987). Race, class and gender: Prospects for an all-inclusive sisterhood. In M. J. Deegan & M. Hill (Eds.), *Women and symbolic interaction* (pp. 95-110). Boston: Allen & Unwin Inc.

DuBois, W. E. B. (1918). *The souls of black folk: Essays and sketches.* Chicago: A. C. McClurg.

Fonow, M. M., & Cook, J. A. (1991). Back to the future: A look at the second wave of feminist epistemology and methodology. In M. M. Fonow & J. Cook (Eds.), *Beyond methodology: Feminist scholarship as lived research* (pp. 1-15). Bloomington: Indiana University Press.

Foster, M. (1995). "Are you with me?" Power and solidarity in the discourse of African American women. In K. Hall & M. Bucholz (Eds.), *Gender articulated: Language and the socially constructed self* (pp. 330-350). New York: Routledge.

Ganguly, K. (1992). Accounting for others: Feminism and representation. In L. Rakow (Ed.), *Women making meaning: New feminist directions in communication* (pp. 60-79). New York: Routledge.

Garner, T. (1983). Playing the dozens: Folklore as strategies for living. *Quarterly Journal of Speech, 69,* 47-57.

Garner, T. E., & Rubin, D. L. (1986). Middle class blacks perceptions of dialect and style shifting: The case of southern attorneys. *Journal of Language and Social Psychology, 113,* 217-229.

Giles, H., Bourhis, R. Y., & Taylor, D. (1977). Towards a theory of language in ethnic group relations. In H. Giles & R. St. Clair (Eds.), *Language, ethnicity and intergroup relations* (pp. 307-348). London: Academic Press.

Goffman, E. (1981). *Forms of talk.* Philadelphia: University of Pennsylvania Press.

Graham, H. (1984). Surveying through stories. In C. Bell & H. Roberts (Eds.), *Social researching: Politics, problems, practice* (pp. 42-64). London: Routledge & Kegan Paul.

Gumperz, J. J. (1982). *Discourse strategies.* Cambridge: Cambridge University Press.

Harris, T. (1982). *From mammies to militants: Domestics in black American literature.* Philadelphia: Temple University Press.

Hecht, M. L., Collier, M. J., & Ribeau, A. (1994). *African American communication: Ethnic identity and cultural interpretation.* Newbury Park, CA: Sage.

Heritage, J. (1984). *Garfinkel and ethnomethodology.* Cambridge: Polity.

hooks, b. (1981). *Ain't I a woman: Black women and feminism.* Boston: South End Press.

hooks, b. (1989). *Talking back: Thinking feminist, thinking black.* Boston: South End Press.

hooks, b. (1994). *Teaching to transgress: Education as the practice of freedom.* New York: Routledge.

Houston, M. (1983). *Codeswitching in black women's speech.* Unpublished doctoral dissertation, University of Massachusetts, Amherst.

Houston, M. (1985). Language and Black women's place. In P. A. Treicheler, C. Kramarae, & B. Stafford (Eds.), *For Alma Mater: Theory and practice in feminist scholarship.* Urbana: University of Illinois Press.

Houston, M. (1992). The politics of difference: Race, class and women's communication. In L. Rakow (Ed.) *Women making meaning: New feminist directions in communication* (pp. 45-59). New York: Routledge.

Klein, R. D. (1983). How to do what we want to do: Thoughts about feminist methodology. In. G. Bowles & R. D. Klein (Eds.), *Theories of women's studies* (pp. 88-104) London: Routledge & Kegan Paul.

Kochman, T. (1981). *Black and white: Styles in conflict.* Chicago: University of Chicago Press.

Lather, P. (1991). *Getting smart: Feminist research and pedagogy with / in the postmodern.* New York: Routledge.

Lincoln, Y., & Guba, E. (1985). *Naturalistic inquiry.* Beverly Hills, CA: Sage.

Moraga, C., & Anzuldua, G. (Eds.). (1983). *This bridge called my back: Writings by radical women of color.* New York: Kitchen Table Women of Color Press .

Nelson, L. W. (1990). Codeswitching in the oral life narratives of African American women: Challenges to linguistic hegemony. *Journal of Education, 173*(3), 142-155.

Oakley, A. (1981). Interviewing women: A contradiction in terms. In J. Roberts (Ed.), *Doing feminist research* (pp. 30-61). London: Routledge & Kegan Paul.

O'Connor, M. (1991). Subject, voice and women in some contemporary black American women's writing. In D. M. Bauer & S. J. McKinstry (Eds.), *Feminism, Bakhtin and the dialogic* (pp. 199-217). Albany: State University of New York Press.

Phillipsen, G. (1975). Speaking "like a man" in Teamsterville: Culture patterns of role enactments in an urban neighborhood. *Quarterly Journal of Speech, 61,* 13-22.

Rakow, L. (Ed.). (1992). *Women making meaning: New feminist directions in communication.* New York: Routledge.

Raymond, J. (1979). *The transsexual empire: The making of the she-male*. Boston: Boston University Press.

Reinharz, S. (1983). Experiential analysis: A contribution to feminist research. In G. Bowles & R. D. Klein (Eds.), *Theories of women's studies* (pp. 27-49). London: Routledge.

Romaine, S. (1994). *Language in society: An introduction to sociolinguistics*. New York: Oxford University Press.

Scott, K. D. (1995). *"When I'm with my girls": Identity and ideology in black women's talk about language and cultural borders*. Unpublished doctoral dissertation, University of Illinois at Urbana-Champaign.

Scott, K.D. (2000). Crossing cultural borders: "Girl" and "look" as markers of identity in black women's language use. *Discourse and Society, 11*(2), 237-248.

Smitherman, G. (1977). *Talkin and testifyin': The language of black America*. Boston: Houghton-Mifflin.

Smitherman, G. (1994). *Black talk: Words and phrases from the hood to the Amen corner*. New York: Houghton-Mifflin.

Smitherman, G., & Cunningham, S. (1997). Moving beyond resistance: Ebonics and African American youth. *Journal of Black Studies, 23*(3).

Stanback, M., & Pearce, W. B. (1981). Talking to "the man": Some communication strategies used by subordinates and their implications for intergroup relations. *Quarterly Journal of Speech, 67*, 21-30.

Williams, R. L. (1997). The Ebonics controversy. *Journal of Black Studies, 23*(3).

Zook, K. B. (1990). Light skinned-ded naps. In G. Anzuldua (Ed.), *Making face, making soul, haciendo caras: Creative and critical perspectives by women of color* (pp. 85-96). San Francisco: Aunt Lute Books.

PART II

CASE STUDIES

FOUR

Triumph Stories: Caring and Accountability in African American Women's Conversation Narratives

Marsha Houston
University of Alabama

In *Black Feminist Thought,* Collins (1990) proposed four dimensions of an alternative Afrocentric feminist epistemology: concrete experience as a criterion of meaning, use of dialogue in assessing knowledge claims, an ethic of caring, and an ethic of personal accountability. Each of these, she suggested, is apparent in the everyday talk of ordinary African American women and is continually reproduced and reinforced by African American women writers and orators (see Davis, chap. 2; Orbe, Drummond, and Canara, chap. 6, this volume). Expressions of the two ethical dimensions of this alternative epistemology in conversations among African American women are the subject of this chapter.

The metaphor, "talking from the heart" captures the ethic of caring, which validates personal expressiveness, emotions, and empathy in the expression and assessment of knowledge claims (Collins, 1990). Recognizing that "every idea has an owner and that the owner's identity matters" is central to the ethic of personal accountability (Collins, 1990, p. 218). Collins conceived the two ethical dimensions as a convergence of African American and feminist epistemologies; she sees ethical motives and discourse styles found in Black women's slave narratives and blues music as strikingly similar to alternative forms of women's moral development and "connected knowing" described in the work of Gilligan (1982) and Belenky, Clinchy, Goldberger, and Tarule (1986).

Call-and-response discourse in traditional African American church services is an expression of the ethic of caring. Relying on Smitherman's (1977) analysis of this speech event, Collins noted that congregants' "Amens" and other supportive utterances validate the minister's message point by point as it is presented; the dynamic, rhythmic style of call-and-response makes "it nearly impossible to filter out the linguistic-cognitive abstract meaning from the sociocultural psychoemotive meaning" (p. 216). Expressions of the ethic of personal accountability seem at once more pervasive and more difficult to illustrate. Drawing from Kochman's (1981) analysis of working-class Black speaking styles, Collins suggested that Black women expect speakers to advocate rather than merely present issues by expressing their "personal positions" and assuming "full responsibility for arguing their validity" (p. 218). This ethical motive becomes apparent whenever one questions whether there is a disconnect between a speaker's "core beliefs" and her (or his) actions and opinions.

Collins conceived the two ethical dimensions as unproblematically connected:

> Neither emotion nor ethics is subordinated to reason. Instead, emotion, ethics, and reason are used as interconnected, essential components in assessing knowledge claims. In an Afrocentric feminist epistemology, values lie at the heart of the knowledge validation process such that inquiry always has an ethical aim. (p. 219)

I suggest a somewhat more complicated relation between caring and accountability in a particular genre of conversation among African American women. As they share stories of triumph over personal difficulties, African American women negotiate a tension between caring and accountability. The two dimensions are expressed through different language features and serve different communicative functions for narrators and listeners.

MAKING BLACK FEMINIST SENSE OF BLACK WOMEN'S
CONVERSATIONS

Crawford (1995) reminded us that, "Like music, talk is a set of skills and a performing art. It's rich and subtle nuances are open to many interpretations. It unfolds in 'real time,' and written representations can capture only a small part of its meaning" (p. xi). Thus, whenever we analyze talk, we have to remember its plurivocal nature: Conversations mean many different things at once because, as human communicators, we are always doing many things simultaneously as we engage in interpersonal encounters. The conversation analyst's focus depends on his or her theoretical lens. Issues of focus and selection are particularly slippery when studying gender:

> Analysis is never done without preconceptions; we can never be absolutely non-selective in our observations, and where the object of observations and analysis has to do with gender it is extraordinarily difficult to subdue certain expectations. . . . [T]he behavior of men and women, whatever its substance may happen to be in any specific instance, is invariably read through a more general discourse on gender difference itself. (Cameron, 1997, p. 48)

Similarly, the behavior of African American women and men invariably is read through discourses that inextricably link gender *and* race in constructing our "difference" (hooks, 1989).

Feminist and other postmodernist theorists (e.g., Butler, 1990; Hall, 1996; Minh-ha, 1989) have influenced scholarly discourse on gender and race by revealing the central role of language and communication in constructing social categories. As a result, gender and communication scholars have turned their attention from cataloguing discrete differences between the features of men's and women's talk to analyses of the situated performance of gender identity (Cameron, 1998; West, Lazar, & Kramarae, 1997). Studies of "performing gender" or "doing identity work" (for examples see Johnson & Meinhof, 1997; Wodak, 1997) demonstrate the extent to which gender identity is fluid, variable, and contingent as well as the ways in which long-entrenched definitions of social groups and the power relationships among them are either resisted or reasserted in daily interactions (Gal, 1994). As Cameron (1997) noted, a performative focus also "obliges us to attend to the 'rigid regulatory frame' within which people must make their choices—the norms that define what kinds of language are possible, intelligible and appropriate resources for performing masculinity and femininity" (p. 49) within particular social and cultural groups.

In this discussion, I inquire into how African American women perform and negotiate gender as they share stories about troubles and triumphs during conversations with other African American women friends and acquaintances. All conversations are spaces where speakers jointly create and negotiate interpretation, identity, ideology, emotion, and other culturally meaningful realities (Jacoby & Ochs, 1995). Because the dominant discourse in the United States devalues African American women in both subtle and overt ways, we often experience conversations outside our own gender and cultural group as hostile spaces where our standpoints and identities are silenced, demeaned, or erased (Essed, 1991; St. Jean & Feagin, 1998). Talk among Black women friends provides "safe spaces" where, "through serious conversations and humor, . . . as sisters and friends [we] affirm one another's humanity, specialness, and right to exist" (Collins, 1990, p. 97). Sharing personal experience stories is one way in which speakers accomplish these conversational goals. In her analysis of everyday talk among African Americans, Smitherman (1977) pointed out that our propensity to "render [our] general, abstract observations about life, love, [and] people, in the form of a concrete narrative" has led to a common saying within black communities, "[black folks] always got a story" (p. 147). Smitherman defined the form of narrative she called "testifying" as Black people's "lifelike" retelling of personal experiences during everyday conversations; testifying is not "plain and simple commentary but a *dramatic* narration and a *communal reenactment* of one's *feelings* and experiences . . . [through which] one's humanity is reaffirmed by the group and his or her sense of isolation diminished" (p. 150, italics added). Her point, that the outcome of sharing personal stories is a deeper connection to the conversational group and the larger community, is reinforced by Johnstone's (1993) argument that people tell stories about their everyday lives during ordinary conversations "not simply to perpetuate social reality, but to create and manipulate it" (p. 69); women's stories, especially, are "statements about the world-creating power of discourse" (p. 76). Thus, sharing stories within the "safe space" of conversations with one another is one way that African American women express the ethic of caring. In our in-group conversations we use narratives to collaboratively create and manipulate affirming visions of self and community.

In a study of a radio discussion involving African American women and African American and White men, Bucholtz (1996) found Black feminist epistemology useful in understanding the women's expectations for talk and explaining their interaction patterns. Other studies of African American women's talk (e.g., Foster, 1989; Morgan, 1991; Scott, chap. 3, this volume) also support Collins' dimensions of a

Black feminist epistemology. Because Collins grounded her epistemic model in "historically rooted patterns of experience rather than essentialized social categories" (Buchlotz, 1996, p. 273), it reflects the reciprocity between social reality and recurrent communication practices. In addition, like all African American feminist theory, Collins' model accords African American women a voice of authority on our communication that is absent from most other theoretical frameworks (see Introduction and Allen, chap. 1, this volume).

The two narratives discussed in this chapter (see full texts in the appendices) are taken from a corpus of five conversations among African American women friends and acquaintances that were audiotaped by me or my students between 1981 and 1990.[1] Totaling 5 hours and 45 minutes of talk, and including 24 participants, this corpus contains many stories that are similar in theme and structure to those examined here. Narratives that I call "triumph stories" have as their central theme overcoming a personal difficulty. They are "how I got ovah"[2] stories, always told in the past tense about minor obstacles surpassed or major adversities defeated. Both "The Overall Man," shared during a conversation among women at a senior citizens center, and "If you can't deal with that, . . ." shared during a conversation among married professional women in their 30s, concern unsuccessful first marriages. More important than the topic of the stories is the way in which they are structured and woven into the conversation. Triumph stories are co-created by the interaction of the conversational group in ways that not only validate the speaker's interpretation of her experience but affirm a worldview shared by her conversation partners.

CARING TALK

Collins argued that caring inheres in both the "expression and assessment" of discourse, that is, in the behavior of both speakers (narrators) and listeners. Triumph stories are, by definition, a form

---

[1]Conversations were arranged among groups of four to six African American women friends who gathered in familiar, informal settings to talk about the general topic, "Growing Up and Surviving as a Black Woman in the U.S." They are part of a larger corpus that includes cross-race and cross-gender conversations among mostly middle-class women and men ranging in age from college students to retirees. For another example of analysis related to these data, see Houston Stanback (1985).

[2]Gloss: "how I got over." Smitherman (1994) defined the African American English phrase "git ovah" as "to overcome any obstacle on the way to your goal" (p. 124).

of discourse in which narrators express a high degree of emotional involvement. The narrators of the stories discussed here indicated both their emotional involvement in their stories and their construction of the conversations as "safe spaces" by using their most casual, relaxed, in-group speaking styles, primarily indicated by their incorporation of features of African American English (AAE; Baugh, 1983; Smitherman, 1977). The two narrators came from different socioeconomic and geographic backgrounds and were at different points in their personal and working lives. Dot[3] grew up in working-class circumstances in the South, and at the time of her narrative was retired from a long career, first in domestic service then in social services; Eve, who grew up relatively middle class in the northeast, was in the midst of a career in public service. Throughout her series of conversations, Dot uses more AAE than does Eve, for whom AAE is more an emblem, expressed through intonation and a few lexical items, than a primary linguistic code. Both women tend to use AAE language or style at points when emotion is highest. For example, Dot uses multiple negation to emphasize her determination to have a life different from her mother's: "I said, 'I **ain't gon' NEVER** get married to a man gon' do hard labor!'" (lines 21-22; features under discussion are printed in boldface type).[4] Because all participants readily switched language styles, AAE was not stigmatized and did not present a problem of intelligibility or create a barrier to interaction (see Scott, chap. 3, this volume). A brief backchannel exchange between Gloria and Jo in lines 9-10 of "The Overall Man" indicates the shifting language styles used in the conversations:

---

[3]All names are pseudonyms.

[4]Transcription Conventions:

. . .	Ellipsis indicates talk omitted.
[]	Brackets indicate the beginning and end of overlapping talk.
=	Latching: indicates that the talk on two different lines follows immediately without even a momentary pause.
he	Underlining indicates emphasis.
HE	Words or syllables in capital letters indicate extreme emphasis.
: :	Colons indicate elongated syllables. The number of colons roughly corresponds to the extent of the elongation.
—	A dash indicates a sudden breaking off of speech.
(( ))	Double parentheses indicate transcriber comments.
? . !	Punctuation indicates pitch changes; question marks signify rising intonation.
Gon'	Modified spelling is used to suggest pronunciation variants.

Gloria: I didn't never want no kids! (Uses multiple negation, an AAE feature)

Jo: I didn't want any either. (Uses only Standard American English)

In addition to their casual language style, the narrators used contrasting discourse strategies to indicate the depth of their feelings about the experiences they recounted. Dot makes it explicit that her story ("The Overall Man") is "the truth, from my heart" (line 6), perhaps because she realizes that the childhood fantasy with which she introduces the narrative sounds frivolous:

When I was growing up I always imagined that I was gonna get married to a tall, handsome guy. And the sucker wasn't gon' NEVER wear no overalls, and he wasn't gon' never be dirty. (lines 2-4)

In addition, because Dot's presentational style is intentionally humorous (e.g., referring to her ideal husband as "the sucker"), avowing the heartfelt truth of her narrative alerts her listeners to its serious themes (Crawford, 1995). In telling "If you can't deal with that" Eve uses emphatic, categorical statements to underscore the determination and resolution she feels about creating an egalitarian marriage:

There are a lotta things that um, I feel like doing and I just do 'em because it's what I wanta do. (line 11)
I'm not gonna change! (line 14)
I can't deal with that right now . . . (lines 26-27)

Thus, the narrators expressed the ethic of caring through both language code and style and discursive indicators of emotional involvement.

Because the participants in each conversation were four African American women friends, it is not surprising that caring is frequently conveyed by the other women in the conversations through expressions of empathy and support as the narrators tell their stories. Co-participants encourage the narrator to continue speaking and validate her point of view through frequent supportive minimal responses ("Umhmm," "Yeah," "Right" as in Examples A and C), semantic repetition[5] (Example A), and sentence completions (Examples B and C):

---

[5]Coates (1996) defined semantic repetition in women's conversations as utterances that preserve another speaker's meaning but vary the words. "In other words, repetition is total at the semantic level but not absolute at the lexical level" (p. 214).

A

Dot: And, uh, I wanted to go to college. I wanted to be just like my father; I wanted to be very, very educated, so I could tell people what to do, and be able to relate, and tell things, get up in-in Sunday School and Conference and, you know, be "Miss Big," you know?
Lil: **Yeah.**
Gloria: **"Miss Chairperson"** ((Laughs lightly))

B

Dot: . . . I said, "I ain't gon' NEVER get married to a man gon' do hard labor. Unh-uh! This guy gon' have a office job, an' he gon' wear a collar an' tie everyday. The FIRST thing I got married to-
Lil: **Was a overall man!**

C

Eve: . . . my whole life shouldn't revolve around my son and [this house and then to have another job too.]
Jean: **[The house, umhmm. Ri::ight!]**

Coates (1996) identified each of these features as indicators of how "in tune" friends are with each other during conversation, and as key to the "collaborative floor" that characterizes conversations among women friends (see also Edelsky, 1981): "the collaborative floor is a shared space, and therefore what is said is construed as being the voice of the group rather than that of the individual" (p. 135). As a result of these discourse features, both stories are the collaborative creations of narrators and their conversation partners.

Yet co-participants seem to assess the content of the two narratives slightly differently. Eve's conversation partners express deeper agreement and identification with her story, as indicated by the frequency, style, and content of their responses. A minimal response occurs an average of every two lines during Eve's narrative as compared to every four lines during Dot's narrative.[6] Eve's conversation partners offer mostly supportive comments, what Hewitt (1997) called "linguistic hugging" (p. 29). In contrast, Dot's conversation partners make "listening noises," encouraging her to complete her story, but not necessarily agreeing or identifying with its content. In their brief backchannel exchange, quoted earlier, Gloria and Jo go so far as to challenge Dot's childhood fantasy about motherhood by disclosing their own childhood desires *not* to become mothers (lines 7-10).

Despite these differences in agreement and identification, I argue that each set of conversationalists equally expressed the ethic of caring. Co-participants' encouraging responses to the narrators indicated that they assessed both stories as coming "from the heart." The responses to Dot's narrative indicate as well that the ethic of caring is not always concerned with agreeing or identifying with narrative content, but with validating the storyteller's interpretation of her experience. Because their conversations are safe spaces, women friends feel free to challenge one another and even to express alternative constructions of womanhood. Disagreements expressed in the context of a collaborative floor allow speakers to simultaneously challenge and support one another (Coates, 1996).

TALKING PERSONAL ACCOUNTABILITY

Both Dot and Eve express personal accountability by emphasizing their agency in improving their lives. Although one might reasonably suspect that they consulted and relied on a network of family and friends for support and advice, much like that offered by the women in their conversation group, in telling their stories they represent themselves as autonomous actors. For example, neither woman blames her ex-husband for the failure of her marriage; these are not "male-bashing" stories. Instead, each woman holds herself accountable for choosing a relationship that was not right for her.

The two narratives are organized similarly in that each contrasts an undesirable situation in the past with the more desirable circumstances of the present. In constructing this contrast, the narrators also construct contrasting images of themselves. Dot contrasts the life she desired, both as a naive girl and later as a young wife, with the life she was born to as a member of a working class African American family in Florida in the 1920s:

---

[6]"If you can't deal with that . . ." has 34 lines of which 14 are minimal responses; "The Overall Man" has 30 lines of which 8 are minimal responses.

Dot: Yeah. An' I used to tell my mother, when I was washin'
and ironin'-ah-them dirty clothes of my father's, and then my
mother used to take in-ah-washin' and ironin'--she worked
nights, but then she did all them crackers' clothes, them ol'
railroad overalls and all that, you-you'd have to get out there
and soak 'em in kerosene. I said, 'I ain't gon' NEVER get
married to a man gon' do hard labor!' (lines 13-22)

Dot's mother worked three jobs—paid employment outside her home
at night, doing laundry for White laborers ("them crackers'[7] clothes"),
and caring for her own family during the day. Dot had not simply
witnessed her mother's "triple shift," she had played the role of
"mother's helper," as is often required of working-class girls, and
knew firsthand the drudgery of doing the family laundry in the days
before automatic washing machines. She uses the dirty overalls worn
by laborers employed by the railroads as a metaphor for the life of
unrewarding labor that she shared with her mother and rejected for
herself as a young wife.

In "If you can't deal with that, . . ." Eve contrasts her choice
to conform to dominant social expectations for marriage and family
life during her first marriage with her choice to defy those
expectations in her second. As a young woman of 18 in her first
marriage, she was employed outside the home, but was also "the
perfect housewife" (line 1), centering her life on taking care of her
house and her son. But she did not find happiness in the roles of
housewife and mother. She sees herself as having chosen a lifestyle
that was wrong for her because of her youth and inexperience: "I
hadn't lived long enough and experienced enough not being married
to know that . . . my whole life shouldn't revolve around my son and
[the] house . . ." (lines 5-7). In Eve's story, the marital home, "the
house," signifies a space of restriction and confinement. Jean's
supportive comment in line 19 accurately summarizes Eve's
evaluation of "the house" as a suffocating space:

Eve: Now with Arthur, I make sure that everything's taken
care of there, but I can't sit in that house.
Jean: **Yeah, oh, I'd die!** (lines 17-19; emphasis mine)

---

[7]Gloss: African Americans in the South often refer to poor Whites using the
derogatory label "crackers."

To "sit in [the] house," to be restricted to family obligations, is for Eve, and the other women in the conversation who validate her vision, a sort of psychological death. It is important to note that Eve, like most African American women, was employed outside the home in her first marriage, so her unhappiness was not the result of the "bored housewife syndrome." It was not merely the "opportunity" to work that Eve desired, but a balance between obligations to work and family and her personal interests and pleasures.

Both narrators construct themselves as proactive in changing the undesirable situations of their pasts. Dot describes her childhood dream as "shattered" and herself as stagnated by her marriage to a man who "worked on the railroad." Reflecting on that period in her life, she refers to herself in the second person (as "you"), suggesting the psychological distance between that young wife and the woman she is at the time she tells her story:

> my dream was all shattered right then, you know. An' **you** had to come in and wash them overalls, iron the bib and crease and all that. Right back where I started from. (lines 27-29)

Dot represents herself as making a conscious decision to "get up from that marriage and leave it" (line 29). She need only allude to happier circumstances after ending the marriage, because her conversation partners know of the life she has had with her second husband.

In contrast, Eve spends a longer time detailing the differences between her first marriage and her present, more egalitarian and satisfying marriage, justifying what she perceives as her current violations of dominant marital norms:

> and you know people are always constantly worried about how other people see them or how other people perceive them, but you know I can't deal with that right now because that maybe isn't necessarily what's makin' me happy. (lines 25-27)

Eve is defiant in her resolve to conduct her marriage in a way that is best for her, rather than according to how "people" think she should. Using "you" to refer to the arbiters of community standards, she asserts, " . . . if **you** can't deal with that well . . . I'm sorry 'cause I'm not gonna change" (lines 14-15). Her apparent apology ("I'm sorry," line 14) belies her satisfaction with her current marital situation and her resolve to sustain it.

Although her determination to pursue an alternative marital style is obvious, Eve expresses that determination in hedge-marked language. For example, in lines 10-33, she uses "you know" seven times along with a variety of other hedge-words: "I think," "I feel," "like," "maybe," "necessarily," and "might." Lines 26-27 are a clear example of the extent to which Eve hedges in advocating her position:

> but **you know** I can't deal with that right now because that **maybe** isn't **necessarily** what's makin' me happy.

Eve's hedging should not be interpreted as a sign of uncertainty about her relational choices. Viewed in the context of the content of her narrative, it is clearly a strategy for maintaining the collaborative floor of the conversation. Hedges are among the strategies women use to accomplish such interpersonal goals of informal talk as "avoiding playing the expert," that is, opening a space for others to challenge or disagree with their viewpoint. As Coates (1996) pointed out:

> Talk is never just the exchange of bits of information. Talk always involves . . . interpersonal interaction. Hedges are a key means to . . . take account of the complex needs of speakers as social beings. . . . [They] are a resource for doing friendship. (p. 172)

Eve's conversation partners, married, professional women and mothers like herself, validate her vision of an egalitarian marriage, offering minimal responses to support her every claim in a manner resembling call-and-response in the traditional African American church:

> Eve: And I think that, you know, I've grown over the years and I feel a lot differently about myself and there are a lotta things that um, I feel like doing and I just do 'em because it's what I wanta do.
> Jean: **Yes.**
> Gail: **That's right!**
> . . . .
> Eve: —and I feel that because I have a full-time job outside the home, there're lots of things that he should not expect from me. Like if I don't feel like cooking . . .
> Jean: **Oh yeah, you know, hey!**
> . . . .
> Eve: And I might not even wake up tomorrow, [so tough!]
> Rose: [**That's right.**]

Jean: [**That's it,**] and you know-
Gail: [**That's it!**]

Coates (1996) explained that "[t]hrough signaling the active participation of all participants in the conversation, minimal responses play a significant role in the collaborative construction of text and of the maintenance of a collaborative floor" (p. 145). Eve is both passionate about her "core beliefs" regarding marriage, and willing to bear the responsibility for enacting them. Although she perceives herself as defying social norms by not making home and motherhood the center of her life, she is obviously not out of step with other African American women in her situation, at least not with her conversation partners.

As mentioned earlier, sentence completions are another way in which women friends collaboratively create their conversations. Rose demonstrates how "in tune" she is with the argument Eve develops in her narrative by completing her sentence in line 34:

Eve: If you don't like it—
Rose: That's ri- **that's yo' problem!** (lines 33-34)

Rose's sentence completion serves as the final evaluative statement that concludes Eve's story, repeating and summarizing Eve's defiance of dominant norms.

In summary, the ethic of personal accountability is expressed in triumph stories through an emphasis on agency and autonomy in overcoming personal difficulties. Dot and Eve speak as advocates for their personal decisions, representing themselves as situated knowers who have learned from experience how to define and pursue life choices that are right for them as individuals. But they do not tell their stories alone; they collaborate with their conversation partners to produce narratives that validate both their individual experiences and the groups' beliefs that Black women should be accountable for past errors and active in creating and sustaining positive changes in their lives.

"DOING GENDER" IN TRIUMPH STORIES

Because speakers express both emotional investment and individual agency in recounting triumph narratives, this discourse genre illumines interconnections between caring and accountability in

African American women's everyday talk. The supportive responses of listeners demonstrate that triumph stories are more than simply a memory recounted by a single individual; they are a collaborative creation of the conversational group (Coates, 1996; Edelsky, 1981). Thus, as co-participants validate the speaker as a voice of authority on her individual experience, they simultaneously construct a shared vision of African American women as autonomous, active agents who are personally accountable for the quality of their lives.

This vision contradicts the dominant cultural stereotype that African American women routinely and inappropriately view themselves as passive "victims," for example, of (gendered) racism, and that we are not proactive in bettering our own lives. Research on African American women's experience of everyday racism has demonstrated just the opposite. Black women only label actions "racist" after they have exhausted all other possible explanations for another's (usually recurrent) behavior; even then, they see gendered racist actions as obstacles to be overcome rather than rationales for defeatism (Essed, 1991; St. Jean & Feagin, 1998). Similarly, Dot and Eve envisioned failed first marriages as obstacles to their self-defined goals for satisfying, fulfilling lives. In telling their stories, they did not construct their first husbands as villains or themselves as "victims," but emphasized their agency in overcoming undesirable circumstances.

By framing themselves as triumphant, African American women tell strikingly different stories than those told by White women. Research that looks at gender differences in personal narratives told by White women and men has found that "[White] women's stories are more often about experiences that are embarrassing or frightening than about personal skill or success" (Coates, 1996, p. 106). For example, Coates found that the White women friends she studied in Great Britain told stories that reinforced their sense of themselves as "objects, as powerless, as reactors rather than actors" (p. 116). In contrast, as the two examples presented here illustrate, the African American women in my corpus of conversations more often told stories of determination and triumph that presented them as proactive rather than reactive. Finally, in telling their triumph stories, Black women narrators appear less communal than the midwestern White women studied by Johnstone (1993). Johnstone pointed out that narrators in her study emphasized "community over contest:"

> I show that women's personal experience stories in the Indiana city
> I have been studying, do in fact tend to revolve around *joint action
> by communities of people*, whereas men's stories tend to be about
> acting alone . . . . (p. 67, italics added)

Not only were most of the women's stories Johnstone gathered focused on collaborative action, in 7 of the 10 stories the women in her study told about acting alone, "the outcome [was] bad: embarrassment, fright, pain, or failure. In one case, not consulting others is explicitly the reason for the bad outcome." In contrast, the African American women whose stories are in my corpus most often presented themselves as acting alone, and the outcome of their autonomous actions is uniformly good: an improved lifestyle, a more satisfying relationship, higher self-esteem, pleasure, safety, and success.

Does this mean that African American women actually value community less than White women or that the "sisterhood" discussed by Jones and Varner (chap. 7, this volume) and numerous other Black women scholars and writers is a meaningless concept in our everyday lives?[8] Both structural features of the narratives in my corpus, as illustrated by the two analyzed here, and research on African American women's presentation of self argue against this reading of narrators' emphasis on autonomy. The role of co-participants in collaboratively creating the narratives through the variety of caring, supportive strategies discussed earlier, suggests that sisterhood (i.e., supportiveness and community) is expressed through the interaction patterns in Black women's everyday talk, not merely its content.

On the other hand, narrators' emphasis on autonomy in the content of their stories is a reflection of an important dimension of African American women's presentation of self. The women in Hecht, Ribeau, and Alberts' (1989) study of African American communication described this dimension as "talking tough"; they suggested that African American women "have had to be so tough as the head of the household throughout history that they 'tend to talk tough and make fun of white women who are soft'" (p. 402). I prefer the label "talking fortitude" to suggest the high value African American women place on presenting themselves not only as determined and resilient but also as candid and unpretentious. The following are typical of responses to an open-ended questionnaire in which I asked African American women to describe "talking like a Black woman:"

> . . . talking with dignity, experience, and determination.
> . . . speaking with wisdom and confidence as the result of her experiences.
> Not beating around the bush; getting straight to the point.
> Positive, strong, straightforward speech. (Houston, 2000)

[8]I am indebted to Ike Adams for raising this question following my presentation of a paper related to this chapter at the University of Alabama, and thus for my rethinking the tension between autonomy and community for African American women.

One might reasonably argue, based on Johnstone's data, that White women have learned to avoid presenting themselves as autonomous actors because this is not a valued representation of womanhood in Euro-American culture. In fact, the White women in Coates' (1996) study, expressed reluctance and ambivalence toward framing themselves as powerful or strong. In African American culture, on the other hand, with its long history of women's autonomy (Lebsock, 1983) such self-presentations are valued. Thus, among the culturally legitimated communicative resources available to African American women are ways of presenting oneself as autonomous and personally accountable, such as those expressed by Dot and Eve.

We should keep in mind, however, that accounts of behavior are not necessarily isomorphic with actual behavior. Although Black women's emphasis in their narratives on autonomous action informs us about preferred ways of performing womanhood (of discursively presenting oneself as Black and woman) in African American culture, it does not inform us about the extent to which African American women actually seek and receive both material and communicative support during times of trouble; sociological studies of women's networks in African American communities suggest that they routinely do both (e.g., Ladner, 1971; Stack, 1974). One strategy for enacting sisterhood while retaining one's self-definition as autonomous is captured in a kernel of wisdom that a student shared with me from her grandmother: "When you have a hard decision to make, get everybody's opinion, then make up your own mind."

The tension between autonomy and collaboration, individuality and sisterhood, evident in this grandmotherly advice and the narratives discussed in this chapter, suggests that in our everyday lives, African American women often negotiate a complex relationship between caring and accountability. Yet both ethical dimensions are expressed and validated in the triumph stories we tell in our conversations with one another. Collins (1990) suggested that our lived experience of negotiating Blackness and womanhood, identities with different meanings and consequences in the African American and dominant cultures, has resulted in Black women's rejection of binary categories, of what she called "either/or dichotomous thinking." By adopting a "both/and conceptual orientation" African American women reconcile and embrace the many contradictions of our lives, including the tensions between the ethic of caring and the ethic of personal accountability (p. 207).

APPENDIX A: DOT'S STORY

The Overall Man

1 **Dot:** Well lemme tell ya'll about this while it's on my mind, then I'll let somebody else have the

2 floor. I always dreamed when I become an adult . . . when I was growing up I always imagined

3 that I was gonna get married to a tall, handsome guy. And the sucker wasn't gon' never wear no

4 overalls, and he wasn't gon' never be dirty.

5 ((Protracted laughter by the group))

6 **Dot:** This is the truth, from my heart! And I was gon' live in a big white house, and I was gon

7 be able to drive my car and go where I wanted, and pick up my kids from school cause I always

8 wanted me two kids. [And that was my-]

9 **Jo:** ((Softly))[I didn't never want no kids!]

10 **Gloria:** I didn't want any either.

11 **Dot:** And that was gon be my lifestyle.

12 **Lil:** Umhmm.

13 **Dot:** And, uh, I wanted to go to college. I wanted to be just like my father; I wanted to be very,

14 very educated, so I could tell people what to do, and be able to relate, and tell things, get up in-in

15 Sunday School and Conference and you know be "Miss Big," you know?

16 **Lil:** Yeah.

17 **Gloria:** "Miss Chairperson" ((Laughs lightly))

18   **Dot**: Yeah. An' I used to tell my mother, when I was washin' and ironin'-ah-them dirty clothes of
19   my father's, and then my mother used to take in-ah-washin' and ironin'--she worked nights, but
20   then she did all them "crackers" clothes, them ol' railroad overalls and all that, you-you'd have to
21   get out there and soak 'em in kerosene. I said, "I ain't gon' NEVER get married to a man gon' do
22   hard labor. Unh-uh! This guy gon have a office job, an' he gon wear a collar an tie everyday.
23   The FIRST thing I got married to-

24   **Lil**: Was a overall man!

25   **Dot**: Was a overall man, a railroad-((Laughs))

26   ((All laugh heartily))

27   **Dot**: Worked on the railroad. So tha-tha-my dream was all shattered right then, you know? An'
28   you had to come in and wash them overalls, iron the bib and crease and all that. Right back
29   where I started from. That's the reason I said, "Unh-uh," I had to get up from that marriage and
30   leave it. That was too much ha::ard work like I had been used to.

APPENDIX B: EVE'S STORY

If You Can't Deal With That . . .

1   **Eve:** . . . in my first marriage I was like the perfect housewife because I was young. I was

2   eighteen, you know, when I got pregnant–um–you know I took care of my house, and um, I

3   worked, though; my son he went to a day care center when he was a little baby.

4   **Jean:** Umhmm

5   **Eve:** Because of the fact that I was so young I didn't even realize, I hadn't lived long enough

6   and experienced enough not being married to know that um my whole life shouldn't revolve

7   around my son and [this house and then to have another] job too.

8   **Jean:** [The house, umhmm. Ri::ight!]

9   **Rose:** Umhmm!

10 **Eve:** And I think that you know I've grown over the years and I feel a lot differently about

11 myself and there are a lotta things that um I feel like doing and I just do 'em because it's what I

12 wanta do.

13 **Jean:** Yes.

14 **Gail:** That's right!

15 **Eve:** You know if you can't deal with that well–you know, I'm sorry 'cause I'm not gonna

16 change.

17 **Jean:** Yeah.

18 **Eve:** Now with Arthur, I make sure that everything's taken care of there, but I can't sit in that
19 house.
20 **Jean:** Yeah, oh, I'd die!
21 **Eve:** You know. Plus I work too, you know [and I=
22 **Rose:** [Yeah.]
23 **Eve:** = feel that because I have a full-time job outside the home, there're lots of things that he
24 should not expect from me. Like if I don't feel like cooking [he would never say anything to me.]
25 **Jean:** [Oh yeah, you know, hey!]
26 **Eve:** And you know people are always constantly worried about how other people see them or
27 how other people perceive them, but you know I can't deal with that right now because that
28 maybe isn't necessarily what's makin' me happy.
29 **Jean:** Umhmm
30 **Eve:** And I might not even wake up tomorrow, [so tough!]
31 **Rose:** [That's right.]
32 **Jean:** [That's it], and you know-
33 **Gail:** [That's it!]
34 **Eve:** If you don't like it–
35 **Rose:** That's ri–that's yo' problem

REFERENCES

Baugh, J. (1983). *Black street speech*. Austin: University of Texas Press.

Belenky, M. F., Clinchy, B. M., Goldberger, N. R., & Tarule, J. M. (1986). *Women's ways of knowing*. New York: Basic Books.

Bucholtz, M. (1996). Black feminist theory and African American women's linguistic practice. In V.L. Bergvall, J.M. Bing, & A. F. Freed (Eds.), *Rethinking language and gender research: Theory and practice* (pp. 267-290). London: Longman.

Butler, J. (1990). *Gender trouble: Feminism and the subversion of identity*. New York: Routledge.

Cameron, D. (Ed.). (1998). *The feminist critique of language* (2nd ed.). London: Routledge.

Coates, J. (1996). *Women talk*. Oxford, UK: Blackwell.

Collins, P. H. (1990). *Black feminist thought: Knowledge, consciousness, and the politics of empowerment*. New York: Harper Collins.

Crawford, M. (1995). *Talking difference*. London: Sage.

Edelsky, C. (1981). Who's got the floor? *Language in Society, 10*, 383-421.

Essed, P. (1991). *Understanding everyday racism: An interdisciplinary theory*. Newbury Park, CA: Sage.

Foster, M. (1989). It's cookin' now: A performance analysis of the speech events of a black teacher in an urban community college. *Language in Society, 2*(1), 1-29.

Gal, S. (1994). Between speech and silence: The problematics of research on language and gender. In C. Roman, S. Juhasz, & C. Miller (Eds.), *The women and language debate* (pp. 407-431). New Brunswick, NJ: Rutgers University Press.

Gilligan, C. (1982). *In a different voice*. Cambridge, MA: Harvard University Press.

Hall, S. (1996). "Who needs identity?" In S. Hall & P. du Gay (Eds.), *Questions of cultural identity* (pp. 1-17). London: Sage.

Hecht, M., Ribeau, S., & Alberts, J. K. (1989). An Afro-American perspective on interethnic communication. *Communication Monographs, 56*, 385-410.

Hewitt, R. (1997). "Box-out" and "taxing." In U.H. Meinhof & S. Johnson (Eds.), *Language and masculinity* (pp. 27-46). Oxford, UK: Blackwell.

hooks, b. (1989). *Talking back: Thinking feminist, thinking black*. Boston: South End Press.

Houston, M. (2000). Multiple perspectives: African American women conceive their talk. *Women and Language, 23*, 11-17.

Houston Stanback, M. (1985). Language and black woman's place: Evidence from the black middle class. In P. A. Treichler, C. Kramerae, & B. Stafford (Eds.), *For Alma Mater: Theory and practice in feminist scholarship* (pp. 177-193). Urbana: University of Illinois Press.

Jacoby, S., & Ochs, E. (1995). Co-construction: An introduction. *Research on Language and Social Interaction, 28*, 171-183.

Johnstone, B. (1993). Community and contest: Midwestern men and women creating their worlds in conversational storytelling. In D. Tannen (Ed.), *Gender and conversational interaction* (pp. 62-82). New York: Oxford University Press.

Johnson, S., & Meinhof, U. H. (Eds.). (1997). *Language and masculinity*. Oxford: Blackwell.

Kochman, T. (1981). *Black and white: Styles in conflict*. Chicago: University of Chicago Press.

Ladner, J. (1971). *Tomorrow's tomorrow: The black woman*. Garden City, NY: Anchor.

Lebsock, S. (1983). Free black women and the question of matriarchy. In J. L. Newton, M. P. Ryan, & J. R. Walkowitz (Eds.), *Sex and class in women's history* (pp. 146-166). London: Routledge & Kegan Paul.

Minh-ha, T. T. (1989). *Woman, native, other*. Bloomington: Indiana University Press.

Morgan, M. (1991). Indirectness and interpretation in African American women's discourse. *Pragmatics, 1*(4), 421-451.

St. Jean, Y., & Feagin, J.R. (1998). *Double burden: Black women and everyday racism*. Armonk, NY: M.E. Sharpe.

Smitherman, G. (1977). *Talkin' and testifyin': The language of black America*. Boston: Houghton Mifflin.

Smitherman, G. (1994). *Black talk*. Boston: Houghton Mifflin.

Stack, C. (1974). *All our kin: Strategies for survival in a black community*. New York: Harper & Row.

West, C., Lazar, M. M., & Kramarae, C. (1997). Gender in discourse. In T. van Dijk (Ed.), *Discourse as social interaction* (pp. 119-143). London: Sage.

Wodak, R. (Ed.). (1997). *Gender and discourse*. London: Sage.

FIVE

"We Be Strong Women": A Womanist Analysis of Black Women's Sociolinguistic Behavior

Denise Troutman

Michigan State University

Some African American scholars have adopted feminism as the ideological framework for examining Black womanhood, whereas others have collapsed womanism and feminism, with a modicum of variance in the definition and resulting ideology. In this chapter, I argue for a new analysis of Black womanhood through a newly constructed definition and ideological stance of womanism. Such an ideological stance and analysis aims to highlight the teachings and lives of real African American women of various social classes who have passed on womanism through specific rites of passage. Womanism, from the present perspective, is one vehicle with which African American women can acknowledge, give back, and revere that which we have received from the Mama Lloyds, the Big Mommas, the aunties, and the sistuhs. I examine the language usage of five African American women, in particular, locating the linguistic analysis within a womanist perspective, one element of which is the replacement of "denigrated images of Black womanhood with self-defined images" (Collins, 1990, p. 23). One central question addressed is how African American women identify and construct their social and linguistic selves.

WOMANISM AS IDEOLOGY

Alice Walker is most often credited as implementing the term and ideology of *womanism*. In her book, *In Search of Our Mothers' Gardens*, Walker (1983) identified the contents as "womanist" prose. She provided an explicit definition of womanist, breaking the term down into four sections. According to Walker, a *womanist* is:

1. From womanish. (opp. of 'girlish,' i.e. frivolous, irresponsible, not serious.) A Black feminist or feminist of color. From the Black folk expression of mothers to female children, 'You acting womanish,' i.e., like a woman. Usually referring to outrageous, audacious, courageous or willful behavior. Wanting to know more and in greater depth than is considered 'good' for one. Interested in grown-up doings. Acting grown up. Being grown up. Interchangeable with another Black folk expression: 'You trying to be grown.' Responsible. In charge. Serious.

2. Also: . . . Appreciates and prefers women's culture, women's emotional flexibility (values tears as natural counterbalance of laughter), and women's strength. . . . Committed to survival and wholeness of entire people, male and female. Not a separatist, except periodically, for health. Traditionally universalist, as in: 'Mama, why are we brown, pink, and yellow, and our cousins are white, beige, and Black?' Ans.: 'Well, you know the colored race is just like a flower garden, with every color flower represented.' Traditionally capable, as in: 'Mama, I'm walking to Canada and I'm taking you and a bunch of other slaves with me.' Reply: 'It wouldn't be the first time.'

3. Loves music. Loves dance. Loves the moon. Loves the Spirit. Loves love and food and roundness. Loves struggle. Loves the Folk. Loves herself. Regardless.

4. Womanist is to feminist as purple to lavender. (pp. xi-xii)

Walker provided an authentic definition in Sections 1 and 2 from the perspective of African Americans (in the United States). Indubitably, the term womanist has linkages to the African American speech community, reflecting Walker's real-time experiences as a member of that community. Within the African American speech community, the term *womanish* has existed and been used for centuries. Many African American women remember the admonishment, before they reached the age of adulthood, from grandmothers and mothers, "Don't be so womanish!" or "You acting too womanish." If an African American young girl or teenager interjected comments into a conversation held among adults, most typically women, she could expect the admonishment. Yet, these same grandmothers and mothers expected and reared their daughters and granddaughters, at the appropriate age level, to be the precise opposite of the earlier warning (i.e., to be a "woman"). Particularly of interest, Walker has effectively raised the term from its colloquial usage within the African American speech community to broader, national usage within women's speech communities and gives the term *legitimacy* beyond that of a specific speech community.

Currently, the term *womanist* and the ideology it encompasses have spread, especially within U.S. academic settings. Many African American women academics and nonacademics refer to themselves as "womanists," especially as the ideology has become more pronounced. The Womanist Studies Consortium (WSC) represents one example of "academic womanism." Founded in 1994 at The University of Georgia, the WSC seeks "to promote the production, visibility and impact of womanist scholarship within all disciplines of the academy" (WSC Web site, Fellowships 1997-1998). The WSC identifies itself as "an interracial, intergenerational, regional affiliation of womanist scholars" (WSC Web site, Fellowships 1997-1998), adopting Walker's (1983) first definition given earlier of womanist as "a Black feminist or feminist of color" (p. xi). As part of its charter statement, the WSC positions itself as follows (WSC Charter Members, 1995):

> The Womanist Studies Consortium . . . supports and facilitates feminist research on women of color in all disciplines and at all possible stages of development. . . . [I]t bridges the isolation, social exclusion, silence, and intellectual desuetude among women-of-color researchers, students, and independent scholars within their home disciplines and home institutions. Members of the WSC participate in a legacy of individuals and coalitions that, since the late 1970s, have privileged, authenticated, and reciprocated experiences of women of color. . . . The womanist goal of the WSC is to preserve and appreciate difference within the context of coalition-building as a strategy for overcoming problems of racial, sexual, class, and power-based conflict.

The WSC may be the most extensive agency publicly promoting and advocating womanism currently, yet other vehicles for womanism exist. Based on a list of womanist events published by WSC on its web pages, other practitioners of womanism can be identified. In the instances given here, both academic and nonacademic practitioners appear. The editors of this volume have required that book chapters be grounded in womanist or feminist theory. The call for contributors specifies that "[c]ritical essays and empirical research studies must combine a Black feminist or womanist conceptual framework with contemporary communication concepts and theories" (Davis & Houston, 1997).

Fryar, editor of a forthcoming encyclopedia, the *Historical Encyclopedia of Black Feminism / Womanism*, has issued a call for contributions to the volume. She indicates in a Web site "Call for Papers" an interest in "words, events, or people depicting the essence of [Black feminism/womanism as a] movement" (WSC Web site, Womanist Theory and Research Events and Publications: Historical Encyclopedia, 1998b). G.I.R.L.S. SPEAK OUT, a conference scheduled for teenagers and college students, fits within the womanist ideology defined by Walker (1983). Sponsored by a community organization that seeks to enable (i.e., strengthen the abilities of) young women and teenagers, the conference focuses on one aspect of "survival and wholeness" (Walker, 1983, p. xi) for one portion of the community. G.I.R.L.S. SPEAK OUT is a component of the project "Voice*Vision*Action." The mission of this community project is "to create a comfortable space for girls and young women to express themselves, learn new skills, build allies, celebrate girls' achievements, and increase public awareness about issues of importance to [the girls and young women]" (WSC Web site, Womanist Theory and Research Events and Publications: G.I.R.L.S. 1998a, p. 1).

WHAT'S IN A NAME?

In this section, I highlight my rationale for use of and preference for the term *womanism*; I provide an operational definition of the term and present an ideological framework for the present analysis, following Collins' (1990) discussion. hooks (1981) wrote that "feminism as a political ideology advocating social equality for all women was and is acceptable to many black women" (p. 148). For many of the exact reasons that hooks indicated, however, many African American women, including myself, do not accept feminism.

Historically and even up to today, feminism does not advocate equality for all women socially, politically, economically, spiritually, or mentally. Feminism has and continues to be exclusionary. hooks (1981) explained the feelings of many African American women accurately, even though she published these ideas in the early 1980s:

> [Black women] rejected the women's movement when it became apparent that middle and upper class college-educated white women who were its majority participants were determined to shape the movement so that it would serve their own opportunistic ends. . . . white women liberationists used the power granted them by virtue of their being members of the dominant race in American society to interpret feminism in such a way that it was no longer relevant to all women. And it seemed incredible to black women that they were being asked to support a movement whose majority participants were eager to maintain race and class hierarchies between women. Black women who participated in women's groups, lectures, and meetings initially trusted the sincerity of white female participants. . . . As they participated in the women's movement they found, in their dialogues with white women in women's groups, in women's studies classes, at conferences, that their trust was betrayed. (pp. 148-149)

Collins (1990) provided a recent discussion of the rejection of feminism:

> Even though Black women intellectuals have long expressed a unique feminist consciousness about the intersection of race and class in structuring gender, historically we have not been full participants in white feminist organizations. Even today African-American, Hispanic, Native American, and Asian-American women criticize the feminist movement and its scholarship for being racist and overly concerned with white, middle-class women's issues. (p. 7)

The rejection of feminism by many African American women and women of color is understandable given the historical and social context. As an African American woman, my definition and construction of womanism differs slightly from Walker's (1983) and the WSC (WSC Web site, Fellowships 1997-1998). Womanism and feminism are not synonymous, although, like Walker and the WSC, Steinem and Hayes (1998) claimed that "womanist and womanism are culture-specific and poetic synonyms for Black feminist and Black feminism" (p. 637). The exclusion of other women and the lack of trust begin to separate the ideological approaches for me: "A house divided cannot stand," according to the book of Proverbs. Another aspect of my definition, which diverges from Walker's (1983), is the absence of homosexuality. Contrary to Walker's idea that a womanist "loves other women, sexually and/or nonsexually" (p. xi), many African American womanists abide by a nonsexual love of other African American women. Thus, I love my (nonblood related) "sistuhs" because of GOD's love (agape) and because we have similar struggles and "go through" similar experiences.

I have selected womanism as the ideological framework used in this chapter, instead of Black feminism, for two reasons. First, womanism emerges from African American culture itself, emanating from and relating to women in particular. The phrase *Black feminism* appears only to colorize an ideology grounded in a different set of historical events, a different reality. Both Smith's (1998) and Collins' (1990) ideological framework underscored for Black feminism accurately reflects the historical reality for African American women, yet their preferred phrasing modifies a European American social reality (feminism) superficially with an adjective (Black). Thus, there is a mismatch linguistically. Although Walker (1983) identified womanism and feminism synonomously, she expressed the inadequacy of the phrase Black feminism:

> I chose [womanism] because I prefer the sound, the feel, the fit of it; because I cherish the spirit of the women (like Sojourner) the word calls to mind, and because I share the old ethnic-American habit of offering society a new word when the old word it is using fails to describe behavior and change that only a new word can help it more fully see. (Steinem & Hayes, 1998, p. 640).

Walker stated further, "I dislike having to add a color in order to become visible, as in black feminist. Womanism gives us a word of our own" (Steinem & Hayes, 1998, p. 640). Womanism, then, is centrally located in the sociohistorical and linguistic worldview of African American women. A different term than Black feminism, I believe, behooves those interested in accurately reflecting this speech community and its contributors.

Second and most important, womanism, as ideology, allows discussants to highlight the teachings and lives of real African American women of various social classes who have passed on womanism through specific rites of passage; thus, these women's thoughts, actions, and behavior form a primary component of this ideological framework. Theory, then, takes a secondary position, proceeding from the concrete teachings and experiences embedded in womanism (cf. Collins, 1990, p. 33). With the concrete, I wish to emphasize the everyday stories of women beyond those standardly told. The stories of African American women, such as Sojourner

Truth, Ida B. Wells, Fanny Lou Hamer, and Rosa Parks, have become more visible now than in previous decades. Besides these women of national stature and repute, I would also like to make more visible the experiences of those everyday African American women within our own home communities and families. I think of women, like Mama LLoyd, Mama Willie—my grandmothers, my mommie, Aunt Lilla, Sister Geneva Smitherman, Mrs. Simmons (my brother's Godmother), a coal Black woman with the adeptness of a thousand alchemists. Jordan (1985) expressed this obligatory, preferential tribute:

> Just yesterday I stood for a few minutes at the top of the stairs leading to a white doctor's office in a white neighborhood. I watched one Black woman after another trudge to the corner, where she then waited to catch the bus home. These were Black women still cleaning somebody else's house or Black women still caring for somebody else's sick or elderly, before they came back to the frequently thankless chores of their own loneliness, their own families. And I felt angry and I felt ashamed. And I felt, once again, the kindling heat of my hope that we, the daughters of these Black women, will honor their sacrifice by giving them thanks. We will undertake, with pride, every transcendent dream of freedom made possible by the humility of their love.

Womanism is one vehicle with which African American women can acknowledge, give back, and revere that which we have received from the Mama Lloyds, the Big Mommas, the aunties, and the sistuhs. Collins (1990) presented a very detailed exposition of African American womanhood and intellectual thought. She identified four core themes that have been given longstanding attention by African American women: analyzing African American women's work, challenging stereotypical images of African American women (e.g., as mammies, Jezebels, matriarchs, and welfare recipients), African American women's activism, and sexual politics. Of these four core themes that she identified, I focus on one, the stereotypical images of African American women. The following treatise is a developing womanist analysis of African American women's language. It is womanist in its focus on concrete experiences of African American women with an emphasis on their deeds, sacrifices, lessons taught, struggle for equality and empowerment, activism in behavior (especially linguistic), and the positive manifestations of strength, courage, endurance. I share the experiences (some through stories) of African American women, discussing womanism as displayed in the experiences.

THE SOCIAL CONSTRUCTION OF AFRICAN AMERICAN
WOMEN'S LANGUAGE

How is African American women's language socially constructed? In part, it is socially constructed through the lives and experiences of African American women themselves. That is, African American women have forged the creation and existence of a womanish language in their daily lives (e.g., see Scott, chap. 3; Houston, chap. 4; Orbe et. al., chap. 6; Jones and Varner, chap. 7, this volume). They have lived, taught, and demonstrated womanism through their differently manifested behaviors: social (including the linguistic), spiritual, emotional, physical, and financial. African American mothers, who are also daughters and sisters, have passed on confidence, boldness, determination, persistence, courage, independence, and more through language. Language, in general, is also socially constructed by broader society members. Thus, real people, in-group and out-group members, contribute to the social construction of language, as with other social phenomena. For example, race has a different social construction in the United States than in South America due to decisions and categorizations made by people, usually those in power. Rothenberg (1998) explained this idea of social construction in relation to "race" and other social traits:

> far from reflecting natural and innate differences among people, the categories of gender, race, and class are themselves socially constructed. Rather than being "given" in nature, they are culturally constructed differences that reflect and perpetuate the prevailing distribution of power and privilege in a society, and they change as other aspects of social, political, and economic life evolve. . . . The claim that race is a social construction takes issue with the once popular belief that people were born into different races with innate, biologically based differences in intellect, temperament, and character. . . . Michael Omi and Howard Winant . . . maintain that race is more a political categorization than a biological or scientific category. They point to the relatively arbitrary way in which the category has been constructed and suggest that changes in the meaning and use of racial distinctions can be correlated with economic and political changes in U.S. society. Dark-skinned men and women from Spain were once classified as "white" along with fair-skinned immigrants from England and Ireland, whereas early Greek immigrants were often classified as "Orientals" and subjected to the same discrimination that Chinese and Japanese immigrants experienced under the laws of California and other western states. (pp. 8-10)

Scientists have given substance to the view that there is only one race, the human race. According to Rothenberg (1998), they "have long argued that all human beings are descended from a common stock" (p. 10). Scholars, usually European American males, during the 18th and 19th centuries contributed significantly to the construction of race categories that have residual effects still today (Omi & Winant, 1998).

Like "race," language is constructed, partially, by the participation of broader society members, not only those persons using a particular linguistic code. Within U.S. sensibilities, the language of African American women has derived some specific characteristics based on perceived and real notions of the women themselves and their linguistic behavior. One example of language construction influenced from the outside is of enslaved African women in 18th-century South Carolina marketplaces. Olwell (1996) described the role of enslaved African women, who experienced a degree of autonomy in their selling and trading of goods. A 1747 petitioner expresses this autonomy in a complaint to the South Carolina Assembly (Olwell 1996):

> [Their masters] give them all imaginable liberty, not only to buy and sell those commodities, but also, . . . to forestall the markets of Charles Town by buying up the Provisions, &c. which come to town for sale, at dear and exorbitant prices, and take what other indirect methods they please, provided they pay their masters wages, which they seldom or never enquire how they came by the same, . . . [further] those Negroes and other slaves, being possessed of large sums of money, purchase quantities of flour, butter, applies, &c., all [of] which they retail out to the inhabitants of Charles Town, by which means leading lazy lives, and free from the government of their masters. (p. 101)

Enslaved African women dominated Charles Town marketplaces. More of them traded in the marketplace than enslaved men because, Olwell (1996) conjectured, they could not perform other day labor. "They soon outnumbered and displaced white traders and made the Charleston market their own domain. By mid-eighteenth century in terms of race, . . . the public marketplace of Charleston might be justly termed a 'black market'" (Olwell 1996, p. 101). One of the prevailing comments of petitioners and observers of the marketplace during this time was of the behavior of the marketplace African women, especially their linguistic behavior (Olwell, 1996):

Ridicule, bluster, and wit were the market women's strongest
weapons. In 1741, the clerk of the market complained that the
"insolent abusive Manner" of slave marketeers rendered him "afraid
to say or do anything in the Market." I have known these women to
be so insolent as even to wrest things out of the hands of white
people, pretending they had been bought before, for their masters or
mistresses, yet expose the same for sale again within an hour after,
for their benefit. (p. 104)

Olwell's paper title, in part, derives from the complaint that these
African women marketeers were "loose, idle, and disorderly." Here is
an example of the intricate relation between language and behavior.
Is the language of the women "loose" and "disorderly" as a result of
the ascribed behavior? Would the enslaved African women describe
their actions and language as the petitioners? The workings of social
constructionism can be gleaned in addressing these questions. The
marketplace was one locale where people felt that the enslaved
African women displayed strength and assertiveness in behavior,
particularly language, even though these women were subject to the
abominable institution of slavery. In this instance of the social
construction of language, African American women's language
becomes marked as offensive and strong, as labeled by outsiders.

Data collected by Houston (1997) and that I have collected on
the topic of African American women's language helps to examine the
social construction of language more closely. Houston (1997)
administered open-ended questionnaires to 135 African American
and 100 European American women, asking them to describe the
talk of specific social groups. She found that these two groups of
women respondents evaluated their own speech patterns positively,
while negatively evaluating each others' speech. Although Houston
did not use a scientific sampling design, she was able to establish the
characterizations presented here. (I report her findings for the
African American women only.) The African American women
respondents most frequently characterized their speech as:

- standing behind what you say, not being afraid to speak
  your mind;
- speaking with a strong sense of self-esteem;
- speaking out, talking about what's on your mind;
- getting down to the heart of the matter;
- speaking with authority, intelligence, and common sense;
- being very sure of oneself;
- being very distinguished and educated;

- reflecting black experience as seen by a black woman in a white patriarchal society.

These women constructed a positive view of their language behavior, whether that construction, like race, is real or perceived. The descriptions that these women generated help in delineating one way that African American women's language is socially constructed. They contribute to the development and social reality of an African American women's way of talk (see also Scott, chap. 3, this volume).

I conducted an informal survey of undergraduate students who had had no formal linguistics training, asking them to describe African American women's language. This class consisted of 34 females and 8 males on the day of data collection. Although the ratio of female to male was 17:4, I examined equal numbers of responses based on gender, seven for both groups. Interestingly, both the African American women participants in Houston's study and the student participants in my study use similar descriptions (see Table 5.1).

The findings from Table 5.1 indicate that a subset of features describing African American women's language is identifiable in mutually agreeable terms, regardless of differences in geographical location, age, race, or gender. Among the mental representations mapped on the brain for some U.S. speakers, then, there appears to exist a socially constructed representation of African American women's way of talking, partially identified here. Is there further evidence of the social reality of these descriptions? The remainder of this chapter aims to address this question, especially the data analysis section.

Table 5. 1. African American Women's Students' Responses.

speaking with authority	authoritarian
speaking out; talking about what's on your mind; not being afraid to speak your mind	direct; opinionated; vocal; voice their opinions; assertive
speaking with a strong sense of self-esteem; being very sure of oneself	self-assured; confident; powerful; cocky

RECONSTRUCTING BLACK WOMANHOOD THROUGH WOMANISM

One of the four themes identified by Collins (1990) as central to a true depiction and ideological analysis of Black women is the replacement of "denigrated images of Black womanhood with self-defined images" (p. 23). Beginning with enslavement and with each century thereafter, African American women have been negatively stereotyped as loose, sexually promiscuous, and immoral (Collins 1990; Smith 1998). These stereotypical images, "from the mammies, Jezebels, and breeder women of slavery to the smiling Aunt Jemimas on pancake mix boxes, ubiquitous Black prostitutes, and ever-present welfare mothers of contemporary popular culture" (Collins, 1990, p. 7), were consciously and purposely created by elite European American males, as one vehicle of Black women's oppression in the United States (Collins, 1990). With African American women in the forefront of reconstruction, these images must be refuted. Using the theme of "refutation and reconstruction of negative images" as one construct of womanism, I focus on a different image of African American women as I have witnessed and experienced it directly. My goal is to help replace the negative images and to focus on self-definition, doing so from a Black woman's standpoint. In the fashion of Etter-Lewis (1993), I share the words, especially the stories, of African American women themselves, allowing their words to reveal their power and the women's socially constructed selves.

In order to synopsize the ideological approach that I view as inherent in a womanist analysis, I list features I have applied in the following analysis. Among other tenets, womanism:

- Highlights the teachings and lives of African American women of various social classes; these women's thoughts, actions, and behavior form a primary component of this ideological framework.
- Presents positive, concrete, authentic, and real images of African American women (thus, refuting and replacing denigrated images of Black womanhood).
- Emphasizes the struggle for equality and empowerment, activism in behavior (including linguistic), and positive, nonstereotypical manifestations of strength, courage, endurance.

In addition to these principles, my womanist analysis highlights characteristics identified by Walker (1983):

- Displays audacious, courageous, responsible, willful, in charge, capable, and serious behavior.
- Values women's strength and emotional flexibility (values tears as natural counterbalance of laughter).
- Demonstrates a commitment to the survival and wholeness of an entire people, especially African American males and females.
- Displays language usage that is characteristic of African American females, such as: "Mama, why are we brown, pink, and yellow, and our cousins are white, beige, and black?" Ans.: "Well, you know the colored race is just like a flower garden, with every color flower represented." Or "Mama, I'm walking to Canada and I'm taking you and a bunch of other slaves with me." Reply: "It wouldn't be the first time." (pp. xi-xii)

"We Be Strong Women": Analysis of Data

The following is an excerpt from "Lucy" in *Good Woman: Poems and a Memoir, 1969-1980*, Written by Lucille Clifton (1987).

> "They named his daughter Lucille," my Daddy would say. They say she was a tall skinny dark-skinned girl, look just like her mother. Mammy Ca'line. They say they couldn't get her to work as hard as the rest and she was quiet and thought she was better than the rest. Mammy Ca'line taught her that, they say, and I wouldn't be surprised if she did. They tell me she was mean. Lucy was mean always, I heard Aunt Margaret Brown say to Mammy Ca'line one time. And Mammy just said no she wasn't mean, she was strong. "Strong women . . .," is what she said, "sister, we be strong women . . ." (p. 4).

In various settings, many African American women—through their own words, through situations endured, through their successes—embody positions of strength. In the words of the pastor of my church, Pastor Erlene B. Sudduth (1998): "Black women have always been strong. It was Big Momma who knelt and prayed, who took us to church, who planted and weeded the garden. Strong men want strong women!" The strength of African American women is manifest in many ways; one of which is through stories. The rest of Clifton's story "Lucy," about the woman for whom she was named, recounts Lucy having a relationship with a Eur-American man, Harvey Nichols. They both fell in love fiercely.

The story continues:

. . . Lucy had this baby boy by this Connecticut Yankee named
Harvey Nichols.

They named the baby Gene Sayle. He was my Daddy, Lue [i.e.,
Lucille Clifton].

Your own grandfather and Mammy Ca'line's grandson. But oh, Lue,
he was born with a withered arm.

Yes, Lord, he was born with a withered arm and when he was still
just a baby Lucy waited by the crossroad one night for Harvey
Nichols to come to her and when he rode up on a white horse, she
cocked up a rifle she had stole and shot him off his horse and killed
him, Lue. And she didn't run away, she didn't run away, she waited
right there by the body with the rifle in her hand till the horse
coming back empty-saddled to the stable brought a mob to see what
had become of Harvey Nichols. (p. 6)

This description of the "first Black woman legally hanged in
the state of Virginia" (Clifton, 1987, p. 3) is powerful, first of all,
because of the time frame in which it occurs, just after the signing of
the Emancipation of Proclamation when people of African descent
still were considered as less than human, with little respected rights.
Regardless of the time, Lucy Sayle exudes strength in her behavior.
Clifton (1987) shows this strength in the repetition of the phrase,
"she didn't run away" (p. 6) and, most poignantly, by Lucy Sayle's
actions. Boldly, she shot and killed a White man, remaining next to
the dead body with the rifle in her hands until the mob appeared—
and she didn't run. The fear of being lynched or hanged—
instantaneous death—measured minutely in Lucy's psyche.

Mammy Ca'line, Lucille Clifton's great, great grandmother,
speaks very clearly of the strength of her daughter, Lucille Sayle,
who "didn't do nothing she didn't want to do and nobody could force
her" (Clifton, 1987, p. 6), and of the strength of other Dahomey
women. Mammy Ca'line's voice is the one that asserts, "We be strong
women" (Clifton, 1987, p. 4). Clearly, she has taught her daughter
about conviction in beliefs, to stand on her beliefs, and pride in
herself during a reprehensible time in the lives of African Americans.
Thus, Lucille Sayle acted as she was taught. Mammy Ca'line
undoubtedly is a strong woman, too, having taught her daughter to
think and behave as she did. Clifton (1987) recounted her father's
words, "They say they couldn't get her to work as hard as the rest
and she was quiet and thought she was better than the rest. Mammy
Ca'line taught her that, they say, and I wouldn't be surprised if she
did" (p. 4). Here is an inkling of the strength-in-spite-of-conditions-
experienced that some African women in U.S. contexts instilled in
their daughters. Maintaining pride and self-esteem in oneself during

harsh circumstances highlights a positive, desired feature of Black womanhood that many African American women have learned and experienced and continue to do so. Such rites of passage contribute to African American women's social construction of themselves and impacts their language and identity (as Houston's, 1997, study demonstrates).

Another testament of the strength exemplified by African American women is shared in Marable's (1983) *How Capitalism Underdeveloped Black America*. Many African American women "carried the scars of their [psychological and physical] rapes . . . with them for the rest of their lives" (p. 74), yet many of them resisted sexual depravity. "Many Black women fought . . . repeated sexual assaults, . . . an untold number sacrificed their lives to retain their humanity. . . . Black women . . . [even] ran away from their plantations or farms in search of freedom" (Marable, 1983, p. 74). One story recorded of a young enslaved African American woman, Caroline Gordon or "Caddy" demonstrates the strength of African American women during the end of the enslavement period. According to Marable (1983, pp. 75-76):

> Caddy had been sold to a man in Goodman, Mississippi. It was terrible to be sold in Mississippi. In fact, it was terrible to be sold anywhere. She had been put to work in the fields for running away again. She was hoeing a crop when she heard that General Lee surrendered . . . that meant that all the colored people were free! Caddy threw down that hoe, she marched herself up to the big house, then, she looked around and found the mistress. She went over to the mistress, she flipped up her dress and told the white woman to do something. She said it mean and ugly: Kiss my ass!

Caroline Gordon exudes a powerful stance on receiving the word of General Lee's surrender. In one centrifugal and historical moment, she has the opportunity to communicate her feelings precisely, without fear of repercussion. Caroline Gordon seizes that moment with urgency. She seeks out, finds, and informs her mistress very directly of what the mistress can do. Gordon's strength is manifest also in her running away from the plantation/farm again, which is indicative of her rejection of a condition of servitude. Her first attempt obviously failed, yet that failure did not deter Caroline Gordon, who tried again.

As Marable indicated, Black women, in general, fought and resisted many instances of sexual attacks. To fight and resist, even under conditions of servitude, speaks clearly of the strength of these women. They are the unsung heroines of African American womanhood. Through their stories, often passed on orally (sometimes with skepticism), African American women have learned of an historical legacy, perpetuated still today—just stand.

Mary Ellen Pleasant, according to Lerone Bennett, Jr., "was a mother to thousands of troubled women and put-upon men and children. She was, as she told a census taker in 1890, a 'capitalist' by profession . . ." (Bennett, 1993, pp. 56-64). In another interview, Mrs. Mary Ellen Pleasant, at age 87, told a reporter:

> I don't like to be called mammy by everybody. Put that down. I'm not mammy to everybody in California. I got a letter today from a minister in Sacramento. It was addressed to Mammy Pleasant. I wrote back to him on his own paper that my name was Mrs. Mary E. Pleasant . . . they shan't nickname me at my age. If he didn't have better sense he should have had better manners . . . (Bennett, 1993, p. 58).

Mrs. Mary E. Pleasant upheld womanist principles in her activism: giving to needy persons within her community. As a result of her giving, Mrs. Pleasant appears to be looked on and referred to as a mother figure ("was a mother to thousands"). Clearly, some individuals took the referent "mammy" too far and Mrs. Pleasant puts an end to the use of the nickname, especially through the reporter whom she directs to get it written down. The interview serves as a vehicle for her message, "I don't like to be called mammy by everybody . . . they shan't nickname me at my age." Mrs. Pleasant displays lucid, cogent reasoning. She leads the reporter and puts necessary persons in their "proper" places through the use of "smart talk" (Houston Stanback, 1982; a combative style of language, consisting of apt, spontaneous, wise retorts that are a reflection of the speaker's mental acuity).

In one of her rap songs called "360 Degrees of Power," Sister Souljah (1992) wrote of the strength of African women, a depiction that must have concrete social reality for Sister Souljah; otherwise, she would not be able to write about it:

> Being both feminine and strong represents no conflict!
> African women have always been powerful,
> decisive and strong
> And in a state of war, we must be even stronger!
> . . .
> Ancestors blessed me with the power of spirits
> Dominate my thoughts, I'm not tryin' a hear it
> I'm stronger than that, too bold deep and black

On a feminine curve with nerve
You thought I was a noun, but no way I'm a verb
An action word
A secret for centuries but now the cat's out the bag
Strong Black woman you should be glad
You have 360 degrees of power girl, you bad

In this instance, Sister Souljah presents a number of positive constructions of African American women. Strength is a positive and historical element of Black womanhood. As Lucille Clifton presented in her father's story of Dahomey women, Sister Souljah refers to strength of African women as an historical trait. This historical inheritance finds some substantiation in Olwell's (1996) historical analysis. Furthermore, Sister Souljah refers to other positive traits of African women, decisiveness and power, femininity and strength, interestingly, traits not typically associated with European American women during 18th-century U.S. contexts.

Finally, Margaret Walker wrote of the strength of African American women in her poem, "Lineage":

My grandmothers were strong.
They followed plows and bent to toil.
They moved through fields sowing seed.
They touched earth and grain grew.
They were full of sturdiness and singing.
My grandmothers were strong.

My grandmothers are full of memories
Smelling of soap and onions and wet clay
With veins rolling roughly over quick hands
They have many clean words to say.
My grandmothers were strong.
Why am I not as they? (cited in Thompson, 1993)

Here, again, a member of the African American women's speech community self-selects "strength" as a characteristic with which to define African American women, in the present case, grandmothers. Walker operationally defined the strength that she observed firsthand in her grandmothers: They toiled—a verb that in itself conveys profuse sweat and hard labor, even struggle; they planted and plowed fields; they possessed an uncanny ability, almost magical, of growing grain by their special touch; they were sturdy women, full of clean words and songs; they were strong. I discovered that Margaret Walker is just as strong as the grandmothers she described. She finished high school at age 14, college at 19 (and

would have finished earlier if she did not have to stay out a year).
When Walker was 16, Langston Hughes read his work at her school,
encouraging Walker to continue writing after she had approached
Hughes. With four children and a differently abled husband,
Margaret Walker supported her family financially and completed her
doctorate in creative writing at the University of Iowa and handed in
her final creative work, her critically received book, *Jubilee,* which
was translated into six languages, made into an opera, and is still in
print (Thompson, 1993).

In these examples, the African American women identify
themselves as "strong" or they display "strong" behavior. They have
constructed this feature as a part of their identity, their experiences.
They have selected the linguistic and sociocultural behavior of self-
portrayal.

DISCUSSION

As creators and speakers of a particular linguistic style, African
American women, in general, have developed their own language
patterns based on their belief systems and social, cultural, historical,
political, and religious reality. "Language . . . is a major component in
any human culture. It encodes the culture's values [, beliefs,]
preoccupations . . . (Cameron, 1990, p. 12). "It is language which
determines the limits of our world. [It is language] which constructs
our reality" (Spender, 1990, p. 103). Thus, a society that is racist/
sexist/classist will use words to reflect that racism/sexism/classcism;
it will use words to encode that behavior into its language.
Researchers, then, should expect that the language of African
American women is a reflection of who they are. Their language will
encode their self-proclaimed identity; their behavior will be reflected
in their language. Is this the case?

One overwhelming deduction that can be drawn from both
the responses in Houston's (1997) survey and the samples from the
African American women speakers/writers/actors is that these
women identify their language and themselves positively. The
African American women respondents (Houston, 1997) see their
language in very positive terms:

- standing behind what you say, not being afraid to speak
  your mind;
- speaking with a strong sense of self-esteem;
- speaking out; talking about what's on your mind;

- getting down to the heart of the matter;
- speaking with authority, intelligence, and common sense;
- being very sure of oneself;
- being very distinguished and educated;
- reflecting black experience as seen by a black woman in a white patriarchal society. (p. 135)

Mammy Ca'line, Sister Souljah, and Margaret Walker affirm the behavioral strength of African American women, which is manifested in the speech of Caroline Gordon and Mrs. Pleasant. Thus, this subset of African American women identify with strong, positive self-images and the impact and interrelationship of language in thought and action becomes apparent. These women view or display strength as an aspect of their existence; they have established it as one common denominator in their lives as women of African descent. They have self-selected this feature (including others, as well) out of a host of descriptive features from which to select. They have constructed strength as one parcel of their identity. One result of this self-selection and construction is that their language and actions have become attached to the identity of strength. Language in thought has become language in action. The data presented here, then, aligns with the data shown in Table 5.1. Both sets of African American women have self-selected strength as descriptive of their behavior, linguistic and social. The students (see Table 5.1) also ascribe strength (associated with power, assertiveness, directness, vocalness) to African American women's language. Therefore, strength appears to hold social reality for African American women within the U.S. based on data analyzed here.

CONCLUSION

One goal embedded in my thinking is the avoidance of stereotyping African American women. hooks (1981) discussed the strength of Black women in the United States during one historical moment in the 19th century, yet her discussion shows feminists' misuse of this assigned social trait, while simultaneously ignoring the sexual victimization of Black women:

> When feminists acknowledge in one breath that black women are victimized and in the same breath emphasize their strength, they imply that though black women are oppressed they manage to circumvent the damaging impact of oppression by being strong—and

that is simply not the case. Usually, when people talk about the "strength" of black women they are referring to the way in which they perceive black women coping with oppression. They ignore the reality that to be strong in the face of oppression is not the same as overcoming oppression, that endurance is not to be confused with transformation. . . . The stereotypical image of the "strong" black woman was no longer seen as dehumanizing, it became the new badge of black female glory. (p. 6)

Here, hooks showed 19th-century feminists' socially constructed view of Black women as oppressed—BUT! Strength, in their construction, overrides any kind of oppression. In this way, the strength of African American women has negative repercussions and interpretations. African American women receive glory in an artificial way. My focus on the strength of African American women aims to glorify these women in the positive ways that I have seen their strength manifested. I believe that exuding strength, as hooks (1981) suggested, entails facing trials and difficulties, sometimes without success. A semantic deconstruction of strength shows that it entails semantic properties such as endurance, resistance, and vigor. One does not endure easy situations, resist easy circumstances, or apply vigor to easy opponents. Collins (1990) expressed the point that "all African American women share the common experience of being Black women in a society that denigrates women of African descent. This commonality of experience suggests that certain characteristic themes will be prominent in a Black women's standpoint. For example, one core theme is a legacy of struggle" (p. 22). To assert that Black women are strong embeds in that assertion the encountering of struggle and adversity.

Langston Hughes' (1996) poem, "Mother to Son," conveys a sense of the struggle for African American women due to oppressive societal conditions, yet who nonetheless continue to keep on climbing. The continuing to climb in the face of struggle is one juncture where strength enters:

Well, son, I'll tell you:
Life for me ain't been no crystal stair.
It's had tacks in it,
And splinters,
And boards torn up,
And places with no carpet on the floor-
Bare.
But all the time
I'se been a-climbin' on,
And reachin' landin's,

And turnin' corners,
And sometimes goin' in the dark
Where there ain't been no light.
So, boy, don't you turn back.
Don't you set down on the steps\'Cause you finds it's kinder hard.
Don't you fall now-
For I'se still goin' honey, I'se still climbin',
And life for me ain't been no crystal stair.

In this discussion, then, I aimed to avoid negative applications of strength, as hooks (1981) indicated has been the historical reality at one juncture in the Black woman's experience. This chapter focused on showing that African American women's strength in their behavior is manifest both in language usage and everyday demeanor. The idea of strength appears to be constructed by African American women themselves and has social reality as manifest especially in the stories of everyday African American women. Walker brought to the forefront an ideology with longstanding application in the African American women's speech community. Now, African American women can begin to show Black womanhood in the many positive ways that we have learned and experienced it.

REFERENCES

Bennett, L., Jr. (1993). The mystery of Mary Ellen Pleasant: Was she a public benefactor or a public menace? *Ebony, XLVIII*(8), 56-64.

Cameron, D. (Ed.). (1990). *The feminist critique of language.* New York: Routledge.

Clifton, L. (1987). *Good woman: Poems and a memoir, 1969-1980.* Brockport, NY: BOA Editions.

Collins, P. H. (1990). *Black feminist thought: Knowledge, consciousness, and the politics of empowerment.* London: Routledge.

Davis, O., & Houston, M. (1997). Call for contributors.

Etter-Lewis, G. (1993). *My soul is my own: Oral narratives of African American women in the professions.* New York: Routledge.

hooks, b. (1981). *AIN'T I A WOMAN: Black women and feminism.* Boston, MA: South End Press.

Houston, M. (1997). When black women talk with white women: Why dialogues are difficult. In A. Gonzalez, M. Houston, & V. Chen (Eds.), *Our voices: Essays in culture, ethnicity, and communication* (2nd ed., pp. 133-139). Los Angeles: Roxbury.

Houston M. S. (1982). *Language and black woman's place: Toward a description of black women's communication.* Paper presented to the Speech Communication Association.

Hughes, L. (1996). Mother to son. In A. Young (Ed.), *African American literature: A brief introduction and anthology* (pp. 391-392). New York: HarperCollins College.

Jordan, J. (1985). *On call.* Boston: South End Press.

Marable, M. (1983). *How capitalism underdeveloped black America.* Boston: South End Press.

Olwell, R. (1996). "Loose, idle and disorderly" slave women in the eighteenth-century Charleston marketplace. In D. B. Gaspor & D. C. Hine (Eds.), *More than chattel: Black women and slavery in the Americas* (pp. 97-110). Bloomington: Indiana University Press.

Omi, M., & Winant, H. (1998). Racial formations. In P. Rothenberg (Ed.), *Race, class, and gender in the United States: An integrated study* (4th ed., pp. 13-22). New York: St. Martin's Press.

Rothenberg, P. (1998). *Race, class, and gender in the United States: An integrated study* (4th ed.). New York: St. Martin's Press.

Smith, B. (1998). Black feminism. In W. Mankiller, G. Mink, M. Navarro, B. Smith, & G. Steinem (Eds.), *The reader's companion to U.S. women's history* (pp. 202-204). Boston: Houghton Mifflin Company.

Souljah, Sister (1992) *360 Degrees of Power.* Souljah's Story/Grand Cuts Music. ASCAP.

Spender, D. (1990). Extracts from man made language. In D. Cameron (Ed.), *The feminist critique of language* (p. 103). New York: Routledge.

Steinem, G., & Hayes, L. (1998). Womanism. In W. Mankiller, G. Mink, M. Navarro, B. Smith, & G. Steinem (Eds.), *The reader's companion to U.S. women's history* (pp. 639-641). Boston: Houghton Mifflin.

Sudduth, E. B. (1998). *Teachings on GOD's word* [tape recorded sermon].

Thompson, K. (1993). Margaret Walker. In D. C. Hine, E. B. Brown, & R. Terborg-Penn (Eds.), *Black women in America: An historical encyclopedia* (pp. 1219-1220). Brooklyn, NY: Carlson.

Walker, Alice (1983). *In search of our mothers' gardens: Womanist prose.* San Diego: Harcourt Brace Jovanovich.

Womanist Studies Consortium. (1995). Womanist Studies Consortium Charter Members. http://www.uga.edu/~womanist/1995/wsc.html.

Womanist Studies Consortium. (1997-1998). Rockefeller Foundation Humanities Fellowships. http://www.uga.edu/~womanist.

Womanist Studies Consortium (1998a) Womanist Theory and
  Research Events and Publications: G.I.R.L.S. SPEAK OUT.
  http://www.uga.edu/~womanist/speakout.html.
Womanist Studies Consortium. (1998b). Womanist Theory and
  Research Events and Publications: Historical Encyclopedia of
  Black Feminism/Womanism. http://www.uga.edu/~womanist/
  histenc.html.

SIX

Phenomenology and Black Feminist Thought: Exploring African American Women's Everyday Encounters as Points of Contention

Mark P. Orbe
Western Michigan University

Darlene K. Drummond
University of North Carolina-Charlotte

Sakile Kai Camara
Otterbein College

Black feminist thought constitutes a conceptual approach that reflects the special standpoints that African American women use to negotiate their positioning of self, family, and society. Collins (1986) explored three specific themes that articulate the sociological significance of this conceptual stance: (a) African American women's self-definition and self-evaluation, (b) the interlocking nature of oppression, and (c) the importance of African American women's culture (Collins, 1986). Although some of Collins' (e.g., 1986) work focuses on the marginal positions of African American female professors in the field of sociology, the conceptual framework of Black feminist thought renders an insightful vantage point into the experiences of all African American women. Collins documented observations, interpretations, and standpoints of African American women, and demonstrated that "there is a long and rich tradition of Black feminist thought" (Collins, 1986, p. S17). In fact, she exposed the inspiration of her intellectual writings as "ordinary Black women" (p. S17) who have fulfilled a number of crucial roles in history (mothers, teachers, preachers, orators, etc.). Although the contributions of more visible African American women activists have been recorded, Collins (1986) noted that "Their actions were nurtured by the support of countless, ordinary African-American women, who through strategies of everyday resistance, created a powerful foundation for this more visible Black feminist activist tradition" (pp. 745-746).

Black feminist thought is grounded in the premise that African American women, as a group, share certain commonalties of perception (themes). "The diversity of class, region, age, and sexual orientation shaping individual Black women's lives [however] has resulted in different expressions of these common themes" (Collins, 1986, p. 16). The focus of this chapter is to gain insight into the ways that the everyday communicative experiences of a diverse set of African American women reflect Black feminist thought. In doing so, we aspire to accomplish three related objectives: (a) to explore, what Collins (1986) described as an unexplored area of Black feminist thought, the "interpersonal relationships that Black women share with each other" (p. 22); (b) to utilize the strengths of a communication perspective in the explication of Black feminist thought or talk; and (c) to demonstrate the utility of phenomenology as a methodological tool consistent with the ideas comprising the social construction of Black feminist thought (Collins, 1989).

PHENOMENOLOGICAL INQUIRY

Phenomenology represents a rigorous human science approach that focuses on the conscious experiences of persons as they relate to the lived world (Lanigan, 1979). Initially employed by European scholars such as Husserl (1962) and Merleau-Ponty (1962), phenomenology has more recently been embraced by scholars in the United States as an effective foundation for feminist research (Langellier & Hall, 1989; Nelson, 1989), including an increasing number of studies specifically on African American women (see, e.g., Ford-Ahmed, 1992; Kapoor, 1992; Peterson, 1992). The value of phenomenological inquiry to critical or cultural studies is found in its fundamental tenets, several of which appear to be especially relevant to scholarship on Black feminist thought. Intertwined within phenomenology are several fundamental principles that directly relate to the four dimensions of an Afrocentric feminist epistemology (Collins, 1989; Houston & Davis, Introduction, this volume).

Collins (1989) described four specific dimensions of Afrocentric feminist epistemology: (a) knowledge versus wisdom, (b) use of dialogue in assessing knowledge claims, (c) the ethic of caring, and (d) the ethic of personal accountability. Each dimension correlates with a number of similar aspects central to phenomenological inquiry. First, both frameworks treat "co-researchers" (as opposed to "subjects") as experts of their life experiences. In this regard, personal experience, or "the consciousness that emerges from personal participation in events" (Foss & Foss, 1994, p. 39), is considered as solid evidence. Second, phenomenological inquiry involves co-researchers who are viewed as persons whose particular social, cultural, and historical life circumstance is acknowledged (van Manen, 1990). Similar to assertions about an Afrocentric feminist methodology, phenomenology contends that personal expressiveness and emotion are central (as are logic and reason) to knowledge, theory, and research. Third, the effectiveness of both Afrocentric feminist epistemology and phenomenology focus on the value of dialogue in creating knowledge. Phenomenological inquiry creates a discursive space where African American women can give voice to the circumstances that are central to the ways in which they experience life. Through a general conversational approach to interviewing and focus groups (Nelson, 1989), the synergistic connection of women's oral narratives becomes the core of evidence (Etter-Lewis, 1991). In addition, co-researchers, as well as the primary researchers, are compelled to recognize their respective standpoint(s) on issues related to the phenomenon under exploration and assume full responsibility for their interpretations. Although this brief summary of the consistent fundamental facets of Afrocentric feminist epistemology and phenomenology does not address all of the similarities between both approaches (for a more indepth treatment, see Collins, 1989, 1990; Nelson, 1989; Orbe, 1998), it clearly demonstrates the potential of using a phenomenological framework for exploring Black feminist thought or talk. In order to develop a greater understanding of the ways in which both approaches collaboratively shaped the foundation of our research, some brief comments about our methodology are needed.

Phenomenological inquiry entails three interrelated steps: the collection, reduction, and interpretation of lived experiences (Lanigan, 1979; Nelson, 1989). First, descriptions of the communicative experiences of African American women were collected from 19 co-researchers in two different midwestern cities. Five indepth interviews, ranging from 30 to 60 minutes, were conducted at one location. These interviews utilized a conversational approach to interviewing (Nelson, 1989) and focused on a number of general questions concerning African American women's communication (i.e., "Do you communicate differently in different settings?" "As you communicate each day, how aware are you of racism and/or sexism?" and "Who do you have your most meaningful communication with?"). Four focus group discussions were facilitated at the second location utilizing a similar topical protocol. Each session included between three and six African American women and lasted between 60 and 120 minutes.[1] The objective of including these specific women in the research project was not to achieve a scientifically determined "random" sample; however, the co-researchers did represent the wide diversity within the heterogeneous group classification of "African American women." For instance, the dialogue generated by the interviews and focus group discussions indicated diverse sets of lived experiences in regard to age, religion, sexual orientation, family background, professional standing, marital status, and socioeconomic status.

The second stage of phenomenological inquiry involves a thematization (reduction) of oral narratives. Following the completion of each interview or discussion, audiotapes of each session were transcribed verbatim. This transcription process served as the inaugural review of transcripts. Following an initial independent review by each researcher, transcripts were reviewed collectively with a conscious eye on the similarities and differences among descriptions of lived experiences. This process was repeated until several themes emerged as central to the issue of African American women's communication (these are explicated in subsequent sections).

---

[1]Co-researchers for these sessions were grouped together according to similar characteristics. The focus groups, respectively, were comprised of (a) three undergraduate students at a large midwestern university, (b) four young mothers who were also undergraduate students at a large midwestern university, (c) three young adult/middle-age gay women, and (d) six undergraduate students at a large midwestern university who had received an academic scholarship. This final group included an eclectic group students (i.e., in terms of age, marital and parental status) at various levels of their education.

The third stage of phenomenology involves an interpretation of themes, which Peterson (1992), in her work on African American women, described as steeped in African American tradition. At this point of analysis, additional reviews of transcripts typically reveal one or two central ideas that appear to illustrate the interconnectedness of themes as they relate to the larger phenomenon (Merleau-Ponty, 1962, used the term *hyper-reflection* to refer to this process). Following our initial interpretation, the descriptions of communicative experiences of African American women were subsequently reviewed or reinterpreted in terms of their applicability to Black feminist thought.

THEMATIC REVELATIONS

The three stages of phenomenological inquiry are not linear in nature; instead the process takes on a spiraling, interdependent form where each stage pre- or postreflectively informs the other stages. Our preliminary analyses of the 79 pages of single-spaced descriptions of lived experiences collectively produced over twenty possible themes of African American women's communication. However, during an extended period of greater review or reflection (where some themes were combined with others or recognized as redundant), several specific themes emerged as especially salient to the self-described lived experiences of African American women. The following sections provide insight into these themes as they represent the ways in which the African American women involved in this research project described their communicative experiences. This can be best understood within two main ideas: multiple consciousness and a "natural connection."

Multiple Consciousness

Existing Black feminist scholarship has given significant attention to the idea that, in order to survive or succeed, African American women must develop a multiple consciousness in their everyday lives (Collins, 1990; Houston Stanback, 1985; King, 1988; Scott, chap. 3, this volume; Smith & Stewart, 1983). It is important to recognize that the effects of racism, sexism, classism, heterosexism, and other forms of oppression are not simply additive in the ways in which they affect African American women (Essed, 1991). In this regard, multiple jeopardy may sometimes be misunderstood. "The modifier 'multiple' refers not only to several, simultaneous oppressions but to the multiplicative relationships among them as well" (King, 1988, p. 47).

Our interviews and focus group discussions were filled with oral narratives that spoke to the issue of multiple consciousness. Most often, however, co-researchers did not name it as such, but instead utilized varying metaphors or analogies in identifying the ways in which a multiple consciousness informed their interpersonal communication with others. Some described it as like "automatically cutting on and off a switch" or when "you throw down one dictionary and pick up another one." One African American woman, who was part of a focus group of young adult and middle-age lesbians, described it as "the ability to put ourselves on different levels at different times." Another member of the group provided the following explanation for how the effects of multiple consciousness pervades the lives of African American women:

> I think that Black women are some of the most real people I've encountered. But you do . . . become an expert at shifting constantly to fit in. And not just to fit in, but to protect yourself, to survive. And so you adapt. You give what you have to give or take or whatever, in order to make it through that interaction.

Through the reduction or interpretation process, the theme of multiple consciousness emerged as a central aspect of African American women's communication. Given the existing literature, this should not have come as a surprise. However, of specific relevance to this research project were the ways that this phenomenon plays out in everyday lives of African American women. Several issues emerged through the analysis of the communicative experiences of our co-researchers.

Communicating in the Midst of Multiple Oppressions. The interlocking nature of oppression is at the heart of Black feminist thought (Collins, 1986). However, "what is often missed are the multiple and creative ways in which black women address their independent concerns of racism, sexism, and classism" (King, 1988, p. 70). When asked about their awareness of racism and sexism, co-researchers described an acute awareness of the existence of these and others oppressive forces in their lives. "You have no choice but to be aware," explained one African American woman. Sometimes, however, it is difficult to ascertain where one form of oppression stopped and others began (see, e.g., Essed, 1991). For instance, some African American women described negative past experiences that left them wondering if the problem was caused by racism, sexism, both, another issue (i.e., classism or heterosexism) or a simple personality conflict. Such was the case with one undergraduate student who recalled a problematic relationship with a Euro-American female professor.

> I just don't understand. You know, what is it? Is it me? Do you have a problem with me? Do you have a problem with my color? I mean I just don't understand. But something like that is soooooo . . . you can't put your finger on it. . . . How can I tell if somebody is being prejudice[d] or they just don't like me?

A number of communication strategies, used to respond to a simultaneity of oppression, were depicted by our co-researchers. The selection of specific strategies was contingent on several factors like one's relationship with others, situational context, "mood," as well as the ways in which these responses would affect their future. Some women described specific ways in which they have confronted oppression. Others recounted more subtle ways to make others aware such as humor. "I'm constantly aware [of racism and sexism], but I try not to wear it on my sleeve," one co-researcher explained. Some co-researchers acknowledged being aware of prejudice, discrimination and stereotypes, but choose to avoid confrontations unless absolutely necessary. These African American women described instances where they "did nothing," "didn't say a word," or "just sit back and go with the flow." Many of these women explained that although they did not have the mental energy or time to confront all of the issues that they face, their mere presence in certain contexts indirectly served to counter racist, sexist, and classist ideologies. Again, many of the strategic responses to oppression were informed by a variety of factors. One African American woman who prefers to "go through on another level" made this point:

> I just don't spend a lot of mental energy with [confronting racism]. If I'm in a one-on-one conversation and a person comes off like that, I just may say something to elevate their thinking. And I may not. It just depends. I don't dwell in that space with people . . . that's not just where I am. Now if they get me on a bad day . . . on one of those hormonal days. Well that could be a different story.

Communication With Euro-Americans. In the opening paragraphs of this section, significant attention was given to the multiple consciousness of African American women and code-switching (Scott, 1996, chap. 3, this volume; Houston Stanback,

1983) that occurs throughout their daily interactions. Often times throughout the interviews and focus groups, the African American women involved in this study compared their interactions with other "Black" women to their communication with "White" women. This point of reference crystallized their vast differences between *intra*racial and *inter*racial women's communication.

A number of superlatives were used by our co-researchers to characterize their interactions with Euro-American women. Although many acknowledged "no choice but to have some kind of communication with White females," they described those interactions as "superficial," "awkward," and/or "shallow." One undergraduate student at a mid-sized university lives in a residence hall comprised of mainly Euro-American women, yet she finds herself not interacting with any non-African Americans beyond the "hi-and-bye" stuff. When asked about this, she shared:

> This is like so funny to me . . . how we interact. I will come out of my room and walk to the bathroom or whatever. And then I will see somebody and I'll say "hi," and she'll say "hi." And then I'll be coming back from the bathroom and they'll be coming back from their room . . . then we'll say "hi" again. The very same person. We do that all day and [sentence is interrupted by laughter] I know she doesn't know my name—and I don't know her name either. Why don't we just ask names?

Although a few researchers questioned the existence of such superficial interaction, other co-researchers attributed it to a lack of trust of Euro-Americans. Others alluded to a general sense of "competing" with Euro-American women as a factor. One undergraduate student at a large midwestern university gathered that some women seem threatened by her presence on campus. "They'll just, you know, kinda look at you like—'Don't jump on me!'"

One issue regarding intergroup communication that was discussed in several interviews and focus groups was how some Euro-Americans attempt to communicate with African American women with a familiarity that is not fully established. Co-researchers cited a number of experiences where co-workers, fellow students, or even strangers would initiate interactions with an assumption of informality that was perceived by many African American women as presumptuous, disrespectful, or insulting. Examples included using phrases like "kiddo," "girl," or "shortening one's name" without asking. The use of "girl" between African American women has clear meaning (see, e.g., Scott, 1996); however, when this term is used in interactions with Euro-American women, it becomes problematic, as seen in the following example of a student who prepared to question a comment made in class:

> when I raised my hand, a couple of white girls behind me were like, "GET 'EM GIRL!" and I just turned around and looked . . . it was like they expected me to roll my head and snap my fingers and tell someone off . . . I'm trying to be intellectual and join in a conversation or discussion in a class and they are like, "GET 'EM GIRL." I really wanted to turn around and say, "I'M NOT *YOUR* GIRL."

Expectations From Others. Following her recollection of the class incident, the woman went on to attribute the Euro-American women's comments to "something that they heard on TV" that prompted them toward a specific expectation as to how she would respond to the situation. Throughout their daily life experiences, African Americans are in the midst of negotiating a complex multiple consciousness around issues of race, gender, class, sexual orientation, and other elements of social identity. However, a consistent theme ran through the communicative experiences of the African American women involved in this study: Others interact with me based on social stereotypes. "It is only until that person gets to know me that I become an individual and not just a Black female," asserted a co-researcher part of a focus group of single mothers. Unfortunately, given characterizations of their communication with Euro-Americans, advancement beyond interactions based on stereotypes seldom occurs for African American women.

According to African American women, what stereotypes do others have of them? Throughout the 79 pages of descriptions of lived experiences a variety of stereotypes were identified and discussed. These included, "having an attitude," "being tough," "very assertive," "being a sexual being"/"super whore," "being poor," and "not knowing what you're talking about." Interestingly, these stereotypes were attributed to African American women with no acknowledgment of the diversity within this large, heterogeneous group. The importance of challenging the "externally defined, stereotypical images of African American womanhood" (Collins, 1986, p. 16) is crucial in promoting self-definition or self-evaluation for African American women. Often, these stereotypes target those African American female behaviors most threatening to Euro-Americans (White, 1985).

The stereotypes unconsciously held by Euro-Americans often reduce the experiences of African American Womanhood to those of a monolithic category. Interracial interactions subsequently involve no clear consciousness of the ways in which African American women negotiate a multiple consciousness based on race and gender and other cultural elements such as class, age, sexual orientation, religion, and physical abilities. Clearly, all African American women are expected to be the same. When they do not communicate based on the stereotypical expectations of others difficulties, based on the others' anxiety and uncertainty, arise. Co-researchers explained that it is as if most Euro-Americans do not know how to communicate with African American women who do not fit *their* stereotypes. Several co-researchers described instances like this when others characterized their speech or dress as "White"—meaning not stereotypically "Black."

> [This happens] all of the time. My supervisor who hired me . . . I had a telephone interview. What a surprise! He had a copy of my resume . . . and I had gotten some academic achievement awards—some minority student academic achievement awards—so they were on it. He called . . . I found this out later . . . the minority affairs director and said, "I'm really confused. I talked to my candidate on the phone and she sounds white, but I looked at her resume and it says minority, so she may be black. I'm not really sure what she is."

Another expectation that African American women face, especially those who work in dominant cultural professional settings, is that they represent "exceptions" to the general population of African American women. In some instances, the expectation is that one's socioeconomic status, educational achievements, or professional standing makes African American women more "like Whites." Co-researchers report that this perception can derive from both African Americans and Euro-Americans and contributes to a greater consciousness in their communication with others. One African American female graduate student reported a specific incident (one of many) that worked to inform a complex multiple consciousness.

> There was a program somewhere on campus and they were talking about Ebonics and standard English, and I said "Oh, I ought to go to that." And [a fellow graduate student] said, "Why? You don't speak that way." And I said that I don't speak the same way around everyone. She goes, "I can't even picture you talking like that . . . that's not you." It's like they have a different perception of people like that. I don't think they realize they are offending me . . . "You aren't like other Blacks," is what they are really saying. I don't think that they do it to hurt me, they do it to let me know that I fit in . . . "You're one of us; you aren't like *those* Black people."

Resisting the Hegemonic Messages of Dominant Society. One aspect of the multiple consciousness of African American women is the cognizant resistance of the hegemonic messages of dominant society. For several co-researchers this meant "not buying into the system" and rejecting societal definitions of what constitutes "success," "beauty," "competence," or "the Black experience." Most central to this theme was the dialogue between African American young women in two focus groups, one of undergraduate students and the other of young parents. In both groups, part of the discussion focused on the competition between young African American women. The group of young mothers discussed issues of beauty, attraction, and relationships and the ways in which European standards ("'good' hair" and "lighter skin") negatively affected relationships within African American communities. "We tend to be racist against each other either blatantly or we don't realize that is what we are doing," explained one woman. At one point in the discussion, a co-researcher interrupted with an intriguing question: "May I ask a question? I just want to know . . . Why are we our worst enemies?" The following explanation, offered by another African American woman, describes the power of hegemony in the lives of African Americans: "I think it came from the beginning. The racism that White people inflicted upon us . . . and it just became an inside thing [which] expresses itself on the outside . . . and that's a shame."[2]

A similar conclusion was drawn in the other focus group discussion of undergraduate students. Stemming from a discussion about differences between interactions with African American women and Euro-American women, a discussion arose that spoke to the issues of competition and success. According to one co-researcher, some African American women's competitive energies were geared toward accomplishing success—as defined by the standards of Euro-Americans.

> I see some African American women trying to be like a White woman . . . their stereotype of the best thing to be was White . . . Here is this White woman and she has a Coach bag . . . and wears Chanel. And then you have these Black women who look up to that and . . . start getting the same type of things . . . I don't think that the African American women who started wanting to be like—I'm not going to say "be white"—but they just wanted to fit that image of what they think is pretty . . . I don't think they understood where [it] is coming from . . .

---

[2]For an in-depth discussion of the impact of internalized racism and sexism on African American women, see Lorde (1984a, 1984b).

Throughout the oral narratives of our co-researchers was the recognition of the different standpoints that African American women occupied in terms of their multiple consciousness. Clearly, the co-researchers involved in this project varied in their levels of awareness in terms of the role that hegemonic socialization played in their daily lives. In this regard, multiple consciousness is not seen as a "point of arrival or departure," but instead, a dynamic process of constant negotiation. Each African American woman's life contains a series of critical incidents that serve as sudden intuitive realizations in terms of her self-concepts. These events, regardless of time passed, continue to influence everyday interactions. Such was the case for one co-researcher whom recalled an interaction with an African American professor, who she approached for assistance in a poetry reading assignment during her undergraduate days on a predominantly Euro-American campus:

> He got out some Black poetry . . . it was like Black English and slang everywhere. And I said "I can't go reading that—all of those white people are going to think I'm stupid!" . . . He pulled me into his office . . . I mean he grabbed me, pulled me into his office, and said "Sit down." I mean he just let me have it. And that is when I realized that it was acceptable to use Black English. Up until then, from my French teacher [in high school]—who was a white woman— I had learned that I should never use it, that it's not appropriate, and there are times when I wished that my family hadn't taught me to speak in that way. . . . When that teacher told me that it was inappropriate and wrong, I think I started to judge people who spoke that way. I mean I didn't go up and say anything, but I would think, "they aren't educated . . ."

A "Natural Connection" Among African American Women

Collins (1986) asserted that the communication among African American women is crucial to survive or succeed in a society where they experience a simultaneity of oppression. Throughout the transcripts, the African American women involved in our research project described the great importance of relationships with other African American women: mothers, daughters, aunts, sisters, friends, and lovers. They shared that their interactions with other African American women were like "communicating at a different level"; it often involved "comforting talk," "mutual respect and admiration," "being completely honest," and "a sense of acceptance." These communicative experiences reflect an established—yet often ubiquitous—sense of sisterhood, defined by Collins (1986) as "generally understood to mean a supportive feeling of loyalty and attachment to other women stemming from a shared feeling of oppression" (p. 22). African American sisterhood, in the words of one co-researcher, is "unconscious, yet undeniable."

One African American woman, who participated in a focus group of "women in the life,"[3] attributed the natural connection of African American women with the comfort of the mirror: "See[ing] someone who looks like you makes[s] you feel comfortable." A natural connection is automatically there based on the shared similarities inherent in being an African American woman. In one of the interviews, a graduate student shared her experiences of being the only African American student in a graduate program and the importance that another African American woman played in her survival/success.

> I walked up to her because she was Black—and I hadn't seen any Black people yet—so I walked up to her, introduced myself, and we hit it off. I connected with [her] right away . . . even though I've only known her since August, it's like we've known each other longer than that. I mean we have prayed together, we go to church together, we go to the library together . . . I mean there is no one else that I could do that with. And I don't even know her that well. It's like we have this life history together . . . I don't even think that I could make it [without her.] . . . it's hard for me to be here. But it's like I know that when I go home in the evenings, I can call her and say, "This is what happened today . . ." We just go back and forth . . . she has challenges that she has to face as well. And it's just so helpful to have each other.

Again, a natural connection inherently forms the basis of interaction between African American women. "[In] my communication with other African American womyn,[4] I feel and I expect a sisterhood. So when I'm in the company of a sister, I expect sisterhood from her. I don't always get it, but I expect it . . ." explained one African American woman.

---

[3]In the African American community, "in the life" is a term used by gay, lesbians, and bisexual persons as a means of self-description.

[4]In one of our focus groups, the co-researchers explicitly discussed their consciousness of choosing particular words to describe themselves and others, including the spelling of these words. As a means to honor their distinct voices, we use these words in direct quotes even though they are not necessarily consistent from other African American women involved in our project. In fact, this point—acknowledging the diversity within African American women/womyn's experiences—is central to the essence of our chapter.

According to our co-researchers, a number of key issues are central to sisterhood and communication. When asked about the sisterhood between African American women, several co-researchers described a number of issues that illustrated how this natural connection informed their communication; these are explained in the next sections.

A Distinction Between Connection and Bond. One important distinction made by several co-researchers was between a natural connection among African American women and a bond between African American women. The natural *connection,* according to one woman, "goes back to our very beginning. Even when they don't see it, it's there because we were connected before we got over here [U.S.]." The connection, according to some of our co-researchers, manifests itself in terms of elements of culture that comprise the African American women's experience. These could be concrete cultural items, like food, hair, church, or music, or more abstract experiences related to their multiple jeopardy/consciousness as African American women. However, for other African American female co-researchers, the connection is a "macro thing" that does not always affect the day to day interactions between African American women in the same manner.

> I think that you're talking more on a metaphysical level and maybe I'm playing semantics . . . [but] I would say I feel connected with that woman based on us being Black women, but I don't know if I can say right off I have a bond with her.

In this regard, the natural connection among African American women was apparent, however, the development of a bond was result of a process and not automatically assumed nor advanced.

In a number of the focus group discussions, African American women gave voice to their desire for sisterhood—to feel that special bond with other African American women—and their dismay that it was not always present in daily life interactions. One source that disrupts the sense of sisterhood was that of competition between African American women for the good things in life (love, success, happiness). This intense sense of competition and jealousy hinders the relationships between some African American women—especially, it seems among our younger co-researchers. One aspect that illustrated this phenomena was how some African American women communicate about their heterosexual relationships.[5]

---

[5]See Lorde's (1984b) discussion on the competition among women for male attention.

> I think we as women are our worst enemies at times. . . . In relationships when there is a man involved, knowing good and well the man was in the wrong, we will cuss that girl up one row and down the other. . . . Sometimes I give them the benefit of the doubt—they don't even know about you—but we will go after the woman.

Other women in this focus group echoed similar sentiments; one co-researcher attributed the lack of sisterhood directly to "men."

> I think we are jealous of one another to be honest. Sometimes I get jealous of pretty females. I think men are the biggest thing. You got to fight with all of your sisters, all black females, just to get this one man. And I really think that this the reason, the main reason that we can not bond.

Following these comments, other co-researchers acknowledged that African American women will "bond if something is wrong." For instance, in terms of the competition for Black men, one woman asked, "But do you notice how we will bond together if we see a Black man with a White woman?" "Girl, we the best of friends!" replied another. In this regard, feeling threatened by competition from European American woman or diminished by African American men who choose Euro-American women as their partners triggers a sense of camaraderie among African American women.

Although some of the younger African American women in our study appeared to find the "answer" hindering true sisterhood (men), other co-researchers recognized other factors that impact the development of bonding between African American women. For some, simply being an African American and a woman is not always enough to elicit a sense of sisterhood. Other aspects of one's cultural identity, as described in the next section, appear to arise as salient issues.

The Diversity of African American Women. For the vast majority of African American women involved in our study, the quest for sisterhood was constantly negotiated. They often sought out meaningful relationships with other African American women, but, in some cases, recognized that you always do not "hit it off" due to personal differences.

> I feel like I want to think of myself as being part of Black wommonhood, so when the communication works well, I feel good about it. But, if I get in a group and . . . for whatever reason, you

> just don't hit if off. . . . You just think that because we're Black
> womyn, maybe that would be enough to at least start with, but
> sometimes it isn't. Sometimes, just being a Black wommon isn't
> enough.

In addition to differences of personal characteristics, a number of
cultural differences may impact the communication and relationships
among African American women. When recognizing the great
diversity among such a large, heterogeneous group, the vastly
different standpoints that African American women may occupy can
make it difficult to develop a bond. In some instances, other cultural
differences—like those based on socioeconomic status, educational
background, sexual orientation, age, or geographical differences—can
emerge as barriers to sisterhood.

We found a number of oral narratives in the transcripts that
spoke to the issue of diversity among African American women. One
African American woman shared how her identity as a lesbian
directly impacts the interaction with family, especially around
holiday time when the entire family gets together. Topical areas that
seem of great interest to other female relatives (men, relationships,
hair, nails) do not interest her. Speaking about her experiences
interacting with other African American women, she explains that
"sometimes I feel like I don't fit in . . . and I don't try to fit." The
experiences of another co-researcher, in her role as an administrator
at a small predominately Euro-American college, addressed how the
issue of one's background can also become a salient issue. Her
relationships with some of the African American female
undergraduate students are hindered by their perceptions of her
"blackness." Raised in a predominately Euro-American neighborhood,
she explained that to some African American women, "I'm not Black
enough. I don't talk that much slang, I don't kick it with them . . . I'm
not from the 'hood'."

One oral narrative appears especially telling, in terms of the
ways in which cultural differences impact how African American
women communicate with other African American women. The two
women, whose experiences were discussed in the previous paragraph,
assumed a communicative stance where they did not attempt to meet
the expectations of others in order to facilitate more meaningful
communication. However even when there is a desire to transcend
cultural barriers, differences—like those based on education—still
remain divisive.

> If I go into the ghetto—whatever that means, let's just use the
> phrase "the ghetto"—and there are a bunch of hard core sisters . . .

you know, just looking like they are ready to fight somebody. . . . For whatever reason, [it's different], whether it be due to the way I might talk or the way I look or if they know about my educational background. You know the higher you go up, especially in education, the more suspect you are. They're gonna associate you with white folks until you show them differently. And even then, there is still sometimes resentment. . . . Even though I might want desperately to be a part of that . . . there is always something that is going to keep me on the fringes or feeling like I'm on the fringes.

Sense of Spirituality. The difficulty of achieving a sense of true sisterhood with all other African American women notwithstanding, the natural connection among African American women seems apparent in most initial interactions. According to several co-researchers, this sense of kinship includes a certain aspect of spirituality. Some discussion focused on the important role that women have played in the traditional African American churches. One focus group of African American women, in some dialogue about a connection that they felt among one another, invoked the words of the gospel song "I Don't Feel No Ways Tired" by James Cleveland. In their comments, they acknowledged that some African American women who did not grow up in "that religious tradition" wouldn't have necessarily the same reference point. However, they did believe that African American women as a whole could identify with the powerful lyrics: "I don't feel no ways tired. I come too far from where I started from. Nobody told me that the road would be easy. I don't believe He brought me this far to leave me." It was this sense of spirituality—of resiliency, perseverance, and destiny—that characterizes a natural connection for many African American women. As one co-researcher explained:

[It's] this spiritual kind of thing that I think you're kind of getting at when you say you walk into a room and [immediately connect with other African American women]. . . . It's that whole other realm that Black women . . . operate on. . . . Somewhere in their life, they've interacted with a woman . . . or they know a woman like that [referring to women in the traditional Black church] . . . I think that also informs how we deal with each other too.

Other comments throughout the interviews and focus group discussions also pointed to a sense of spirituality for African American women that extended beyond simple religious or denominational designations. For many of the African American women who shared their stories with us, it was this sense of spirituality that allowed them to deal with the simultanity of oppression that permeates into their daily life experiences. This feeling that their lives were guided by a higher being allowed some to "go through life on another level" and to continue to persevere through the obstacles that were placed in their ways toward a role that only African American women could fulfill. Instead of viewing their lives as a multitude of oppressions, many African American women opted to view their unique positioning as a blessing (see, e.g., Allen, 1995). In many instances, this spiritual sense of being was instilled in them through the communication with other African American women. One African American woman shared that she got some valuable insight as she entered graduate school: "Business before pleasure, but neither before God." A focus on the power or plan of a higher being has enabled her to endure the struggles of graduate school and working on a campus in a town that is so small it doesn't appear on most maps. "At first, I was upset that I had to move . . . I was like 'God, why are you doing this to me?' But there is a reason why I am [here]; I'm not going to worry about it."

The sense of spirituality articulated by African American women seemed to cut across other cultural differences, such as age, socio-economic status, and geography. Struggling with the rigors of graduate school, professional responsibilities, or the daily adversities of being a single parent were all possible through the identification of a spiritual source. For one African American woman, it also encouraged her to reevaluate what she perceived as "success." "When I think about being successful," she shared, "I think about being married, being happy, and having the bills paid. But I'm finding that that's just not it." In recent months, this woman has begun an afterschool program in her home that serves a number of children in the HUD housing complex in which she lives. This God-inspired endeavor has given her a renewed sense of purpose, direction, and fulfillment.

> [F]or the first time in my life, I feel happy. And I am still poor, I am still a single parent, I am still a black heavy set woman . . . who doesn't get a fair break. But still, right now, I am a happy woman because I feel like I am doing something that God wants me to do. And He used all of that stuff that I went through . . . and turned that around and used [it] . . . to His good. And I'm happy, I am so happy that there is something that actually came out of all that junk that I went through.

The commitment to serving others displayed by this woman was also shared by many of the other African American women involved in this project. Several were in fields or active in projects that served others. Some were educators, nurses, or counselors or working on degrees toward these careers. Others utilized a variety of professional, church, civic, or other community-based organizations in assuming a keen sense of social responsibility in helping others. In fact, several of the African American women made their desire to "make a difference in this world" explicitly clear. This desire was clear, not only in the careers that they chose, the service organizations that they are a part of, but also in the ways in which they communicate with others in their day-to-day lives.

CONCLUSION

Black feminist thought explicates a consciousness that has existed among African American women throughout the history of the United States (i.e., White, 1985). In fact, "many ordinary Black women have grasped [the] connection between what one does and how one thinks" (Collins, 1989, p. 748). If we believe that everyday conversations are simply microcosms of the larger social and political relationships of a specific place in history (Houston, 1997), exploring the communicative experiences of African American women is fertile ground for future research on Black feminist thought and talk. "Women's personal and existential choices, both conscious and preconscious, necessarily carry political implications that more or less confirm or disconfirm existing structures of experience" (Nelson, 1989, p. 225). As such, scholarly inquiries that seek to gain insight into the everyday lives of African American women should be of great interest to communication, phenomenology, and feminist scholars.

Specifically, the research described in this chapter offers clarification to existing literature associated with Black feminist thought. Two specific themes central to the communicative experiences of African American women were presented. First, the reality of a multiple consciousness was explicated through four motifs:

1. Communicating in the midst of multiple oppressions.
2. Communication with Euro-Americans.
3. Expectations of others.
4. Resisting the hegemonic messages of dominant society.

Second, attention was given to the natural connection among African American women. Specific to this theme were three additional features:

1. A distinction between connection or bond.
2. The diversity of African American women.
3. Sense of spirituality.

Throughout this chapter, these themes were presented as a means to add clarification to the existing work on Black feminist thought or talk. Specifically, these ideas tie directly with the central ideas of Collins' work (1986): self-definition/evaluation, interlocking nature of oppression, and the importance of African American women's culture.

The insights contained in this chapter represent a collaborative interpretation of communicative experiences of African American women involved in a study on African American women's communication. However, it is important to recognize that in phenomenological inquiry, such an interpretation is hardly definitive. According to de Lauretis (1984), the intersubjective nature of interpretative work is best seen as "an ongoing construction, not a fixed departure or arrival" (p. 159). For phenomenologists who are consciously engaged in their own lifeworlds, this means that their interpretations are immediately altered the instant that they view the "finished" product and begin to reflect on it. In this regard, our insights simply reflect one point of analysis in a tradition and future of Black feminist scholarship. The promise of Black feminist scholarship is readily apparent in its relevance to a vast array of disciplines and in the immeasurable ways in which each discipline can contribute unique insights to the growing body of literature. This chapter represents how phenomenological inquiry, utilized via the collaborative lens of three young communication scholars, can make just such a contribution.

REFERENCES

Allen, B. J. (1995, November). *Twice blessed, doubly oppressed: Women of color in academe.* Paper presented at the annual convention of the Speech Communication Association, San Antonio, TX.

Collins, P. H. (1986). Learning from the outsider within: The sociological significance of black feminist thought. *Social Problems, 33*(6), S14-S23.

Collins, P. H. (1989). The social construction of black feminist thought. *Signs, 14*(1), 745-773.

Collins, P. H. (1990). *Black feminist thought: Knowledge, consciousness, and the politics of empowerment.* Boston, MA: Unwin Hyman.

de Lauretis, T. (1984). *Feminist studies/critical studies.* Bloomington: Indiana University Press.

Essed, P. (1991). *Understanding everyday racism: An interdisciplinary theory.* Newbury Park, CA: Sage.

Etter-Lewis, G. (1991). Black women's life stories: Reclaiming self in narrative texts. In S. B. Gluck & K. Patai (Eds.), *Women's words: The feminist practice of oral history* (pp. 43-58). New York: Routledge.

Ford-Ahmed, T. (1992, October). *Exploring lived experiences of African American graduate women during an explosive week.* Paper presented at the annual Midwest Popular Culture Association and the Midwest American Culture Association, Indianapolis, IN.

Foss, K. A., & Foss, S. K. (1994). Personal experience as evidence in feminist scholarship. *Western Journal of Communication, 58,* 39-43.

Houston, M. (1997). When Black women talk with White women: Why dialogues are difficult. In A. Gonzalez, M. Houston, & V. Chen (Eds.), *Our voices: Essays in culture, ethnicity, and communication* (pp. 187-194). Los Angeles: Roxbury.

Houston Stanback, M. (1983). *Code-switching in black women's speech.* Unpublished doctoral dissertation, University of Massachusetts, Amherst.

Houston Stanback, M. (1985). Language and Black woman's place: Evidence from the black middle class. In P. Treicher, C. Kramarae, & B. Stafford (Eds.), *For alma mater: Theory and practice in feminist scholarship* (pp. 177-193). Urbana: University of Illinois Press.

Husserl, E. (1962). *Ideas: General introduction to pure phenomenology* (W. Gibson, Trans.). New York: Collier Books.

Kapoor, P. (1992, October). *A chance of double lives: Study of black female graduate experience.* Paper presented at the annual Midwest Popular Culture Association and the Midwest American Culture Association, Indianapolis, IN.

King, D. K. (1988). Multiple jeopardy, multiple consciousness: The context of a black feminist ideology. *Signs, 14*(1), 42-72.

Langellier, K. M., & Hall, D. L. (1989). Interviewing women: A phenomenological approach to feminist communication research. In K. Carter & C. Spitzack (Eds.), *Doing research on women's communication: Perspectives on theory and method* (pp. 193-220). Norwood, NJ: Ablex.

Lanigan, R. L. (1979). The phenomenology of human communication. *Philosophy Today, 23*(1), 3-15.

Lorde, A. (1984a). Eye to eye: Black women, hatred, and anger. In A. Lorde (Ed.), *Sister outsider: Essays and speeches by Audre Lorde* (pp. 145-175). Freedom, CA: The Crossing Press.

Lorde, A. (1984b). Scratching the surface: Some notes on barriers to women and loving. In A. Lorde (Ed.), *Sister outsider: Essays and speeches by Audre Lorde* (pp. 45-52). Freedom, CA: The Crossing Press.

Merleau-Ponty, M. (1962). *The visible and the invisible* (C. Smith, Trans., F. Williams, Trans. rev.). London: Routledge & Kegan Paul. (Original work published 1948)

Nelson, J. (1989). Phenomenology as feminist methodology: Explicating interviews. In K. Carter & C. Spitzack (Eds.), *Doing research on women's communication: Perspectives on theory and method* (pp. 221-241). Norwood, NJ: Ablex.

Orbe, M. (1998). *Constructing co-cultural theory: An explication of culture, power, and communication.* Thousand Oaks, CA: Sage.

Peterson, E. A. (1992). *African American women: A study of will and success.* Jefferson, NC: McFarland.

Scott, K. D. (1996, June). *Style switching as ideological position in Black women's talk.* Paper presented at the SCA Black Caucus/African American Communication and Culture Division annual summer conference, Frankfort, KY.

Smith, A., & Stewart, A. J. (1983). Approaches to studying racism and sexism in Black women's lives. *Journal of Social Issues, 39,* 1-15.

van Manen, M. (1990). *Researching lived experience: Human science for action sensitive pedagogy.* Albany: State University of New York Press.

White, E. F. (1985). *Art'n't I a woman? Female slaves in the plantation south.* New York: W. W. Norton.

SEVEN

"Take Care of Your Sisters": Communication Among the Women in the Works of Pearl Cleage

Joni L. Jones
Teri L. Varner
University of Texas at Austin

> *That is what theater is for me—a hollering place, a place to talk about our black female lives, defined by our specific black female reality to each other first, and then to others of good will who will take the time to listen and understand.*
> —Cleage (1994, p. 13)

Dramatic texts provide an opportunity to view communication in a distilled form. Playwrights often attempt to set on the page the kind of interactions they believe suggest actual spontaneous communication. With this in mind, examining plays as a way of looking at styles of everyday life communication offers an opportunity to experience communication in a refined form. Plays often employ all the strategies of Everyday Life Performance (ELP)[1]

---

[1]As employed by Hopper (1993), ELP was designed to deepen responsiveness to talk. As employed by Stucky (1993), ELP was a strategy for developing

with more specific focus and goal orientation than ELP, and fewer nonfluencies and incomplete ideas than is typically found in ELP. Everyday Life Performance is a tool used by conversation analysts that allows for the detailed understanding of vocal utterances, and is simulated by playwrights attempting to record human interaction with all of its idiosyncrasies. In so doing, playwrights can offer a window into reality. Canon supported this claim when she wrote "Black women writers skillfully and successfully supply the patterns of conduct, feeling, and contestable issues that exist in the real-lived context that lies behind this literature" (p. 70). The fictive dramas examined in this chapter offer an opportunity to explore the real communication styles of African American women.

Pearl Cleage is currently receiving some attention and acclaim as a playwright, novelist, and essayist. The drama *Flyin' West* (Cleage, 1996b) has been presented at major regional theaters across the United States including Crossroads Theatre, St. Louis Black Repertory Theatre, Long Wharf Theatre, Indiana Repertory Theatre, the New WORLD Theatre, BAM's Majestic Theatre, the Kennedy Center, Plowshares Theatre, Intiman Theatre, The Ensemble Theatre, and First Stage Productions. *Blues for an Alabama Sky* (Cleage, 1996a) is developing a similarly impressive production history at theaters that include Arena Stage, Alliance Theatre, Hartford Stage Company, Huntington Theatre Company, and Pro-Arts Collective. Blues was also presented in Atlanta as part of the 1996 Cultural Olympiad in conjunction with the Olympic Games. *Hospice* (Cleage, 1989), which premiered in New York, won five AUDELCO Awards for achievement Off Broadway in 1983. Cleage's (1997) first novel, *What Looks Like Crazy on an Ordinary Day,* was selected as part of the Oprah Winfrey Book Club. Her essays can be found in her own collections, as well as major feminist anthologies such as *Words of Fire* (Guy-Sheftall, 1995), *Double Stich* (Bell-Scott, Guy-Sheftall, Royster, Sims-Woods, DeCosta-Willis, & Fultz, 1981), and *The Woman that I Am* (Madison, 1994). Much of what has been written about the dramas of this "third-generation black nationalist and radical feminist" (Cleage, 1996b, p. 46) deals with issues of aesthetics and theatrical conventions. In this chapter we shift the focus of the discussion away from aesthetics and toward the communication strategies of the African American women in Cleage's plays.

In Cleage's (1993) two-character drama, *Late Bus to Mecca,* one of the characters reviews a list of rules for sisterhood that includes the declaration "Take Care of Your Sisters." This chapter

---

aestheticized performances and understanding the specifics of character. In both cases, the aim is to explore the subtleties, details, nonfluencies, nonsequiturs, and distinctive patterns of everyday speech.

examines the extent to which the women in Cleage's plays actually take care of each other through their communication choices, which center around three communication strategies—sass, silence, and support. These categories of communication are a modification of the three levels of speech hooks (1989) outlined in *Talking Back*.[2] Although *sass, silence*, and *support* do not exhaust the possible communication strategies between African American women, these features of communication dominate the styles of communication employed by the women in Cleage's plays.

Sass is a way of having voice when other means are not available. Because women have generally been socialized against defending themselves physically, verbal defense mechanisms become essential. Sass is "back talking," "smart mouthing," "womanish" commentary designed to attack an other, protect the self and/or demonstrate verbal agility. It is a variant of signifying, which Smitherman (1977) defined as "the verbal art of insult in which a speaker humorously puts down, talks about, needles—that is, signifies on—the listener" (p. 118). However, unlike signifying, contemporary expressions of sass are not necessarily associated with elements of indirection and subtlety. During the slave era in the United States, enslaved African women were unable to directly challenge the verbal and physical abuse heaped on them; instead they keenly developed the skill of "sassing the master." At that time, circumlocution was important for survival, whereas today, direct scathing commentary is often applauded for its artistry: Enslaved women bold enough to vocally resist their oppression risked the lash if they were to sass openly. In her analysis of slave narratives, Braxton (1984) wrote that the narrators in those works often describe "the spirit of resistance of those who chose to fight back, negotiating for respect through verbal dueling, impertinence, sass and other forms of overt rebellion" (p. 47). As with other African American-based linguistic strategies such as the use of the double negative, the use of the continuous "to be," and the use of proverbs, sass has endured even beyond the immediate context for which it was originally intended.

---

[2]In "Talking Back," the first essay in her widely read feminist commentary of the same name, hooks (1989) discussed various speech strategies employed by African American women. The essay focuses almost exclusively on "talking back" and the empowering potential of that single speech act, although Wallace (1981) derived three very specific categories from hooks' ideas. Wallace argued that hooks illustrated "the three levels of speech that occur among Black women: speechlessness . . . ; self-reflexive speech . . . ; and 'talking back.'" (p. 19) Throughout this chapter we note the ways in which our categories overlap with and diverge from those identified by hooks through Wallace.

Indeed, the persistence of oppression, albeit less stringent than U.S. slavery, makes sass a useful contemporary survival tool.

Sass, in its most potent variation, has a kinship to conjuring as the speaker casts invocations at the listener. The words take on the power of *nommo,* the Dogon expression loosely translated as word force. African American women could then hurl words like punches, trusting that the power invested in the words would strike as surely as a fist. This use of sass differs from hooks' empowering notion of "talking back" in that sass does not always constitute a communication which "transcends and transforms the barriers of race, class, and sex to address the world" (Wallace, 1981, p. 19). Sass is often clever without being transformative, rendering the speaker only temporarily powerful.

Sass also has the capacity to foster bonding between women as sass can reveal or deepen intimacy. The closest of friends can say things to each other that would be off limits for others to express. In this way, sass does not protect one communicator from the other, but instead it joins the communicators in a shared understanding of the relationship and the kind of communication appropriate in that relationship.

Although sass may have been a strategy for keeping one's dignity in the face of assault or for solidifying the closeness in a relationship, it also may have contributed to stereotypic beliefs about African American women. Collins (1981) argued that when an African American woman verbally defends herself "she is labeled aggressive and unfeminine" (p. 44). Because of "pressures incumbent on Black female speech" (Wallace, 1981, p. 19), virtually any response by African American women might be labeled as sass regardless of the structure, tone, or impetus for the comment.

Silence often functions in contradictory ways in communication interactions. Silence can be used as a passive-aggressive strategy to refuse compliance with oppression. Behind such silence is often anger about and vengeance against injustices. The silence masks a wall of strength and power with no viable outlet. This is especially effective when speaking carries with it the threat of violence. Such silence would have been an essential survival strategy during slavery in the United States.

Silence is also a way of protecting the self from the horrors we witness. In discussing Toni Morrison's *Beloved,* Canon (1995) asserts that after experiencing so much ugliness "our minds no longer allow our eyes to see and . . . our mouths to speak" (p. 75). Canon describes the way in which Baby Suggs cannot speak when she sees the bleeding lashes on her daughter Sethe's back. Baby Suggs is "speechless, without words, struck silent" (p. 75). If we don't put words on it we can tuck it away in our spaces of private pain. The words might be replaced with a gasp, a distant look of remembered though unexpressed devastation, or a suck of the teeth. At times, then, the silence is punctuated by a host of nonverbal responses. These direct responses, both the absence of words and the silent nonverbal commentary, are integral to the communication as they vivify interaction.

Although these forms of silence are powerful ways of shielding the spirit from the unspeakable, silence can also have the adverse effect of removing the African American woman from the communication entirely. Too often, when African American women are silent, they are simply ignored. Silence may be misinterpreted and its political implications missed.[3] Some may actually choose the option of silence in order to counter the myth of the "loud Black woman" who, through a quick and angry tongue will emasculate all the men and frighten the White women.[4] Rather than perpetuate such images, some African American women prefer to remain silent. In such instances, where there is no horror witnessed nor an injustice that must be righted, the woman is disregarded with no one seeking her opinion or noticing that she has not contributed any commentary. In her discussion of Black motherhood, Collins (1981) simply wrote, "if she remains silent, she is rendered invisible" (p. 44). The silence might be the learned politeness associated with the socially acceptable performance of femaleness, yet Lorde (1984) reminded African American women that "your silence will not protect you" (p. 41).

Silence, then, can be a conscious tool for commenting on injustice and for protecting the self from unnamable horrors, and an unconscious source for undermining an African American woman's power. Merely raising one's voice, however, does not insure that the message will counter the forces of hegemony. As Wallace (1992)

---

[3]Much has been written on African American women and silence. See Orbe (1998) and Parker (1998) for discussions of silence among African American women in business contexts; see Wallace (1992) for an exploration of the ramifications of African American women's silence; and see Dash (1992) for commentary on the silencing of particular film narratives by African American women.

[4]In the award-winning drama *for colored girls who have considered suicide/when the rainbow is enuf* by Ntozake Shange (1977), the lady in orange declares, "ever since i realized there waz someone callt a colored girl an evil woman a bitch or a nag i been tryin not to be that" (p. 44). These lines reveal the ways in which some African American women participate in a self-policing in order to conform to socially acceptable standards of female behavior.

noted, "the problem of silence, and the shortcomings inherent in any representation of the silenced, need to be acknowledged as a central problematic in any oppositional black feminist process" (p. 663).

Support can be categorized in two primary ways: communication designed to help others, and communication that aids in helping the self. Communication that helps others is characterized by the loving gift of woman truths, those lessons that cover all manner of information including issues of health, etiquette, gender performance, childrearing, personal style, interpersonal relations, aesthetics, food preparation, career development, and sex. Such messages are what Canon (1995) called "liberation ethics" (p. 138), words that advance a woman's sense of self and offer armor against oppression. This is the sort of communication that grows from intimacy between women. It is through these relationships that values about womanhood are transmitted. Because these relationships are so important, Cole (cited in Harper, 1997) offered an important warning when she wrote: "We womenfolk have to keep asking ourselves what kind of messages are we delivering, what kind of lessons are we teaching" (p. 46). Supportive communication as used in this essay is in direct contrast to the "tongues of fire" that hooks (1993) said often come in the guise of love but leave an irrevocable sting (p. 32). There are some uses of sass that might also be classified as support when the sass reveals intimacy between the women communicating. In this way, sass as support both helps the recipient and the sender as each acknowledge their closeness through the communication.

Supportive communication that is designed to help the self often manifests as personal narratives in which one bears witness. In so doing, the speaker describes the trials she has faced and overcome. Such narratives "shape significance" (Langellier, 1989, p. 264) by pointing to the values of the speaker and be revealing her "social process of coping." The telling is cathartic and rejuvenating.

Another important aspect of supportive communication for the self is seen in those personal narratives that connect the speaker to ancestors and to progeny. Such communication gives the speaker roots, allows her to draw on the strength of her ancestors, reminds her that she is well supported by tradition, gives her continuity and place, and situates her in a larger context thereby allowing her to draw on the power she feels through ancestral spirit. In so doing, she increases her own *ase*, a Yoruba concept that refers to life force. She empowers herself through her own narrative. This has a close kinship with narratives that tell history. Historical narratives often serve the same function of connecting the speaker with a spiritual force that goes beyond the immediate circumstances. Invoking the ancestors gives power to the self.

SASS

That initial act of talking back outside the home was empowering. It was the first of many acts of defiant speech that would make it possible for me to emerge as an independent thinker and writer. In retrospect, "talking back" became for me a rite of initiation, testing my courage, strengthening my commitment, preparing me for the days ahead. . . . (hooks, 1989, p. 9)

Hospice centers around a troubled mother-daughter relationship. The mother, Alice, is a former poet and activist who is dying of cancer. As the play opens, Alice is deeply committed to one goal: "I'm looking for a hospice, Sister. A place to die in peace, not in pieces" (Cleage, 1989, p. 52). Jenny, her daughter, is "thirty years old and very pregnant" (p. 46). Jenny is a movie critic/journalist and an aspiring poet who finds herself unexpectedly living once again with Alice after years of a bitter estrangement. Of the four plays examined in this essay, *Hospice* provides the most frequent and biting examples of sass. Alice uses sass to protect herself from Jenny's insistence upon cordiality and intimacy.

Jenny: I want to make the best of it.
Alice: The best of *this*?
Jenny: The best of the time we have together.
Alice: That's not one of my strong points, making the best of it.
Jenny: It's my specialty . . .
Alice: You want to make a fairy tale out of it! You want me to tell you the secret of life and give you my motherly blessing. You want me to make up for twenty years of silence in two weeks. You want the two of us to play mother and daughter. (Cleage, 1989, p. 52)

The mother's communication strategy with her daughter appears to be in opposition to Guy-Sheftall's (1981) concept "mothering the mind," which "refers to the process by which people help to create the conditions for another's creativity" (p. 62). Rather than create conditions that would nurture Jenny's creativity, Alice's sass actively seeks to suppress her daughter's creativity. To Jenny's surprise Alice turns down the option of listening to music and instead asks Jenny to read one of her own poems:

Jenny: (hesitantly): Well, I have been working on something new.
Alice: (raising eyebrow): You're writing poems now?

Jenny: (nervously, fingering the pages): Well . . . sometime . . . I
           hardly ever show them to anybody though. They can't help
           comparing mine to yours. (She laughs ruefully.) You're a
           hard act to follow.
Alice: Then don't try it. And on second thought, don't read
           anything to me either. If I'm a tough act, I'm probably an
           impossible audience. (Cleage, 1989, p. 57)

Once again, Alice rejects an opportunity for closeness by using sass to
attack Jenny.

    Frequently in mother-daughter relationships, it is the
daughter who must learn by listening to the mother's thoughts and
opinions. In the context of African American culture, it is important
to note that "specific information is transmitted from one generation
of adult women to younger females regarding gender role
expectations, child rearing social skills, macrocultural and
microcultural values, norms and belief systems" (Jewell, 1993, p.
163). When sass is the primary mode of communication the daughter
may receive these important lessons as stern critiques of her
behavior. In several essays, Cleage speaks about her relationship
with her mother. Cleage was raised in an environment where
"mothering the mind" was the norm,[5] but explores a mothers' sass
through Alice.

    In discussing the power relations found in literary mother-
daughter relationships, Washington (1991) noted that "the
daughter's story leaves spaces and gaps which only the mother can
fill" (p. 128). Washington built on Marianne Hirsch's analysis which
calls for a "multiple female consciousness, creating the possibility for
the daughter to achieve both autonomy and a healthier relationship
with the mother" (Hirsch, cited in Washington, 1991, p. 128).
Dramatic texts allow for "multiple female conscious" as both mother
and daughter are given voice. The tension between Alice's sass and
Jenny's attempts to deflect the sassy invectives result in the difficult
movement toward a tentative reconciliation at the end of the play.
Near the final moments of the play, before Jenny is taken to the
hospital where she will deliver her child, the two women engage in a
brief mutually supportive interaction:

---

[5]Cleage devoted a considerable amount of her nonfiction writing to a
commentary about her mother. Among these essays are "Heading Home,"
"Lessons," "But Where Are You Now?," "My Mother Hated Being Poor,"
"Mexico Love" in *The Brass Bed and Other Stories*, and "Missing You" in
Deals with the Devil and Other Reasons to Riot.

(*They look at each other. Alice touches Jenny's cheek lightly.*)
(*Suddenly.*) Forgive me, Sister I did what I could. (*They embrace each other very gently. Alexis' car horn blows outside.*)

Alice: (*breaking the embrace and urging Jenny to the door*): Don't try to be brave now, Sister. Scream as loud as you want.

Jenny: (*stops at the door and looks back at Alice*): I love you, Mamma.

Alice: And I was always some place loving you, Baby. I was always some place loving you. (*Jenny exits. Alice sits down slowly in the rocking chair. She looks down slowly at the poem in her hand and all the energy seems to leave her body. She drops the pages to the floor.*)

Alice: Don't fool yourself, Miss Alice. Just don't fool yourself.
(Cleage, 1989, p. 72)

Although the communication between Alice and Jenny might be generally characterized as abrasive and deprecating forms of sass, the play also includes brief and significant instances of support. Indeed, the very brevity of these supportive interactions is a demonstration of their significance.

Late Bus to Mecca is set in a bus station, a liminal space rife with possibilities of movement, destination, and relocation. Ava, "a twentyish black woman" (Cleage, 1993, p. 300), is waiting for a Greyhound bus to transport her from Detroit to Atlanta where she hopes to make some quick money hustling during a major boxing match. While waiting, she attempts a conversation with a mute character known in the script simply as "A Black Woman, also a twentyish black woman" (p. 300). Ava is adept at sass. She is one of the "fast-talking, quick-thinking black women" (p. 13). Cleage says she likes to include in her plays. Through much of the play Ava's sass is directed at her absent friends Sheri and Tony, but out of frustration she uses sass with A Black Woman as well. Ava says rather bluntly to A Black Woman, "Great! I got one on the way who can't tell time and one sittin' here who can't talk. This must be my lucky night!" (p. 311) Ava seems free to use sass as attack because of A Black Woman's inability to verbally defend herself. Such abrasive commentary fits hooks' (1993) description of the "tongues of fire" she feels characterizes many mother-daughter relationships (p. 32). Perhaps Ava is encouraged to make such stiff criticism because she is forced into a mother role with the apparently helpless A Black Woman, and because A Black Woman's silence seems to present no defense, no barrier to ward off attack.

More than the other plays examined in this essay, *Flyin' West* demonstrates how sass can be used as a sign of increased intimacy as well as a way of protecting the self. Set in 1898 in the all-Black town of Nicodemus, Kansas, *Flyin' West* depicts the lives of four African American women who took advantage of the Homestead Act of 1860, which offered hundreds of acres to U.S. citizens willing to settle in the "wild west." Sisters Fannie and Minnie, along with their friend Sophie, fled the racist violence of Memphis, Tennessee after a lynching and subsequent riot in that city in 1892. Miss Leah was already braving the west when the Memphis migrants arrived. As with *Late Bus*, Cleage also set this play in a liminal space. The "wild west" calls forth notions of danger, mystery, and uncertainty along with freedom, independence, and strength. Under such unpredictable circumstances, the certainty offered through sisterhood is particularly welcome. Miss Leah and Sophie frequently engage in loving sass throughout the play:

Sophia: I'll make some coffee.
Miss Leah: I don't know why. Can't nobody drink that stuff but you.
Sophia: It'll warm you up.
Miss Leah: It'll kill me.
Sophia: Well, then, you haven't got much time to put your affairs in order. (Cleage, 1996b, p. 49)

This dialogue could be construed as the kind of mean-spirited communication that hooks' warned against, but it actually serves to lift the spirit rather than demean it. This sass is supportive because both women understand and accept the intentions behind the sass, and both women are equally comfortable offering sass in their interaction. Later in the play, when asked why she agitates Miss Leah, Sophie responds "She'll live longer if she's doing it to irritate me" (Cleage, 1996b, p. 54). Sophie, then, is using sass as a way of keeping Miss Leah on the earth plane, an act of love and appreciation rather than degradation. In such usage, sass is a form of "taking care of your sisters" as it is used to acknowledge intimacy through playfulness and to keep one's wits active through the skill required to participate.

Sass that demonstrates intimacy is found sparingly in *Blues*. When Angel says to Delia "Look at you Deal. You got bags under your eyes like an old woman. All tired and frowned up" (Cleage, 1996a, p. 30), Delia recognizes that the comment is really intended to help her take better care of herself rather than hurt her feelings.

In Cleage's plays, sass is not used as empowerment when exchanged among the women. When the women use sass with one another, it does not break a silence with a penetrating truth. Although this significant linguistic tool does not work in the most insurgent way between the women, such power is wielded against the men in the plays. Perhaps the absence of sass as truth among the women limits the power the women can have in Cleage's plays, but this absence also importantly suggests that the women in her plays are less likely to be in inequitable power relationships with other women that would require sass as truth telling. hooks declares, "For us, true speaking is not solely an expression of creative power; it is an act of resistance, a political gesture that challenges politics of domination that would render us nameless and voiceless. As such, it is a courageous act—as such, it represents a threat. To those who wield oppressive power, that which is threatening must necessarily be wiped out, annihilated, silenced" (hooks, 1989, p. 8).

SILENCE

It is necessary to realize that the voices of black feminism in the U.S. emerge today from a long tradition of the structural "silence" of women of color within the sphere of the production of knowledge worldwide. Rarely addressed by mainstream or radical feminism or by anyone, this "silence" has doomed to failure most efforts to change the black woman's status and/or condition within society. There is a danger that in the proliferation of black female images on TV, in music videos and, to a lesser extent, in film, we are witnessing merely a postmodern variation on this phenomenon of black female "silence." (Wallace, 1992, p. 655)

Cleage's *Late Bus to Mecca* and *Blues for an Alabama Sky* make significant use of silence. In *Late Bus* the silence is represented primarily by the nonspeaking character known as A Black Woman while in *Blues* the silence is the result of the polite conversation that many women are encouraged to speak, even at the expense of life-sustaining support.

Throughout most of *Late Bus,* A Black Woman remains in a near catatonic state while Ava talks to her about the rather standard subjects of men, hair care, sex, and the virtues of independence. Ava establishes a nonverbal communication system with A Black Woman that eventually allows them to move beyond linear communication strategies toward interactional and transactional ones. Although the conversations in the play are dominated by sass and support, Cleage is clearly interested in the power of silence by peopling her two-character play with a woman who remains silent throughout.

Because the silent character is given a generic name, she seems to embody Every Black Woman in Cleage's self-proclaimed "morality play." In a note to the reader, Cleage explains that "[m]y intention is to identify and highlight the values and actions that will be necessary if black women—and by extension black people—are to survive into the twenty-first century" (Cleage, 1993, p. 297). A Black Woman, then, seems a shell shocked image of all African American women who have tried to make sense of the paradoxes and horrors heaped upon them. She is the embodiment of the silence African American women hang onto in order to keep some semblance of sanity. Her ambiguous interaction with Ava pulls her out of her private unnamed nightmare into the beginnings of a union with another human being. This union and support seem to be Cleage's recommendations for the 21st century.

In Scene 9 there are no words spoken. This scene occurs after Ava has been caught rifling through A Black Woman's purse. Out of shame, Ava can only sit in silence smoking a cigarette under the accusing gaze of A Black Woman. Here, the silence has a kinship to Canon's speechlessness that is the result of something too ugly to name. The ugliness in *Late Bus* is the violation of trust and respect, the very gifts Ava offers and A Black Woman guardedly accepts.

Blues for an Alabama Sky takes place in the summer of 1930 in a Harlem brownstone apartment building. The two female characters in the play are Angel Allen, "a thirty-four-year-old black woman who looks five years younger; former back-up singer at the Cotton Club"; and Delia Patterson, "a twenty-five-year-old black woman social worker on staff at the Margaret Sanger family planning clinic" (Cleage, 1996a, p. 23). *Blues* is unlike the other plays in this discussion in a variety of ways. Angel and Delia have limited interaction. In fact there are only two scenes in which the two women engage in dialogue without any of the other characters present, and these scenes are quite short. Despite various social issues the women confront, they spend scant energy engaged in supportive communication. They also minimally participate in the kind of intimate sass that fosters sisterhood. Given Cleage's commitment to "be a part of the ongoing worldwide struggle against racism, sexism, classism and homophobia" (Cleage, 1996b, p. 46), it is surprising that the two women spend very little time together thereby missing the opportunity to "take care of their sisters." Cleage explains that this was the "first play in which I've had a black woman character who didn't triumph at the end. In most plays, if the woman is weak, she gets stronger; if she's confused, she achieves clarity" (Cleage cited in Langworthy, 1996c, p. 22). Indeed, the lack of interaction between the women may lay the foundation for the tragic choices Angel makes at the end of the play. Hecht, Collier, and Ribeau (1993) noted the significance of interaction among African American women in the formation of their identities when they wrote:

> African American women share an epistemological frame of which researchers of identity need to be aware. One characteristic is an emphasis on experience as a criterion of meaning. In addition, African American women use dialogue to assess knowledge claims and are committed to an ethic of caring and an ethic of personal accountability. (p. 78)

Without "dialogue to assess knowledge claims," Angel is left without the valuable dialogue that might mitigate against her perpetually self-destructive behavior.

Delia engages in the polite communication strategy that prohibits honest interaction and personal growth. Like many women she has learned to mask her true responses behind social conventions. During one of the rare intimate moments between the women, Delia retreats just as the conversation becomes deeply personal and challenging.

Angel: (*Massaging Delia's head expertly and gently as she speaks*):
When I was working at Miss Lillie's, as many of those old men would pay me for this as would pay me for the other.
Delia: I don't know how you can talk about it like that.
Angel: Talk about what like that?
Delia: About what happened to you.
Angel: It was better than living on the street.
Delia doesn't respond. (Cleage, 1996a, p. 30)

Delia's decision to remain silent closes off the possibility for solidifying the closeness between the women. Jewell (1993) reminded us "the mutual sharing of concerns related to male/female relationships, parenting, childrearing, birth, death and ongoing forms of societal inequities serve to cement firm relationships between African American women kin and non-kin" (p. 68). Because the sharing is interrupted by silence, the closesness is shunted. Delia's strategy of silence might be the social politeness that is used when one's true feelings could be thought to jeopardize a friendship. Trees and Manusov (1998) pointed out that, "The potential consequences of criticism due to face threat create a quandary for friends, raising the question of how to criticize and yet still remain friends" (p. 572). Although some studies offer evidence that women refrain from making negative comments that could be damaging to the relationship,[6] Tracy and Eisenberg (1990) noted that "Criticizing a person's work, ideas, or personal style is a communicative act that most people find difficult. Giving criticism leaves a person open to negative judgments of being vague or wishy-washy on the one hand, or rude and disrespectful on the other" (p. 37). This is especially true if the relationship is unequal. Guy, one of Angel's closest friends, tells Delia that Angel "treats everybody like they're her little sister" (Cleage, 1996a, p. 25). Delia, as the subordinate in the relationship, may not feel capable of offering support or intimate sass to Angel and instead opts for silence.

Flyin' West is full of talk. The sass Miss Leah and Sophie dole out, and the supportive communication Fannie consistently (and sometimes naively) provides dominate the interactions of the play. The one instance of prolonged silence, however, is a most significant one. After the women learn that Frank has been beating his wife Minnie and that he has coerced her into signing over her share of Sophie's property to him, the women collaborate in his murder. Minnie's silence during the years of abuse in her marriage is a survival strategy akin to the silence of enslaved Africans in the United States. Cloud (1999) described the possible intentions behind a gendered silence when she writes "In a context of male violence against women, one cannot regard silence as a voluntary choice, although it may be a survival strategy and/or a form of counterhegemonic resistance" (p. 182). For Minnie, her year's of silence is neither voluntary nor counterhegemonic as the silence only allows Frank to continue his abuse with the certainty that Minnie will not speak out against him.

When Frank is indeed dead, Cleage provides a long set of stage directions indicating the actions the women perform amid silence. Minnie goes to the body to confirm the death of her husband and the resultant end to her physical and emotional abuse. "We see her move through a complex set of emotions, ending with her knowledge of the monster Frank had become. Her face now shows her resolve and even her body seems to gain strength" (Cleage, 1996b, p. 76). Minnie then hands over her deed of property to Sophie who, in turn, gives it back to Minnie. In this silence much is communicated. As Minnie assumes responsibility for herself, she begins to accept the pledge of self-actualization evoked during a ritual of affirmation enacted by the women. She moves closer to being a free woman when she releases the connection to Frank. Freedom

---

[6]Of particular interest are studies by Baxter (1984) and Hample and Dallinger (1987). These researchers focus attention on the social conventions which may inhibit women when offering criticism.

will mean coming to voice, but her transition to freedom is full of the unnamable coersions, concessions, and physical blows that render her silent. By returning the deed to Minnie's hand, Sophie makes good on her "promise to always remember the day we left Memphis and went west together to be free women as a sacred bond between us with all our trust" (Cleage, 1996b, p. 63). If Sophie were to keep the deed that Minnie under duress signed over to Frank, Sophie would be keeping Minnie in bondage as surely as Frank did by not allowing Minnie to make her own decisions and map her own way. For Sophie, the words of their group ritual were *nommo*, word force, real and binding. Miss Leah and Fannie watch the exchange of the deed and thereby serve as witnesses to the solidification of Minnie's transformation. These silent actions bring each of the women to the freedom their ritual demanded. Rituals are, after all, designed to be efficacious by creating something new or protecting against misfortune. Ritual culminates in action. For all intents and purposes, the play is now over. In the silence, the issues of the play come to rest.

The primary issue of the play is the freedom of African American women, and this freedom is intimately linked with speaking out. By 1898, when the play is set, African American men had the right to vote as granted them by the Fifteenth Amendment which was ratified in 1870. African American women, along with men, gained their legal freedom under the Thirteenth Amendment of 1865, but women would not be allowed to vote until the ratification of the Eighteenth Amendment in 1919. When Sophie exclaims "Two things I'm sure of. I don't want no white folks tellin' me what to do all day, and no man tellin' me what do do all night" (Cleage, 1996b, p. 54), she is identifying the primary constraints on the freedom of African American women during the 19th century. The hardships of living on the plain are offset by living among African Americans; however, even the isolation of the plains does not protect the women from sexist violence. Through the relationship between Minnie and Frank, the play explores the confluence of race and gender in domestic violence. Cleage makes her position on the subject quite clear when she writes:

Surely I am clear that it is not "the brothers" who are the problem. It's "the Man." Right? *Wrong*. It's the brothers. Period. Although all African American insanity, male and female, can ultimately be explained by the long ago presence of the slave ships pulling up on the coast of Africa, that blood soaked presence cannot continue to be an acceptable reason for our current sorry state. We cannot undo slavery. It happened. We cannot ignore racism. It is a fact of our lives. But we can begin to work on the ways that racism makes us turn on each other. Black men must begin to take *personal responsibility* for the way they treat us and the way they treat our children. There is no white man physically present in the house when a black man decides to beat his wife. . . . And, *yes,* I really do understand that white men are responsible for the madness, but who is responsible for the cure? (Cleage, 1987, p. 23)

Given the clarity and passion in this statement, it is no wonder that the women of *Flyin' West* do not wait for Frank to discover his "personal responsibility." The women's actions reflect Cleage's own vehement refusal to accept oppression, no matter who the oppressor might be. The choice the women make, however, does raise important questions about using violence to curb violence. In the world of melodrama, we are encouraged to examine the central issue of the play and accept a rather Machiavellian result. Frank's murder makes clear how sincere the women are about the sanctity of their lives; it is not the act of murder that is to be evaluated on a moral continuum. If it were to be evaluated as such, Frank would have been created with more texture than he is given. As is, it is easy to dispense with Frank because he seems a wholly unlikable, one-dimensional character. Such easy moral positions are common to the genre of melodrama, to which this play owes some allegiance.

Sullivan critiqued the play on the basis of its melodramatic underpinnings. Although Sullivan, and the several reviewers she cited, rightfully situate the play within the dramatic tradition of the time in which the events take place, these writers do not note the importance of minstrelsy to Cleage's creation. In addition to melodrama playing on U.S. stages in the 19th century, black-face minstrelsy was also prevalent. Cleage's depiction of life in the West for 19th-century African Americans is a direct challenge to the malaprop-speaking, coon song-singing, burnt cork-wearing images of African Americans that were indelibly etched on the American psyche. Bert Williams, a major African American minstrel performer, became famous with the creation of the Jonah Man character popularized in the song, "I'm a Jonah Man":

My luck started when I was born,
Leas' so the old folks say.
Dat same hard luck's been my bes' frien'
To dis very day.
When I was young, Mammas' friends—to find a name they tried,
They named me after Pappa—and de same day Pappa died, Fo'. . .
Chorus:

I'm a Jonah. I'm a Jonah man,
My family for many years would look at me and den shed tears.
Why I am dis Jonah
I sho' can't understand,
But I'm a good substantial, full-fledged, real, first-class Jonah man.
A frien' of mine gave me a six month's meal ticket one day.
He said, "It won't do me no good, I got to go away."
I thanked him as my heart with joy and gratitude did bound,
But when I reached the restaurant, the place had just burned down.
(Woll, 1989, p. 35)

Cleage creates people, particularly women, who refused to be Jonahs especially in the coon tradition of minstrelsy. Sophie, Fannie, Miss Leah, and eventually, Minnie are determined to make their own luck. In so doing, they change the way the world perceives of 19th-century African Americans.

Hospice offers a look at the complex silence between a mother and daughter. Washington (1991) noted "While I think black women writers differ from white writers in their treatment of mother-daughter stories, they still tend to be daughters writing about mothers, and in speaking for their mothers, they do, to some extent, silence them" (p. 111). Jenny has not been able to literally silence Alice but in her insistence on a particular kind of mother-daughter relationship, she attempts to silence Alice's true self. Jenny does silence her own feelings frequently in their relationship in the hopes of creating peace.

Alice explains, to some extent, her avoidance of intimacy. She describes being raised in a world of unspoken feelings when she tells Jenny, "The quiet in [my parents'] house used to be so strong it was a part of the conversation" (Cleage, 1989, p. 59). Such a foundation gives her few tools for the kind of communication Jenny is now seeking. Indeed, Alice's favorite song is Billie Holiday's "In My Solitude." After Jenny has reluctantly recited her very private poem to Alice, ironically it is Alice who breaks the silence:

Alice: (quietly): It's too late to be sorry, Sister, but I . . .
Jenny: (stops her): Sometimes the love is enough. When it's all
         you've got. Sometimes the possibility is enough. And we
         don't have to explain it. We just have to be here together
         and try. We only have to try! (A beat.) All I ever wanted to
         tell you was that I understood. I think I always understood.
         (Jenny and Alice look straight at each other in silence. Jenny
         moves to Alice, but stops and winces slightly. She puts her
         hands to her stomach lightly breathing, through her mouth.)
         (Cleage, 1989, p. 71)

Interestingly, Cleage uses silence in more complex ways than she does sass. Silence in Cleage's works sometimes masks true feelings, protects against violence, and replaces the unnameable.

SUPPORT

> Alice: I think when I married your father so young, my mother was afraid she wouldn't have time to get all the women lessons in before I was gone.
> Jenny: Did she?
> Alice: She told me what she knew. I guess that's the best anybody can do. (Cleage, 1989, p. 71)

African American women form solidarity with one another and establish values for survival through their communication. Talking with each other can be a place of safety where one can test one's voice, a voice often silenced in the larger community with African American men and with people of different historical backgrounds. Talking was a space free of male prescriptions for writing, a place where theorizing was a form of material reality in the practice of everyday living. Jewell (1993) described the potential richness of interaction among African American women:

> The mutual support and reinforcement that African American women maintain can be observed on a daily basis as they interact with each other. The discourse between friends and even acquaintances is generally uplifting and supportive. African American women, young and old, are complimentary in their discourse. They frequently invoke a social closeness by interacting in close physical propinquity, touching and offering positive compliments to each other about the most minute accomplishments. (p. 68)

From her essays, it appears as though Cleage benefited from the very supportive kinship that Jewell described. Cleage received indelible woman-lessons from her mother who left a strong legacy of African American middle-classness and decorum. When Cleage (1987) reflects on the anniversary of her mother's death she writes, "What I want to remember are all the things that were the *essence* of her. The things that shaped my own ideas of what a black woman could and should be, to herself and to her family and to her people" (p. 193). Cleage's grandmother and great-grandmother also figured prominently into the development of her sense of womanhood.

Although Cleage creates this kind of female support in *Flyin' West*, she examines less satisfying relationships and more damaging communication styles in her other dramas.

Despite the friction between Alice and Jenny, they share a few rare instances of support.

Alice: You know what your father said when you were born?
Jenny: What?
Alice: I thought he might be disappointed because you weren't a boy, so I said I'd heard that sometimes kings divorce their wives if the firstborn is female. And he laughed and shook his head. "Not in my tribe," he said. "Not in my tribe."
Jenny: (*delighted*): He never told me that!
Alice: It's not a man story. That's a story women tell each other. (Cleage, 1989, p. 55)

Here, support comes in the form of a personal narrative that connects both speakers to their history.

Even though Alice continually wraps her communication in sass as armor against closeness, she paradoxically employs features of supportive communication. Alice frequently uses the appellation "sister" when speaking to. Jewell (1993) pointed out that

> The words "girl," "honey" and "girlfriend" are frequently used by African American women when addressing each other. These forms of address are expanded depending on the popular culture. For example, "diva" is a term which surfaces in the 1980s and 1990s and African American women sometimes address each other in this fashion. (1993, p. 68)

Given this statement, when Alice refers to Jenny as "sister," Alice is using a term of endearment that might soften the sass she offers up so freely.

Unlike Cleage's other plays, the primary support for the female characters in *Blues* comes from the male characters. In a fleeting instance of supportive communication between the women, Angel's mild sass as intimacy directed toward Delia leads to support in the form of advice:

Angel: Look at you, Deal. You got bags under your eyes like an old woman. All tired and frowned up.
Delia: I do look tired, don't I?
Angel: Sit down here for a minute. Can I take your hair aloose?
Delia: Angel. . .

Angel: This will only take a minute. I promise.
(*Delia sits and Angel begins to massage her head expertly. As she talks, we see Delia's body relax.*) (Cleage, 1996a, p. 30)

Because there is so little interaction between Delia and Angel, a brief exchange like the one above is invested with unique significance. Even though Cleage does not give the women much opportunity for private conversation in *Blues,* in this interaction she places them in the close proximity that Jewell believes is common among African American women. Their conversation takes on aspects of Jewell's "social closeness" even though they do not know each other well or spend much time together.

In *Late Bus*, Ava begins with a great deal of sass then quickly moves into supportive communication. Although Ava is fluent with sass, she doles out support in large measure. Her concern for A Black Woman deepens in the play as Ava realizes that A Black Woman is a profoundly disturbed individual who might ease Ava's own frustrations. While asking, "Are you okay?" in Scene 2 may have some hostility laced in it, asking, "You gonna be okay?" in the final scene of the play is filled with the warmth of friendship. Ava's support of A Black Woman comes through the many lessons she offers, the joint development of a communication strategy, and her moments of bearing witness. Cleage closes out the play with a series of slides that gives this advice to the audience:

Slide 1:   The Lessons:
Slide 2:   1. Take care of your sisters.
Slide 3:   2. Be resourceful.
Slide 4:   3. Make a plan.
Slide 5:   4. Make a move.
Slide 6:   5. Don't do animals. (Cleage, 1993, p. 322)

Flyin' West is a pioneer story that closely follows the dramaturgy of melodrama. As such, it is not surprising that many personal narratives are woven into the dialogue. Langellier (1989) argued that personal narratives are "the mundane happenings of an ordinary day and extraordinary events that mark our lives" (p. 243). When the women are alone, they tell stories about their past and present lives. Miss Leah, the elder, recounts the horrors of losing children during slavery. Minnie remembers both her distant past as a child growing up in Nicodemus with the love provided by her family and an all-Black community, and her more recent troubled past in Europe with her husband Frank. Sophie is inclined more toward direct preaching and teaching rather than storytelling, but her communicative style is also a form of personal narrative.

Among the women, Fannie is the self-appointed scribe who wants to keep a record of their lives to pass on to future generations.

Fan: Do you want to work on your stories some tonight?
Miss Leah: I'm too tired.
Fan: Let's just finish the one we were working on Sunday night.
Miss Leah: I keep tellin' you those ain't writin' stories. These are tellin' stories.
Fan: Then tell them to me?
Miss Leah: So you can write 'em!
Fan: So we can remember them.
Miss Leah: Colored folks can't forget the plantation any more than they can forget their own names. If we forget that, we ain't got no history past last week. (Cleage, 1996b, p. 54)

The telling of stories is very much a way of life, but Miss Leah is suspicious of anything that pulls the words away from their source. She worries that doing so will reduce the kind of power the words hold, and worse, that writing will actually facilitate cultural amnesia rather than develop a collective cultural memory.

When Miss Leah finally delivers personal narratives they are examples of supportive communication that teach strength, create cultural continuity, and preserve a very personal perspective on history. These narratives create unity among the women. Miss Leah's descriptions of slavery are an extension of Cleage's commitment to sharing African American women's histories. Cleage writes: "My work is deeply rooted in, and consciously reflective of, African-American history and culture since I believe that it is by accurately expressing our very specific and highly individual realities that we discover our common humanity" (1996b, p. 46).

When the women find themselves outside alone, Minnie takes the opportunity to ask them "to do the ritual again." The ritual is an invocation, the verbal support that binds the younger women in the play:

Sophia: Because we are free Negro women. . .
Fan and Minnie: Because we are free Negro women. . .
Sophia: Born of free Negro women. . .
Both (Fan and Minnie): Born of free Negro women. . .
Sophia: We choose this day to leave a place where our lives, our honor and our very souls are not our own.

Fan:	Say it, Sister!
Sophia:	We choose this day to declare our lives to be our own and no one else's. And we promise to always remember the day we left Memphis and went west together to be free women as a sacred bond between us with all our trust.
Both:	With all our trust. . .
Sophia:	And all our strength. . .
Both:	And all our strength. . .
Sophia:	And all our courage. . .
Both:	And all our courage. . .
Sophia:	And all our love.
Both:	And all our love. (Cleage, 1996b, p. 63)

Here, the women offer each other the supreme support, a bond of freedom, courage, strength, and love that will help fortify them against the uncertainties of living on the plain and brace them for the challenges posed by racism and sexism. It is this intimate pledge of support that makes their dramatic choices at the end of the play all the more plausible.

CONCLUSION

Until the recent black woman's literary and artistic renaissance, to be black, female, and gifted was synonymous with being obscured, frustrated, and invisible. (Hine, 1990, p. 357)

Creating art affords the artist the opportunity to bring into existence that which did not previously exist. In so doing, the artist can yield to the forces of hegemony or create images, ideas, and symbols that challenge prevailing paradigms. Because an artist is an African American woman does not insure that her art will create "a critical oppositional representation of the black female subject" (Wallace, 1992, p. 663). Cleage is committed to the use of theater as her "hollering place" where she might develop such insurgent representations. In Cleage's work, sass, silence, and support are most often used to advance self-actualizing communication, and in this way become methods for "taking care of sisters." The interaction among her female characters demonstrates the fluidity and malleability of these communication strategies. Sass can be used as support or as segue to the intimacy that leads to support; silence might mask the sass that surrounds rage; silence born of socialized politeness might be intended as support. Sass, silence, and support are not discreet styles. These strategies merely mark general tendencies rather than wholly separate entities.

Hine (1990), railed against the "deep, pervasive, and centuries-long conspiracy of silence surround[ing] the creative expressions, strivings and struggles of the African-American woman" (1990, p. 357). Cleage's contribution toward loudly breaking that silence with distinctive images of African American women provides communication scholars with literary and performance data that illuminates everyday life interaction strategies. A next step in this analysis would be to determine how sass, silence and support are actually performed in the productions of Cleage's dramas. In this way the analysis would incorporate an understanding of how the linguistic choices are manifest in the bodies of the performers. Ongoing critique of and debate about the cultural production of African American women adds an essential complexity to any investigation of theater, communication, or cultural studies.

REFERENCES

Baxter, L. A. (1984). An investigation of compliance-gaining as politeness. *Human Communication Research, 10,* 427-456.

Bell-Scott, P., Guy-Sheftall, B., Royster J. J., Sims-Woods, J., Decosta-Willis, M., & Fultz, L. P. (Eds.). (1981). *Double stitch: Black women write about mothers & daughters.* New York: Harper Perennial.

Braxton, J. (1984). *Black women writing autobiography: A tradition within a tradition.* Unpublished doctoral dissertation, Yale University, New Haven, CT.

Canon, K. G. (1995). *Katie's Canon: Womanism and the soul of the black community.* New York: Continuum.

Cleage, P. (1987). *Deals with the devil and other reasons to riot.* New York: Ballantine Books.

Cleage, P. (1989) Hospice. In W. King, Jr. (Ed.), *New plays for the black theatre* (pp. 45-72). Chicago: Third World Press.

Cleage, P. (1991). *The brass bed and other stories.* Chicago: Third World Press.

Cleage, P. (1993). Late bus to mecca. In J. Miles (Ed.), *Playwriting women: 7 plays from the women's project* (pp. 299-323). New York: Heinemann.

Cleage, P. (1994). Hollering place. *The Dramatists Guild Quarterly, 31,* 12-14.

Cleage, P. (1996a). Blues for an Alabama sky. *American Theatre, 13,* 23-43.

Cleage, P. (1996b). Flyin' west. In K. A. Perkins & R. Uno (Eds.), *Contemporary plays by women of color* (pp. 46-78). New York: Routledge.

Cleage, P. (1997). *What looks like crazy on an ordinary day.* New York: Avon Books.

Cloud, D. (1999). The null persona: race and the rhetoric of silence in the uprising of '34. *Rhetoric and Public Affairs, 2*(2), 177-209.

Collins, P. H. (1981). The meaning of motherhood in black culture and black mother-daughter relationships. In P. Bell-Scott, B. Guy-Sheftall, J. J. Royster, J. Sims-Woods, M. Decosta-Willis, & L. P. Fultz (Eds.), *Double stitch: Black women write about mothers & daughters* (pp. 42-60). New York: Harper Perennial.

Dash, J. (1992). *Daughters of the dust: The making of an African-American woman's film.* New York: The New Press.

Guy-Sheftall, B. (1981). Piecing blocks: Identities. In P. Bell-Scott, B. Guy-Sheftall, J. J. Royster, J. Sims-Woods, M. Decosta-Willis, & L. P. Fultz (Eds.), *Double stitch: Black women write about mothers & daughters* (pp. 61-62). New York: Harper Perennial.

Guy-Sheftall, B. (1995). *Words of fire: An anthology of African-American feminist thought.* New York: The New Press.

Hample, D., & Dallinger, J. M. (1987). Individual differences in cognitive editing standards. *Human Communication Research, 14,* 123-144.

Harper, T. (1997, June). Sistah prez. *Sky,* pp. 43-46.

Hecht, M. L., Collier, M. J., & Ribeau, S. A. (1993). *African American communication: Ethnic identity and cultural interpretation.* Newbury Park, CA: Sage.

Hine, D. C. (1990). To be gifted, female, and black. In *Black women in U.S. history.* Brooklyn, NY: Carlson.

hooks, b. (1989). *Talking back: Thinking feminist, thinking black.* Boston: South End Press.

hooks, b. (1993). *Sisters of the yam: Black women and self-recovery.* Boston: South End Press.

Hopper, R. (1993). Conversational dramatism and everyday life performance. *Text and Performance Quarterly, 13,* 181-183.

Jewell, S. K. (1993). *From mammy to Miss America and beyond: Cultural images and the shaping of U.S. social policy.* New York: Routledge.

Langellier, K. (1989). Personal narratives: perspectives on theory and research. *Text and Performance Quarterly, 9,* 243-276.

Langworthy, D. (1996). Making our history: An interview with the playwright. *American Theatre, 13,* 22.

Lorde, A. (1984). The transformation of silence into language and action. In *Sister outsider* (pp. 40-44). Freedom, CA: The Crossing Press.

Madison. D. S. (1994). *The woman that I am: The literature and culture of contemporary women of color.* New York: St. Martin's Press.

Orbe, M. P. (1998). *African Americans in corporate America: Everyday lived experiences as points of negotiation.* Paper presented at the annual meeting of the National Communication Association, NY.

Parker, P.S. (1998). *African American women executives' use of strategic communication within dominant culture organizations.* Paper presented at the annual meeting of the National Communication Association, NY.

Shange, N. (1977). *For colored girls who have considered suicide/when the rainbow is enuf.* New York: Bantam Books.

Smitherman, G. (1977). *Talkin' and testifyin': The language of black America.* Detroit, MI: Wayne State University Press.

Stucky, N. (1993). Toward an aesthetic of natural performance. *Text and Performance Quarterly, 13,* 168-180.

Tracy, K., & Eisenberg, E. (1990). Giving criticism: A multiple goals case study. *Research on Language and Social Interaction, 24,* 37-70.

Trees, A. R., & Manusov, V. (1998). Managing face concerns in criticism: Integrating nonverbal behaviors as a dimension of politeness in female friendship dyads. *Human Communication Research, 24,* 564-583.

Wallace, M. (1992). Negative images: Towards a black feminist cultural criticism. In L. Grossberg, C. Nelson, & P. Treichler (Eds.), *Cultural studies* (pp. 654-664). New York: Routledge.

Wallace, M. (1981). Baby faith. In P. Bell-Scott, B. Guy-Sheftall, J. J. Royster, J. Sims-Woods, M. Decosta-Willis, & L. P. Fultz (Eds.), *Double stitch: Black women write about mothers and daughters* (pp. 12-20). New York: Harper Perennial.

Washington, M. H. (1991). *Memory of kin: Stories about family by black writers.* New York: Anchor Books.

Woll, A. (1989). *Black musical theatre.* New York: Da Capo Press.

EIGHT

The Nobility of Womanhood: "Womanhood" in the Rhetoric of 19th Century Black Club Women

Cindy L. White
Central Connecticut State University

Catherine A. Dobris
Indiana University, Indianapolis

the rape of a negress by the male of her own color is almost unheard of [because the black male] is so accustomed to the wantonness of the women of his own race that it is not strange that his intellect, having no perception of the personal dignity or the pangs of outraged feeling, should be unable to gauge the terrible character of this offense against the integrity of virtuous womanhood.
  —Bruce (cited in Franklin, 1995, p. 74)

Only the Black Woman *can say "when and where I enter, in the quiet, undisputed dignity of my womanhood, without violence and without suing or special patronage, then and there the whole* Negro race enters with me."
  —Cooper (1892/1988, p. 31)

171

Black women's activist heritage is an integral and vital part of Black women's intellectual tradition. Collins' (1991) discussion of the politics, character, themes, and goals of Black feminist thought illustrates that the sources of Black women's intellectual tradition are multiple. Contemporary historians and literary theorists in particular, have recovered a rich body of work that details the centrality and implications of 19th-century Black women's thought to legal, ethical, economic, political, social, and cultural conditions of the 19th- and 20th-century United States (see, e.g., Carby, 1987; Collins, 1991; Giddings, 1984; Guy-Sheftall, 1995; Lerner, 1972). In the area of rhetoric and public address, however, we are lacking rhetorical examinations of this body of work and this intellectual tradition.

This chapter examines 19th-century Black women's rhetorical constructions of identity. In particular, we examine how Black women intellectuals[1] rhetorically negotiated their identity in relation to prevailing ideologies of womanhood, how they used and developed womanhood as a rhetorical strategy for their own emancipation, and how they forged their own ideologies of womanhood in the process.[2]

The rhetoric of Black club women at the turn of the century is an instructive example of the use of identity as a rhetorical strategy in the battle for racial and sexual equality. Moreover, a close analysis of club women's rhetorical strategies in interrogating prevailing sexual and racial ideologies makes explicit the centrality of race in the struggle for women's equality. We examine the work of three influential club women who specifically used "womanhood" as a means for analyzing racialized and gendered social relations. Out of these critiques, Fannie Barrier Williams, Anna Julia Cooper, and Josephine St. Pierre Ruffin crafted a rhetoric of womanhood that laid a strategic groundwork for Black women's emancipation.[3]

---

[1]We employ Collins' (1991) conceptualization of the term *intellectual* as informed by and accounting for a Black feminist standpoint. Collins argued that Black women's tradition of activism, and their artistic, political, and community work in institutions other than the academy necessitate a conceptualization of intellectualism and scholarship that unites theory and praxis. Black feminist thought both emanates from and credits the everyday work of women who seek to illuminate, examine, and represent Black women.

[2]This chapter is part of Cindy White's larger project on the rhetoric of 19th-century Black women and the Black Women's club movement. Ideas and portions of this chapter are taken from this larger work (White, 1995).

[3]See Deborah Gray White's (1999) discussion of Williams, Cooper, and Ruffin in *Too Heavy a Load*, for further background.

RACIAL SPECIFICITY AND THE IDEOLOGY OF WOMANHOOD

Barbara Welter's (1976) influential discussion of "The Cult of True Womanhood," describes the essential characteristics of an ideology of womanhood in antebellum America. The "four cardinal virtues" of "True Womanhood," according to Welter, were, "piety, purity, submissiveness, and domesticity . . ." (p. 21). Popular forms of media, religious, and educational materials all encouraged women and men to measure a woman's worth, value, and happiness against a carefully crafted standard of these virtues. Conformance guaranteed bliss. Deviance assured moral corruption, domestic unhappiness, and worse.

Although historians generally acknowledge the existence of the "cult of true womanhood," and agree as to its basic tenets, many have questioned its power in influencing women's lives and the role it played in the development of a feminist consciousness (see, e.g., Cott, 1977; Scott, 1970). The consensus among women's historians is that most White women's lives in antebellum America did not conform to the prevailing image of the "lady" (Carby, 1987, p. 23). Although historical examinations of White women's conformity to tenets of the ideology focus attention on the material conditions of these women's lives, they obscure the cultural functions of the ideology. Regardless of how closely or carefully White women's lives actually conformed to the ideology, it nonetheless enjoyed huge popularity and was common cultural coinage. The cult was, as Carby noted, a "function[al] ideology" that had enormous "generative power . . . as ideology . . ." (p. 24). It aimed at overcoming the contradictions in women's lived and material existence. Historical investigations that focus solely on the extent of White women's conformity to the prevailing attributes of womanhood not only obscure the cultural functions of the ideology, they ignore its relationship to, and consequences for, Black women (pp. 24-25).

Limited historical treatments of ideologies of womanhood that are impoverished by an inattention to race can mask the necessity and value of historical specificity to rhetorical analysis. Only by careful attention to differentiation in analyses of gender will we begin to understand how women's different responses to current social-sexual ideologies became a site for the negotiation and articulation of womanhood as identity. "Ideologies of white womanhood," Carby noted, "were the sites of racial and class struggle which enabled white women to negotiate their subordinate role in relation to patriarchy and at the same time to ally their class interests with men and against establishing an alliance with black women" (pp. 17-18). The same ideologies were used to justify the exclusion of Black women from economic, social, and political opportunities. The historical record delivers ample evidence of a political legacy fraught with residual tensions between Black and White women from such a rhetorical and material relationship. Ideologies of womanhood were historically and racially specific. The women who lived against their backdrop, in conformity or resistance, confronted them as *racialized* as well as *gendered* beings. It is essential that rhetorical analyses of ideologies of womanhood pay careful attention to the historical subject position of the women who interrogated them.

Equally essential is recognizing the discursive nature of the ideology and rhetorical nature of identity construction. de Lauretis (1986) suggested that an individual's identity is constructed within a historical process of consciousness, a process in which one's history "is interpreted or reconstructed by each of us within the horizon of meanings and knowledges available in the culture at given historical moments, a horizon that also includes works of political commitment and struggle" (p. 8). Those cultural meanings and "knowledges" are discursive constructions. The conscious interpretation, reconstruction, and mediation of identity in relation to historically situated and discursively constructed ideologies, is a rhetorical project.

Black women active in the nascent club movement lived and worked in an age that Ida B. Wells described as "obsessed with womanhood." Much of their rhetoric is a self-conscious examination of Black women's identity as it was rendered by the prevailing ideology of womanhood. For Black women, the rhetorical negotiation of identity in such a rhetorical/ideological milieu was a significant political struggle. Moreover, it was a political struggle *different* than that of White women. Investigating Black women's rhetorical stances in relation to prevailing ideological standards of sanctified womanhood—their negotiation of the standard as simultaneously conformist and subversive—is necessary to the project of deconstructing the ideology and making sense of women's lives.

Collins argued for an understanding of Black women's standpoint that acknowledges the interdependence of thought and action. Activism and intellectualism are joint wellsprings of a tradition of Black feminist thought; considering them as separate entities, as other traditions do, Collins argued, misunderstands and distorts Black feminist thought. Nineteenth century club leaders are important models and progenitors of this tradition. Their critiques and analyses of sources of oppression and emancipation were infused with an activist tradition that grew from women's experiences and illuminated their lives (Carby, 1987; Collins, 1991; Giddings, 1984). Clubs were vital forums for Black women's intellectualism, important outlets for activism, and training grounds for leadership.

The remainder of this chapter examines the work of three prominent club women who actively engaged the ideology of womanhood and used womanhood as an emancipatory topoi. We begin by introducing them and locating their work in the historical context of the formation of a national federation of clubs. Although the women whose voices and arguments are recorded here cannot represent all Black club women, they are representative of leading 19th-century Black women intellectuals (Carby, 1987; Collins 1991; Giddings, 1984; Washington, 1988).

WOMANHOOD AS RHETORICAL STRATEGY

Fannie Barrier Williams was an activist, a club woman, and a teacher. She was a state representative to the National Colored Women's Congress and in 1982 lectured at the World's Colombian Exposition in Chicago. Josephine St. Pierre Ruffin was a member of the White New England Women's Club. She founded the New Era Club, a club for Black women, and edited its newspaper, *The New Era,* which became the official journal of the National Association of Colored Women. Anna Julia Cooper was an educator, a scholar who earned a doctorate from the University of Paris, and an activist. Cooper's (1892/1988) work, *A Voice From the South by a Black Woman of the South,* is an early and important statement of Black feminism. In 1883, Cooper addressed the World's Congress of Representative Women, and in 1900 she spoke at the Pan-African Congress Conference in London (Washington, 1988). The work of all three women is united rhetorically by common themes that coalesce around womanhood and that are the grounds for their articulation of an ideology of womanhood that is imbued with Black women's sensibilities.

Womanhood As Collective Enterprise

The opening quotation of this chapter echoes a common ideological sentiment in 19th-century America. The lynching of Black men accused of raping White women became a routine means for enforcing subjugation of the whole race. Mythologizing Black women's sexuality as wanton and depraved was a necessary building block in a larger ideological edifice that policed Black male power in post Reconstruction America. Black women's lives, bodies, and existence, both materially and ideologically, bounded the sanctity of the image of womanhood. Representations of womanhood that rested on the exclusion of Black women not only served to forge an alliance between White men and White women, they ensured that Black women and Black men were kept in a very specific economic, political, and social position to the White patriarchy.

Following the war, an increase in the numbers of Blacks living in urban areas, a larger population of middle-class women with leisure time, and an increase in the urgency and demand for relief for the poor, all contributed to the growth and development of a national Black women's club movement. The club movement was gaining momentum just as Black Americans were facing and reacting to a decline in their safety and status in the post-Reconstruction years.

In response to the brutal lynching of three successful young Black businessmen in Memphis, Tennessee in March of 1892, Ida B. Wells ran an editorial in her newspaper the *Free Speech* in which she called for a mass migration of Blacks from Memphis. Wells' editorial succeeded in convincing scores of Blacks to leave the area and began her life long campaign against lynching (see Wells, 1991a, 1991b).

In 1893 and 1894, Wells took her anti-lynching campaign overseas to seek the help and support of the English. Although many in England were initially skeptical of Wells' claims about lynching, it was not long before she had enlisted the belief and support of numerous influential Britons. In America, John W. Jacks, president of the Missouri Press Association mounted a defense against Wells' English offensive. In a letter to Florence Balgarnie, Jacks attacked Wells' personal character and impugned the integrity and virtue of all Black women calling them "prostitutes," "thieves and liars" (cited in Lerner, 1972, p. 436). Although this was certainly not the first time Black women had endured assault on their characters, Jacks' letter proved to be the final impetus necessary for the unification of the clubs. It precipitated a call for a national convention that met in 1895 and led to the formation of the National Association of Colored Women (NACW) in 1896. The defense of Black womanhood served as the organizing principle for the NACW and defined its whole mission.

The middle-class leaders of the clubs were acutely aware that prevailing racist ideologies made no distinctions among Black women; all would be judged by the worst. Adopting the motto, "Lifting As We Climb," NACW leaders determined to address the condemnation of any Black woman by elevating all Black women. Margaret Murray Washington (an active member of the NACW and its president from 1914 to 1918), proclaimed the success of the clubs and the NACW, as she identified its primary purpose:

> Nothing has so changed the whole life and personnel [!] of the colored woman and so surely brought her into her own as has the club life to which she has lent herself, inspired by the national association which has for its aim the development of its women, mentally, morally, and industrially, as well as along civic lines, and whose motto is, "Lifting as we climb." (cited in Lerner, 1972, p. 447)

As Washington made clear, "social uplift," captured in the NACW's motto, was the primary agenda of the national association. Rhetorically, the motto "Lifting As We Climb" and the leaders of the movement like Washington and Terrell, adopted the prevailing ideology of womanhood as the grounds by which women should be judged and their activities directed. Although it may seem that this position represents a conservative approach to women's emancipation, much like Catherine Beecher's "social housekeeping," or Frances Willard's "home protection," it cannot and should not be judged on the same grounds.

Womanhood was at issue for Black women in a way it was not at issue for White women. All White women might potentially enjoy the status of womanhood as a means of re-inscribing and enforcing the racial superiority of Whites. Even the lowliest among them, when compared to any Black woman, might be afforded the status and privileges (however temporarily) that the ideology of womanhood conferred. As the boundary points of the ideology, Black women enjoyed no such privilege. Thus for them, asserting themselves as rightful representatives of the ideology was far more than a simple proclamation of the luxury of class distinctions among them—it represented nothing less than the admission of their humanity.

Womanhood's Work

Leading Black women adopted a dual and conflicting role in the community of women. As "representative" women, they were the advocates for masses of poor and disenfranchised Black women. At the same time, they were the representatives of the cultural, moral, and intellectual progress of Black women (Washington, 1988). The ideology of womanhood provided them a rhetorical fulcrum from which they negotiated this position. Terrell's insistence that the educated had a duty to "reclaim" their poorer sisters from the degradation inflicted by racist policies and bring them into the fold of Black womanhood hints at a rhetorical stance that Cooper and Williams specifically develop into a coherent justification for Black women's agency.

No woman made a greater, plainer, or more assertive claim for the moral, social, and political imperatives of womanhood than Anna Julia Cooper. Writing as "A Black Woman of the South," Cooper (1988) added her voice to the chorus of Black women intellectuals who attributed the debasement of the race to a legacy of subjugation:

> We are the heirs of a past which was not our fathers' moulding [sic]. "Every man the arbiter of his own destiny" was not true for the American Negro of the past: and it is no fault of his that he finds himself to-day [sic] the inheritor of a manhood and womanhood impoverished and debased by two centuries and more of compression and degradation. (p. 28)

Resorting to ideological presuppositions of womanhood as a moralizing force in a degraded society, Cooper argued that the effects of racism made Black women's agency a moral and social imperative. "Weaknesses and malformations, which to-day [sic] are attributable to a vicious schoolmaster and a pernicious system," Cooper warned, "will a century hence be rightly regarded as proofs of innate corruptness and radical incurability" (p. 28). The direness of the circumstance and the press of time, she continued, made it necessary to recognize quickly that Black women were necessary to success and to begin training them for their work:

> Now the fundamental agency under God in the regeneration, the re-training of the race, as well as the ground work and starting point of its progress upward, must be the *black woman*. With all the wrongs and neglects of her past, with all the weaknesses, the debasement, the moral thralldom of her present, the black woman of to-day stands mute and wondering at the Herculean task devolving upon her. But the cycles wait for her. No other hand can move the lever. She must be loosed from her bands and set to work. Our meager and superficial results from past efforts prove their futility, and every attempt to elevate the Negro, whether undertaken by himself or through the philanthropy of others, cannot but prove abortive unless so directed as to utilize the indispensable agency of an elevated and trained womanhood. (p. 28)

Cooper's skillful recuperation of the nobility of womanhood allowed her to argue that Black women were uniquely positioned to ensure the elevation of the race. That position of the mother of the race, the guardian of its children, morality, and piety emanated from the ideology of womanhood. But in Cooper's hands, the ideology was remolded by unfettering it from the frivolities that constrained women's agency.

Cooper argued that a history of subjugation and a climate of terror, oppression, and hatred left the Black community in need of all of its resources. As a resource critical to the survival, security, and progress of the race, she reasoned, the community had to give Black women every opportunity to grow, develop, and work on behalf of the community and the race. Cooper's analysis enabled and fortified her primary agenda for enlarging the scope of women's agency: education. If women were to meet the demands of their calling to uplift the race they would need free and equal access to higher education. She observed:

> I ask the men and women who are teachers and co-workers for the highest interests of the race, that they give the girls a chance! We might as well expect to grow trees from leaves as hope to build up a civilization or a manhood without taking into consideration our women and the home life made by them, which must be the root and ground of the whole matter. Let us insist then on special encouragement for the education of our women and special care in their training. Let our girls feel that we expect something more of them than that they merely look pretty and appear well in society. Teach them that there is a race with special needs which they and only they can help; that the world needs and is already asking for their trained, efficient forces. (p. 78)

Although Cooper's argument that girls should be educated in the interest of the race, relied on the ideology of womanhood, it admitted a conscious expansion of woman's agency in the repudiation of the separation of spheres of influence. Black womanhood, the means for authenticating women's agency, had to be unfettered by useless constraints that were tied to the false chivalry of an oppressive Southern ideology. Cooper argued that Black women had to be educated to serve the purpose of their unique womanhood:

> Fifty years ago woman's activity according to orthodox definitions was on a pretty clearly cut "sphere," including primarily the kitchen and the nursery. . . . The woman of to-day [sic] finds herself in the presence of responsibilities which ramify through the profoundest and most varied interests of her country and race. Not one of the issues of this plodding, toiling, sinning, repenting, falling, aspiring humanity can afford to shut her out, or can deny the reality of her influence. No plan for renovating society, no scheme for purifying politics, no reform in church or state, no moral, social, or economic question, no movement upward or downward in the human plane is

lost on her. . . . No woman can possibly put herself or her sex outside any of the interests that affect humanity. All departments in
the new era are to be hers, in the sense that her interests are in all
and through all; and it is incumbent on her to keep intelligently and
sympathetically *en rapport* with all the great movements of her
time, that she may know on which side to throw the weight of her
influence. She stands now at the gateway of this new era of
American civilization. In her hands must be moulded the strength,
the wit, the statesmanship, the morality, all the psychic force, the
social and economic intercourse of that era. To be alive at such an
epoch is a privilege, to be a woman then is sublime. (p. 143)

Cooper's positioning of womanhood as the center of humanity's
progress could only be accomplished by her unique standpoint as a
Black woman at the threshold of the "new era."

Because Black women existed in specific relation to the
patriarchal ideologies of womanhood that denied their humanity by
denying their womanhood, the restoration of both must be
accomplished simultaneously. Cooper's cooptation of the missionary
nobility associated with prevailing ideologies of womanhood was
incorporated into a critical analysis that explicitly recognized the
mutual reinforcement of *racialized* and *gendered* social formations.
As a racialized category, the imperatives of womanhood were
employed to argue for serving to prove the humanity, culture,
morality, and intellectualism of the race. This analysis rejected
separate spheres as an ideological remnant that specifically denied
the *racializing* of womanhood as a social category in order to keep
Black women and men in a subjugated position in White society.
Black women, Cooper argued, had to enter humanity on their own
terms. The race's heralding of a "new era" depended on her unlimited
agency.

Like Cooper, Fannie Barrier Williams used the nobility of
womanhood as a means of subverting ideological condemnations of
Black women. Williams argues that the degraded condition of some
Black women is directly attributable to an inhumane and racist
White patriarchy. Her discussion of "The New Black Woman" begins
with a direct indictment of practices that consciously colonized Black
women outside of the ideology of womanhood in order to demarcate
its boundaries:

Afro-American women of the United States have never had the
benefit of a discriminating judgement concerning their worth as
women made up of the good and bad of human nature. . . . These
women have been left to grope their way unassisted toward a
realization of those . . . standards of family and social life that are

the badges of race respectability. They have had no special teachers to instruct them. No conventions of distinguished women of the more favored race have met to consider their peculiar needs. There has been no fixed public opinion to which they could appeal; no protection against libelous attacks upon their characters, and no chivalry generous enough to guarantee their safety against man's inhumanity to woman. Certain it is that colored women have been the least known, and the most ill-favored class of women in this country. (cited in Lerner, 1972, p. 575)

Williams' analysis maps the nature of gendered social relations that were drawn, formed, and demarcated by race. As White women enjoyed the status and privileges of womanhood, they assiduously ignored ideologies and practices that guaranteed their comfort and superiority on the literal backs of Black women. Moreover, their failure to reach out to Black women, to work on their behalf, ensured that Black women would be prey to man's inhumanity.

Williams' comparison of White and Black women's clubs noted that race and the different conditions it had produced among them, explained the differences in their agendas and progress. The enormity of the task set before the Black club women, Williams argued, was directly attributable to the enormity of the injustice suffered by all Black women:

Colored women organized have succeeded in touching the heart of the race, and for the first time the thrill of unity has been felt. They have set in motion moral forces that are beginning to socialize interests that have been kept apart by ignorance and the spirit of dependence. They have begun to make the virtues as well as the wants of the colored women known to the American people. They are striving to put a new social value on themselves. Yet their work has just begun. It takes more than five or ten years to effect the social uplift of a whole race of people. The club movement is well purposed. . . . It is not a fad. . . . It is rather the force of a new intelligence against the old ignorance. The struggle of an enlightened conscience against the whole brood of social miseries, born out of the stress and pain of a hated past. (cited in Lerner, 1972, p. 576)

Like Cooper, Williams used the ideology of womanhood as the means for justifying Black women's agency as a necessary corrective to the effects of injustice. And like Cooper and other club women, she assumed the validity of the ideology, assumed Black womanhood as reflective of that ideology and, most important, used it as a means of asserting the necessary expansion of the scope of their agency.

Recognizing that racialized social formations did not show class distinctions among them, Black women adopted a rhetorical stance that assumed their womanhood and enhanced their rightful agency. Moreover, the claim to womanhood enabled a full and frank treatment of the causes of degradation of the Black community and the condemnation of the whole race. In negotiating their own womanhood, Black women established their humanity by subverting the prevailing ideology of womanhood.

The Dignity of Womanhood

In order to prove their rightful claim to prevailing standards of womanhood, Black women argued that they had to respond to attacks on their character with quiet dignity and by example, rather than with words. They argued that "social uplift" was necessary to instruct women in the proper displays of womanhood and they urged a strategy of enactment. Through a united display of quiet dignity, they were to stand in stark contrast to false and unfounded attacks on their womanhood. They were to claim and win the privileges of womanhood by strategic enactment of the ideology that denied their humanity, in other words, by being *ladies*.

In her call to arms at the First National Conference of Colored Women (1895) Josephine St. Pierre Ruffin explained the need for, and mapped out the strategy:

> Too long have we been silent under unjust and unholy charges; we cannot expect to have them removed until we disprove them through *ourselves*. It is not enough to try to disprove unjust charges through individual effort, that never goes any further. Year after year southern women have protested against the admission of colored women into any national organization on the ground of the immorality of these women, and because all refutation has only been tried by individual work the charge has never been crushed, as it could and should have been at the first. Now with an army of organized women standing for purity and mental worth, we in ourselves deny the charge and open the eyes of the world to a state of affairs to which they have been blind, often willfully so, and the very fact that the charges, audaciously and flippantly made, as they often are, are of so humiliating and delicate a nature, serves to protect the accuser by driving the helpless accused into mortified silence. It is to break this silence, not by noisy protestations of what we are not, but by a dignified showing of what we are and hope to become that we are impelled to take this step, to make of this gathering an object lesson to the world. For many and apparent reasons it is especially fitting that the *women* of the race take the lead in this movement, but for all this we recognize the necessity of the sympathy of our husbands. (cited in Lerner, 1972, pp. 442-443)

Like Cooper and Williams, St. Pierre Ruffin testified to the interdependency of ideologies of race and gender in the construction of nineteenth century social relations. The force of those ideologies and the figuration of those relations demanded an organized effort that St. Pierre Ruffin predicated on a pro-active rather than a reactive strategy. It is a mistake to assume that this strategy represented a capitulation to the passivity of womanhood or a willingness of club leaders to wait until the world simply came to its senses, shocked into recognition by women's dignity.

Rhetorically, St. Pierre Ruffin and others used the nobility of womanhood as grounds for organizing themselves and moreover as a means of proving the necessity for and value of their own education and work. Although the strategy of quietly proving the charges unjust may appear passive it is important to recognize that it was their bold adoption of the persona of the lady that served as the rhetorical grounds for it. From a Black woman's standpoint this was an act of resistance and subversion that enabled and mobilized further resistance.

Moreover, St. Pierre Ruffin also skillfully asserted the importance of the support of Black men to women's emancipation while carefully reinforcing that women's agency was necessary to their "rightful" representation of the race. St. Pierre Ruffin was joined by Cooper in the task of enlisting the active support of Black men to the cause of women's expanded agency:

> It seems hardly a gracious thing to say, but it strikes me as true, that while our men seem thoroughly abreast of the times on almost every other subject, when they strike the woman question they drop back into sixteenth century logic. They [Black men] leave nothing to be desired generally in regard to gallantry and chivalry, but they actually do not seem sometimes to have outgrown that old contemporary of chivalry—the idea that women may stand on pedestals or live in doll houses, (if they happen to have them) but they must not furrow their brows with thought or attempt to help men tug at the great questions of the world. I fear the majority of colored men do not yet think it worth while that women aspire to higher education. . . . (p. 75)

Black women's analyses of the conditions that denied their admission to womanhood and to humanity revealed the intricacies of mutually reinforcing ideologies of race and gender. These analyses enabled them to argue that Black men should imagine and align themselves in a new relation to Black women. Black men had a responsibility, they argued, to abandon the prevailing constructions of those ideologies and actively support women's emancipatory claims to her own rendering of womanhood.

IMPLICATIONS

This chapter demonstrates the significance of standpoint to the nuancing of rhetorical strategy and the construction of ideology. What is generally treated and accepted as a topoi for oppression—the ideology of womanhood—especially for a "true feminist stance" (i.e., one that only accepts as feminist direct opposition to the ideology), was used by Black women as a strategic means of liberation.

Black women's rhetorical renderings of womanhood demystified gendered and racialized social relations and became the central justification and grounds for the subversion of those relations. The uniqueness of their standpoint enabled them to employ womanhood as topoi for the invention of arguments that removed the camouflage of white superiority and established the grounds for their participation in the world. By locating the causes of the degradation and imperilment of the whole community in ideologies that denied them their humanity by denying them womanhood, Black women successfully expanded the scope and value of their work. Their arguments for "social uplift" validated the demand for the serious education of women and enlisted the support of men on their behalf. The substance of their rhetoric emphasized their place as the representative symbol of the possibilities, dignity, and nobility of the race. Black womanhood, as it was imagined and rendered by 19th-century Black women, guaranteed that Anna Julia Cooper's vision of the Black woman's place in America would forever defy the denial of her humanity.

REFERENCES

Bruce, P. (1995). The plantation negro as freeman. In V. P. Franklin (Ed.), *Living our stories, telling our truths: Autobiography and the making of the African-American intellectual tradition.* New York: Scribner.

Carby, H. V. (1987). *Reconstructing womanhood: The emergence of the Afro-American woman novelist.* New York: Oxford University Press.

Collins, P. H. (1991). *Black feminist thought: Knowledge, consciousness, and the politics of empowerment.* New York: Routledge.

Cooper, A. J. (1988). *A voice from the south.* New York: Oxford University Press. (Original work published 1892)

Cott, N. F. (1977). *The bonds of womanhood: "Woman's sphere" in New England, 1780-1835.* New Haven, CT: Yale University Press.

de Lauretis, T. (1986). Feminist studies/critical studies: Issues, terms, and contexts. In T. de Lauretis (Ed.), *Feminist studies/critical studies* (pp. 1-19). Bloomington: Indiana University Press.

Giddings, P. (1984). *When and where I enter: The impact of black women on race and sex in America.* New York: Bantam Books.

Guy-Sheftall, B. (Ed.). (1995). *Words of fire: An anthology of African American feminist thought.* New York: The New Press.

Lerner, G. (Ed.). (1972). *Black women in white America: A documentary history.* New York: Vintage Books.

Scott, A. (1970). *The southern lady: From pedestal to politics, 1830-1930.* Chicago: University of Chicago Press.

Washington, M. H. (1988). *A voice from the south.* New York: Oxford University Press.

Welter, B. (1976). *Dimity convictions: The American woman in the nineteenth century.* Columbus: University of Ohio Press.

Wells, I. B. (1991a). A red record: Tabulated statistics and alleged causes of lynchings in the United States, 1892-1893-1894. In I. Wells-Barnett (Ed.), *Selected works of Ida B. Wells-Barnett.* New York: Oxford University Press.

Wells, I. B. (1991b). Southern horrors: Lynch law in all its phases. In Wells-Barnett (Ed.), *Selected works of Ida B. Wells-Barnett.* New York: Oxford University Press.

White, C. L. (1995, April). *The rhetorical negotiation of identity: Ida B. Wells' analysis of womanhood and lynching.* Paper presented at the meeting of the Eastern Communication Association, Pittsburgh, PA.

White, D. G. (1999). *Too heavy a load.* New York: Norton.

NINE

The Female Voice in Hip-Hop: An Exploration into the Potential of the Erotic Appeal

Eric King Watts
Wake Forest University

> *The erotic is a measure between the beginnings of our sense of self and the chaos of our strongest feelings.*
> —Lorde (1984, p. 54)

In the opening scene of Spike Lee's 1986 break-out film, *She's Gotta Have It,* our vision sweeps over the rumpled sheets of a starkly made bed surrounded by unlit candles in a black and white room. Lee's protagonist, Nola Darling, a fiery, sassy, "independent" woman, sits up in bed, caresses us with her eyes and states in a coy, yet matter-of-fact voice, "some people call me a freak." Nola flashes a wry smile and invites us into her performative space in the drama. When the camera moves in on her, it is as if we are pulled in bed with her to experience her story. And what a story it is. Lee dramatizes a female life experience where patriarchal notions of sexual need, pleasure, and dominance are inverted and shaped by Nola's attempts to engender and articulate her female subjectivity. While negotiating the tensions inherent in having sexual relationships with three men and trying to meet the nonsexual needs of her loving, lesbian girlfriend, Nola and her candle-lit bedroom become a cinematic site where the potentialities for erotic power to create new forms of sexual pleasure and new aspects of social agency are explored.

Lee's film is noteworthy in this regard because he seems sensitive to how constructions of female pleasure operate as mechanisms of control and attempts to give voice to what hooks (1990) called a politicized "yearning" (p. 12). And so when Nola confides in us that some people label her a "freak," we understand this statement as a reference to the film's core subject: the historical attempt by men to regulate or police the use of the female body (Carby, 1992; Ortner & Whitehead, 1981). Nola dismisses her lovers after deciding that the sexual demands of the men in her life are excessive. But after a lingering, melancholic loneliness, brutally punctuated by a rape at the hands of a former lover, she reclaims the one man she feels she needs only to conclude at the end of the film that she's not a one-man woman after all. Even though sexually "liberated," Nola is dependent on men. If Nola could fuse her three lovers into the "perfect man," she would be dissatisfied because it is not a man she yearns for, but the capacity to critically deploy and enjoy her erotic power *for herself.* This yearning is manifested in invitations to men to perform differing versions of male desire in her performative/transformative space—her bedroom.

Nola's momentary delights ultimately constrain her agency, however. This is so because Lee's strategy for reconstituting her subjectivity pays more attention to the specific and localized means of achieving orgasm than it does to the manner in which Black female eroticism is annexed in service of White patriarchy. Lee's narrative convention of resolving Nola's dilemma through "better" sex rightly critiques impoverished masculinity, but because it is delimited by Black desire, it wrongly exonerates and satiates a White patriarchal pop cultural appetite hungry for displays of Black female sexuality as paradoxically deficient and excessive. In the film, Nola's predicament results from the convergence of her psychic-sexual meditations and the self-centered pursuits of Black men. Nola's "problems" stem from the "failings" of Black love. Yet in a broader sense, her frustrations signify the workings of a market economy for Black bodies. Lee unwittingly binds Nola to a set of patriarchal mass cultural values and beliefs that appear *normal* by representing Black sexual "deviance."

Given this critical reading, I find it an interesting coincidence that *She's Gotta Have It* enjoyed significant success at the same time that Salt 'N' Pepa (SNP) dropped their first hip-hop bomb, *Hot, Cool, and Vicious.* As the first female rap group to tout a gold album (France, 1994), SNP not only demonstrated the financial viability of female rap, they espoused a hip hop sexuality that explicitly made a case for female control over female bodies. Like Nola, SNP and other female emcees emerging in the mid-1980s demanded that they too had to have it. But, unlike Lee's cipher that is isolated in pursuit of "it," the collective struggles of female rap artists over the use/abuse of their bodies highlight the fact that subtle and complex relations mediate the Black female image. Rap artistry amplifies material connections among an urban *ethos,* American values, and corporate strategies, translating them into staggering record sales and cultural influence. Moreover, I argued elsewhere that rap performance provides important lessons about selfhood and community relations (Watts, 1997). As such, the dynamic affiliations among Black female sexuality, subjectivity, and the culture industry require critical interrogation.

In this chapter, I argue that the cultural economy of hip-hop performance brokers competing and complementary orientations toward Black female sexuality and the power of the erotic. These orientations are constitutive of personal and market strategies enacted by female artists to provide symbolic and pragmatic power over their lives and in the rap "game." Accordingly, female sexual display emerges as a site of dynamic disputation where patriarchal erasure of Black female subjectivity is resisted, revised, and exploited. Specifically, I situate Lorde's notion of the Erotic within an exploration of female rap narratives and images with the intention of revealing what they suggest about the character, status, and importance of eroticism in the lives of Black women today. This chapter proceeds in three phases: First, in general terms I discuss Lorde's erotic potential and the norms and practices used in society to administer it in the service of male domination of the female body. Second, I distinguish provocative features of sexual strategies in rap artistry and delineate their rhetorical uses and functions. I argue in this section that in the attempt to make "cream," Black females and males in hip-hop constitute a world of sexual materialism where sexual pleasures and economic ventures have colonized one another to the extent that the truly erotic is threatened. Finally, I perform my own critical act of cultural reclamation by doing a close reading of a selected rap text. In this critical project I hope to identify the terms, practices, and traditions necessary for the erotic to triumph over a surging anti-erotic aesthetic in hip-hop.

THE DENIAL OF THE EROTIC

Sister Outsider is a collection of speeches, essays, and interviews in which Lorde (1984) transformed the silence imposed on marginalized persons into the sources necessary for the constitution of what hooks (1990) called a "radical black subjectivity" (p. 15). Opposing it to the pornographic, Lorde described the erotic as a "depth of feeling" that is simultaneously chaotic, spiritual, and knowledgeable (p. 53). Eroticism is existential in that it is realized as a fullness of being, a joyfulness in sharing ourselves with one another. Playful and serious, erotic sources within us are always urgently requesting that our daily existence materializes, in everything we do, our fullest capacity for love. Eroticism is, therefore, political in the sense that the psychic coherence and power it begets can transform what we imagine as valuable, possible, reasonable, bearable. Locked inside women as an "inferior" source of information compared to a "masculine" scientism, the erotic is creased along a dialectic of fear and desire. "We have been warned against it all our lives by the male world, which values [it] enough to keep women around in order to exercise it in the service of men, but which fears this same depth too much to examine the possibilities of it within themselves" (pp. 53-54). Determined to maintain power in Western societies, men have demanded that eroticism only materialize in gross and obscene fashion—like a jangling raw nerve giving rise to bodily stimulation and base sensation. Put through sexual contortions, Lorde argued that in contemporary society the erotic appears to us disfigured and misnamed.

It is important to recognize the relation between patriarchal suppression of the erotic in the female body and the strategic erasure of female subjectivity. Holland (1988) noted that the negation of a powerful female presence is dependent on the dual task of muting the voice and masking the body. The denial of the erotic brutally accomplishes both. For once, the erotic falls victim to a rationale defining it as merely carnal and in need of severe social sanction, it warrants a belief system oppressing women. The silencing of women using "market models of patriarchy" that exhibit a "capacity for skilled sexual violence" (Printz, 1992, p. 1068) has received much attention in feminist scholarship (Collins, 1990; Davis, 1990). But even in this context, White female bodies tend to represent oppressed "femininity," whereas Black female bodies are absent (Hammonds, 1994).

Scholarship of this sort insinuates that the erotic is encased within pristine and repressive forms of womanhood. Hoagland (1993) suggested "the model for oppression in Anglo-European thinking is the male conception of femininity" (p. 93). In her essay, Hoagland argued that "wimin's" powers have been carefully distorted and "buried" behind the sexist inscription of male authority within the term *feminine*. Women attempting to live up to this prescription find themselves bullied into being frail, emotional, dimwitted, and submissive. Moreover, labeled as merely "irrational," men explain acts of planned female resistance away. "Society attempts to control and limit aggression through social sanctions against those labeled feminine in a way not attempted among those labeled masculine" (p. 90).

An example of the masking force of "femininity" can be found in the film, *M. Butterfly,* where the total elision of the female body takes place. In a kind of coming-out scene, the male Chinese protagonist-as-female-lover acknowledges the patriarchal presumption that "only a man knows what a woman should be like." This story captures the masking power of the male gaze. In "Is the Gaze Male?," Kaplan (1993) revisited some important ground in feminist scholarship concerning the visual construction of femininity. While arguing against early critical approaches that assessed visual characterizations based on their apparent "autonomy," Kaplan sided with scholars like Laura Mulvey by taking issue with the very production of female representation. In terms of American cinematic presence, Kaplan asserted that the woman appears or takes form not as a sign of the signified, but that the "signifier and signified have been elided into a sign that represents something in the male unconscious" (p. 257). Fearing her reality, it is what the man *desires* the woman to be like. And so, "Butterfly" in essence represents the psychological cinematic manifestation of male fear and desire.

The erotic dialectic of fear and desire is also apparent in Bartky's (1993) essay, "Foucault, Femininity, and the Modernization of Patriarchal Power" (1993). Bartky discussed Foucault's analysis of how the rationalization of the Western world produced a system of social, cultural dehumanization and discipline that exerts a great deal of control over the human body, both spatially and psychologically. She took Foucault to task, however, for not examining the ways in which women are subjected to "a modality of embodiment that is peculiarly feminine" (p. 152). According to this argument, men desire women's bodies, but also fear them because the lack of a penis represents castration (Mulvey, 1984). Yet Bartky also demonstrated a kind of fear in her critique of Foucault. That is, her neglect of the specialized manner in which the Black female body is distorted in the attempt to make it docile is in keeping with Christian's (1985) assessment that mainstream (and not so mainstream) feminists perceive the Black woman's body as less important than their own. The point is that the racist fears of some White feminists re-double the negative effect on the Black female voice and body.

The historical and strategic distortions of the Black female body and voice have yielded two related, yet opposing characterizations in patriarchal culture: the mammy and the Jezebel (Christian, 1985; McDowell, 1988). In the former stereotype, the erotic is submerged within a body useful for nurturing White babies—both young and old; in the latter image, the erotic is strategically administered as a sex-driven plaything for White male lusts. In either case, the erotic is mutated into a form useful for White patriarchal domination of Black sex. These mutations thrive as deliberate racist patriarchal icons fostering a black female fiction where "there is no subtlety to our experience. We are always portrayed as lacking in complexity, as transparent . . . all surface, lacking in depth" (hooks, 1995, p. 97). Constructed as a prostrate sign of Black sexual aberrance, the Black female body functions in mass consumer society as a screen on which the taboo fantasies and terrors of White supremacist patriarchy are projected (hooks, 1992). This static fixed, mute, yet hyper-visible poster appears vibrant and energetic, but because it displaces "black female subjectivity as a layered, shifting, and complex reality," it is anti-erotic (Kuenz, 1993, p. 421).

Not surprisingly then, Lorde's notion of eroticism requires a "bridge between language and action, voice and body" to offer its creative energies (Holland, 1988, p. 2). Speaking from multiple margins—those erected by the distancing effect of Black-otherness, female-otherness, and lesbian-otherness—Lorde exhorted the urgent need to resist violence, abuse, and shame in fighting for one's erotic sources (Olson, 1997). In "The Transformation of Silence into Language and Action," the poet constitutes in speech the knowledge necessary to teach us how to keep from being eaten alive (Lorde, 1984). In this address delivered at the assembly of the Modern Language Association in Chicago, Lorde employed her personal battle with breast cancer as a metaphor for women's struggles against being silenced in society. In asserting this associative commonplace between illness and silence, Lorde identified persistent silence with impending death (Olson, 1997). Taken as a powerful utterance within the statement that *Sister Outsider* makes, Lorde's speech suggests that the suppression of the erotic in women is life threatening because it signifies more than mute acquiescence to power, but an internal erosion of being. Rather than a source of shame or embarrassment, "Lorde's words . . . signal the potential for black women's empowerment by showing sexuality and the erotic to be a domain of exploration, pleasure, and human agency" (Collins, 1990, p. 166). Moreover, as Olson (1997) noted, "speech and silence are rife with gendered implications for epistemology and the development of self in relationship to community" (p. 53). Keeping these issues in mind—sexual pleasure, social agency, and subjectivity—this exploration now turns a critical ear and eye toward the titillating, terrific, and terrifying sexual performances of female rap artistry.

MAKING C.R.E.A.M IN THE RAP GAME

Standing at the door of a hip hop house party in progress means surveying dancing, loving, cussing, and backbiting among men and women alike. A massive festival opens before one's eyes and the occasion for frenzied bodies working up a sweat is simply (and significantly) the intensely jubilant celebration of one's self in motion. Rap music has always sponsored "freak-fests" wherever DJs could find some juice. But what is different about this spectacle rocking and rolling before us is that women DJs and emcees are carding folks at the door:

> Give me body/ don't make me wait/ welcome into my Queendom, come one come all/ 'cause when it comes to lyrics, I bring them/ in spring I sing/ in fall I call out to all the one's who had a hard day/ I've prepared a place on my dance floor/ the time is now for you to party/ I thought it would be a good chance for you to move/ one nation under a groove/ house music always soothes/ so get with the flow, let's go/ yo, can you rock to a house groove tempo?/ if so, then shall we let the games begin/ what better off position can you be in?/ I'm on fire/ the flames too hot to douse/ the pool is open/ come into my house.

Queen Latifah's (1989) booming, syncopated serenade greets us with the kind of speech act that can only be taken as an order, "give me body." Her pronouncement of ownership of both the sites of resistive performance and the terms for the celebration set the tone for our exploration into the primary features of disputation with male dominance in female rap music. Rose (1994) identified three major fields of rhetorical action in women's rap that I revisit here: First, artists articulate a distinctly female voice and worldview. Second, artists depict and redefine the sexual and material character of female-male relationships. Third, artists assert female mastery over their bodies and their sexual pleasures. Latifah's affirmation that she controls the dance floor, the music, the lyrics, and, ultimately, when, where, and how we groove our bodies in the spectacle is evidence of this focus. From Lorde's perspective, the capacity to live an erotic life issues from the enunciation and actualization of a female subjective position in regards to one's body, spirit, and social practices. This sense of self-awareness is made possible and is regulated by the norms and values of a rap industry vivified by an urban *ethos* obsessed with the notion of making "cream." In the pages that follow, I characterize the concept of "cream," link it to the sexualized strategies of female artists just noted, and comment on its potential to subvert and undermine the constitution of the erotic by promoting the value of an anti-erotic aesthetic.

Ever since the Wu-Tang Clan exploded onto the hip-hop scene in 1993 with their debut CD, *Enter the Wu-Tang (36 Chambers)*, rap vernacular has been circumscribed by the corporate sign of "cream." On the track called "C.R.E.A.M.," the victory of a thoroughly material existence is affirmed by the sheer omnipresence and omnipotence of capital. Operating as an acronym for a commercialized world, CREAM signifies the depressing fact that Cash Rules Everything Around Me. By no means a new observation, the term *cream* has nevertheless gone from being a provocative reference to the regulatory processes of the American political economy to being THE thing everybody's gotta have. Replacing "juice" as the principal term designating power and status, "cream" conflates a sense of economic necessity with a personal will to power. For female rap artists, "making that cream . . . ain't easy as it seems" (MC Lyte, 1996) because industry power brokers are overwhelmingly male (Power 30, 1997).

In terms of a distinctly female voice, making cream requires that one demonstrate mad verbal skills and take control over one's environment and self. Ever since she stepped to center stage at the ripe old age of 17, Queen Latifah has been involved in the struggle to carve out feminine creative space in hip-hop. Her regal pose and persona make sense when she hands down what Eure and Spady (1991) described as "Latifah's Law" (p. 148) or instructs multiple audiences about the "Nature of a Sista." Latifah centers her voice as a hip-hop authority on the track "Listen to Me" and affirms her power to command respect and attention. In the song, Latifah cites cities and countries from around the world where there are people who listen to her. In the end, the audience is impressed by the expansiveness of her international flavor. We clearly understand why Latifah (1993) boasts of "niggas on my tits. . . ." But, on the hip-hop playground one's "cream" is often acquired through the dissing of others. And so, Latifah has to guard her reign zealously. On "I Can't Understand," Latifah seems genuinely confused as to why anyone would dare question her authority:

> Perplexed and I'm vexed, 'cause everywhere I go/ people be flexin', expectin' me to wanna flow/ I don't play that/ the only way I would be playin' is if I payback and run the play back/ so what you sayin'/ you don't wanna be a sista' in the name of rap?/ yet ya wanna talk shit and your style is wack/ I wouldv'e squashed it before and made the whole issue dead/ now I'm fed, so it's off with your head/ now the moral of the verse is that your career is through/ and don't be fuckin' wit' nobody who ain't fuckin' wit' you/ if I was in your shoes, I'd let them be a start walkin'/ next time there might not be no talkin'. . .

The "dissing" she gets and gives is, of course, a potent derivative of playing the dozens (Garner, 1983). But, by centering women in this public interaction, female norms of exchange have a chance of being established as such. For example, on the track "Just Another Day," Latifah discards her rap persona by saying that she's "just plain old Dana today." Dana Owens embodies the ordinary woman hanging in the 'hood. Dana, therefore, provides stronger identification with her female listeners as she deals with brothers who want to scheme on her for sex or jack her for money. Dana is not unprotected, however. A would-be assailant thinks twice about stepping to her after he sees that she's armed. Dana tells us that the "jacker" ran off because he recognizes that "mine's bigger." By signifying off the penis-centered male bravado, Dana challenges the chief sign of patriarchal sexual domination. Moreover, Dana is able to give real-life lessons to female listeners who walk her urban streets. And so, Dana's narrative adds veracity and depth to the female image in rap because after all, it's just another day.

Coming from the streets of the Bronx, MC Lyte understands the trials of street justice all too well. As an emcee with "street smarts" ("Hard Copy," MC Lyte, 1993) she grasps the need to consistently meet challenges to her autonomous self over and over again by demanding her audiences answer the question, "What's My Name." In an effort to continuously re-make parts of herself to stay central within a culture industry in constant flux, Lyte demonstrates verbal dexterity and originality by introducing us to her own language:

> Kumbaya la face to the tar/ izfar omar tomar so far/ otay earl la searl the teen hime/ I gets mine you know, I gets mine/ a boom to the bang/ a bang to the boom/ so bit, oh shit ela the room/ post to the

pre tix time tex/ her life oh trife comes sex comes becks/ many two
loaves on a leaf four clover/ it ain't over 'til it's over. . . . ("Never
Heard Nothin' Like This," MC Lyte, 1993).

Lyte's language combines hip-hop lingo with some features and
structures of pig Latin. By playing within a primary convention of
rap—making sense out of nonsense—Lyte asserts that not only do
women possess crazy skills, but that their creative energies can alter
the aesthetic and topical conventions of hip-hop. Taken together,
Latifah and Lyte present the female voice in terms of its distinctive
world view and its ability to reproduce itself as an ever expanding
series of utterances. Moreover, a complex and cosmological perspective
on black female subjectivity is engendered: "I use my scales/ positive/
negative/ energy/ male and female emotions within me . . . weighing
souls on the scale/ follow me as we take this trip through astrology/ the
galaxy from Pluto to Mercury . . . though I walk through the valley of
the shadow of death I fear none/ I'm at one with the sun 'till I'm done . .
." ("Zodiac," on *bad as i wanna be*, MC Lyte, 1996). The "cream" these
artists generate is based, in part, on their longevity. Stemming from
talent and marketing savvy they are able to denounce with eloquence
and authority a legacy of silence and submission.

An analysis of the strategies female artists use to transform
female-male relationships brings us face to face with the ways in
which patriarchal pop culture exploits the erotic. Female artists
advocate strategies ranging from cheating on faithless men to
executing brutal revenge fantasies paralleling the revenge narratives
male artists spin about the police (Rose, 1994). After being the object
of male bravado and sexual violence, it is fitting that the phallus, in
its various guises, becomes the site of subversion. For example,
Roxanne Shante (1992) threatens male sexual mythology by using
"voodoo" to "make his dick small, make him see spiders on the wall"
(p. 284). Similarly, Bytches With Problems (1991) denounce the kind
of man "Who always holds his thing in his hand/ talkin' about it all
the time/ lyin' and sayin' it's about size nine . . . the one who claims
to be a real good lover/ usually he's a two-minute brother. . . ."

The terms of sexual relations in the hip-hop community
become even direr for male privilege when men meet artists like The
Conscious Daughters (TCD) and Boss. TCD were the brainchild of
Paris and Scarface Records (Hunt, 1994), but don't expect this pair of
Oakland artists to harp on the strong Afrocentric verse like their
mentor.

These are the gangsta bitches of Apache's dreams: women hard
enough to buck down any man physically or metaphorically, yet

confident enough with theirs to reveal a distinct feminine side . . .
the Daughters' part deals more with their views of themselves as
strong women, as accepting the lessons of their black foremothers
who left them a legacy of survival and pride in a harsh, racist, male-
dominated world. (Coker, 1994, p. 42).

This is certainly true, but those lessons have also come up in a raw
street code that promotes women to pull rank on men by pulling glocks
(A. Jones, 1994). Karryl Smith and Carla Green appear in the driver's
seat with the release of their first single, "Somethin' To Ride To (Fonky
Expedition)." On this track, TCD invert patriarchy by putting the fellas
in the back seat while they take the wheel and cruise through the 'hood.
This narrative is composed of men swinging from TCD's "jocks" because
of their cream while others are intimidated by their feminized version
of going for bad. "Ridin' wit' a gat in my lap and one finger on the zap/
lookin' for some niggas in a cadillac . . ." (Conscious Daughters, 1993).
Assuming that women "can't be soft and make it as a female rapper"
(Coker, 1994, p. 42), TCD announce venomously that they are "comin' at
you all the way live with that gangsta shit" while warning that they're
"fuckin' bitches up, 'cause I ain't no chump . . ." ("Princess of Poetry,"
Conscious Daughters, 1993). On "Wife of a Gangsta," TCD seem to be in
danger of sabotaging their strategies by linking their power to a
spouse's drug trade. In an interview with the Source, Green talks about
the message: "As a female, you know what he's doing; it's just that you
like the material things that yu get out of it . . . [gangstas] take care of
you, you get your nails and your hair done, stuff like that . . ." (Coker,
1994, p. 42). This apparent promotion of the servility of women gets
troubled because the narrative tells us about the real life ambivalence
urban women must experience in the face of abject poverty and extreme
wealth. Moreover, the "wife" enacts all of the central energy of the
narrative. Indeed, the "husband" exists only in the negative—as a
shadow of her action ("Wife," Conscious Daughters, 1993).

In songs like "Recipe of a Hoe" and "Comin' To Getcha'," Boss
(1993) identifies the "fake ass wannabe a pimp mothafucka" who
cheats, abuses, and deceives women with flashy promises. "Recipe"
reveals and belittles the old formula that men use to get laid and
ends the narrative by telling men they are "no good, pussy-hungry
ass niggas. . . ." Similarly, "Comin' To Getcha' enacts the flirtation
and murder of men bent on raping and sodomizing Boss. The chorus
of the song storms toward the listener and seems to compel men to
either join Boss' troopers or change their abusive ways.

Taking the general rhetorical form of womanist
appropriation, these themes and images depict the way in which
some artists virtually *become* "masculine" aggressive voices so as to

invert patriarchy and put men in *their* place. Helene Shugart (1997) discussed the vitality of these kinds of "counterhegemonic acts" in terms of how they operate as critical reflections of patriarchal myth, traditions and values. Reflective appropriation acts as a mirror on the margins of discourse, creating oppositional images which give rise to new ways to view the world. "The specific counterhegemonic function of reflection . . . is the cultivation of a critical awareness of oppression" (Shugart, 1997, p. 225). Boss and TCD flip the script on Black male power strategies revealing a variety of masculine postures as trivial and bombastic. They place women in charge of their own destinies and provide both figurative and practical tactics with which to confront misogyny and neglect. Lorde spent much of her life enacting forms of "human liberation rhetoric" and believed that this particular species of discourse was essential to reconstituting erotic power (Olson, 1997, p. 51). Moreover, Shugart emphasized the fact "that appropriation is *viscerally liberating and invigorating* in its own right, not only or even necessarily as a means to an end" (p. 213, italics added). But, it is this sense of stimulation and pleasure the appropriator feels in the act of resistance that becomes intoxicating, marketable, and serviceable for patriarchy. TCD and Boss transform themselves into gangsta' bitches to make "cream" in the game and in so doing spend more time rapping out an anthem of "the niggas better come correct shit" (Mayo, 1993, p. 48) than they do exploring the varied ways their female sexual pleasures are annexed in the service of patriarchal domination. In the end, "masculine" norms are legitimized as valuable and powerful, further disfiguring the erotic. For a closer examination of the manner in which the erotic is troubled within the transactional nature of sexual pleasure and capital gain, mediated by "cream," let us consider the world of sexual materialism.

Perceived by some to be the "Thelma and Louise of rap music" (Gonzales, 1997, p. 62) Lil' Kim (Kim Jones) and Foxy Brown (Inga Marchand) infuse haute-couture fashion and hyper-sexual sensation into the sort of intriguing hip-hop performances that help put their debut CDs at the top of the charts ("Top R&B Albums," 1997). Hooked up with two of the most powerful musical cartels in the game (Power 30, 1997) Lil' Kim and Foxy Brown's styles and images have enraptured the rap community. Their performances offer a significant arena in which to witness the exhilarating potential of the erotic and the dampening operations of a patriarchal cultural economy provoking an anti-erotic aesthetic.

The "Intro" to Lil' Kim's (1996) CD, *Hard Core*, explicitly denotes the pornographic imagination by locating her persona at the nexus of male fantasy, masturbation, and sexual desire. The price of admission equals the price of her CD and stimulates a young man's (and our) venture into the world of sexual materialism. Calling herself a "diamond-cluster hustler" and a "disease-free bitch," Lil' Kim makes no apologies for centering her narratives on a provocative correspondence between her revved-up sexual engine and a market logic that promises that "I'm rich and I'm a stay that bitch . . ." ("Queen Bitch," 1996). Similarly, Foxy Brown headlines the fact that she's "selling hot pussy" (hooks, 1992, p. 62) by entitling her CD, *Ill Na Na*. On the track, "I'll Be," Foxy Brown swears that she'll "never settle for less/ I'm in excess, not inexpensive . . . that's just the way I'm built/ nasty. . . ." The vulgar financial transaction she alludes to materializes specifically when she addresses a suitor: "What up pop?/ brace yourself as I ride on top/ close your eyes as you ride right out your socks . . . lose his mind as he grind in the tunnel/ wanna give me the cash he made off his last bundle . . ." ("I'll Be," 1996). This sense of sexual insanity is reminiscent of the grotesque malformation of the erotic as it is flattened into trivial pleasure. However, what I mean to suggest in the pages to follow is that these assertions do not plainly attest to a dominated eroticism. On the contrary, they give conflicted testimony to the pressures of patriarchal culture and to the premise that black female subjectivity "remains in excess of the very economy of bodies meant to contain it" (Printz, 1992, p. 1069).

Tucked behind these brief excerpts highlighting sex for cash is the basis for my argument about the rhetorical function of "cream." Specifying a peculiar relationship between female sexual pleasure and capital gain, "cream" operates as a synecdoche. In *Grammar of Motives*, Burke (1969) defined a synecdoche as a trope which, in its most potent enactment, compels an audience to reconstitute one kind of substance in the terms set forth by another kind of substance. Not involving solely the association of a part to a whole (as would be the case if I were to be called "Dr. Rap" because I hold a PhD and research the art form), essentially a *reduction* in substance, a synecdoche irrupts each substance inside the other fully, expansively. In other words, synecdoche features one of the modes in which two substances can become consubstantial with one another.

With this put forth, I contend that in the hip-hop world of sexual materialism "cream" mediates a kind of transmutation of the sexual and the financial. To say that a woman has "cream" is not to simply call attention to her bankroll or to her body, but to recognize that she is involved in a dynamic, fluid set of exchange relations between persons and social practices. "Cream" indexes a phenomenon in which sexual pleasure is shaped by the tantalizing dream of wealth and the pursuit of capital gain becomes a highly sensual and explosively satisfying experience. Whereas prostitution occurs within a context dissociated from female sexual gratification, "cream" is a phenomenon in which *female sexual pleasure is centered and conceived in terms of profit*. Also, the anticipation of profit triggers bodily arousal. Black female sexual pleasure has been referred to as a "bartering chip" (Morgan, 1997, p. 78) in pop culture and of "secondary" importance to an overarching economic strategy (hooks, 1992, p. 69). This sort of commentary assumes, however, that pleasure remains exiled to the margins of female sexual performance. If, on the other hand, we recognize that female rap artists have developed a heightened sensitivity to their own bodily pleasures and how to stimulate them, that Lil' Kim is sincere when she says "I fuck ta bust a nut, Lil' Kim is not a slut," ("Player Haters," 1996) we have to take seriously the implications of "cream."

There are four interrelated issues worthy of brief examination regarding making "cream." First, female artists center their subjective sexual pleasure in their narratives, thus sparking an erotic charge. Second, "cream" mediates the encroachment of female sexual pleasure into a "masculine" economic domain (and the other way around). Third, making "cream" is a cooperative project between females and males fostering a marketable cultural sign of sexualized resistance to patriarchal authority that is important to the economics of the rap game. Fourth, the maintenance of "cream" within a sexual dialectic constitutive of females and males gives rise to an anti-erotic aesthetic.

Female sexual pleasure moves from margin to center by focusing on female mastery over sexual spaces like the bedroom and through an inversion of the male logic that penile penetration drives sexual pleasure. On "Spend a Little Doe" (1996) Lil' Kim seizes control of a sexual encounter with an unreliable lover: "With the dildo I like to play while I'm workin'/ and that's for certain/ keep jerkin' I ain't done with you. . . ." In several scenarios the vagina replaces the penis as the most significant site of stimulation. Both Foxy Brown and Lil' Kim revel in the fact that "pussies fuck dicks" (Brown, "Fox Boogie," 1996) and contemplate "dreams of fuckin' an R&B dick . . ." (Kim, "Dreams," 1996). A sense of sexual proprietorship is evident in Foxy Brown's vow: ". . . and from here on I solemnly swear to hold my own like Pee Wee [Herman] in a movie theater . . . I could do the bad by my damn self" ("Ill Na Na," 1996). And the testament to female awareness and authority over sexual pleasure is voiced through Lil' Kim's displeasure concerning a lover's neglect: "Somethin' I couldn't stand . . . somethin' that couldn't make his ass a real man/ that motherfucker never ate my pussy" ("Not Tonite," 1996). The potential for an erotic explosion is revivified in the re-centering of female sexual pleasure. By concentrating on one's own bodily needs and desires, female artists glimpse their power as sexual subjects.

Viewed from the aspect of female subjectivity, it is precisely this psychic substance which colonizes (and is colonized by) the cultural economy of rap music. Brokered by the synecdochic operations of "cream," the "masculine" means for attaining "juice"— violence and intimidation—are made sensual and vaginal. In pursuit of the dollar, Foxy Brown laments that there's "no where ta rest, nigga/ no where ta hide/ it's a high-speed chase and death is on my mind/ will I fall or fail/ who calls the shots/ it's all real . . . and through this cream my whole team/ lust fiend/ the ghetto dream . . ." ("The Chase," 1996). The velocity for this adventure is produced by the transfiguration of the phallic and vaginal, signified in her "Letter to the Firm" (1996) by the remark that the "gun is our punana." This latest refrain cannot be taken as a strict equation between female genitalia and weaponry, functioning as reflective appropriation (albeit this modality is inclusive of the overall effect). The Firm is a musical cartel featuring Nas and Jay Z, both male artists. In this respect, the gun, usually a "masculine" means of asserting economic control gangsta style, signifies a gender-flexed concept. Foxy Brown's centralized sexual pleasure produces the agency necessary for capital gain and domination of rivals. Meanwhile their shared (female) sexual pleasure ("*our* punana") shapes the terms in which capital gain is defined and sought. In short, lust and greed refer to the same notion—"cream"—and to each other. The phenomenon is circular and transfusing.

The rap cartels in which Foxy Brown and Lil' Kim have been considered affiliates, The Firm and Junior M.A.F.I.A. respectively, give us the structural models essential for appreciating the character of a sexualized dialectic between females and males. These rap collectives are constitutive of an urban *ethos* commercializing a mobster mentality. As such, some misogynous tendencies are re-introduced as a dynamic in "cream." The coexistence of male dominance and female subjectivity provides the substantive ground boosting the sexual dialectic. Earlier I reviewed some strategies women in hip-hop employ to counter male abuse in relationships. In the world of sexual materialism, the personal battles many women wage in their lives against misogyny and neglect become variables in a market calculus defining sexual confrontation for mass appeal. The war between the sexes is pre-figured by "covert" planning sessions that make salient the rationales at work. On Lil' Kim's CD, two tracks operate in tandem to clarify the status of this dialectic. "Take It!" and "Scheamin'" put into play the movements of "cream" as it relates to personal urges and industry needs. On the former track,

The Notorious B.I.G., Lil' Cease, and Trife act out their lusts for Lil' Kim and some of her friends while at a club. The presumably "private" all-male conversation links Lil' Kim's physical beauty and status as a pop icon to their intense desire to "fuck her." Similarly, on the latter track, Lil' Kim and her friends voice their desire to "get with" B.I.G. and his partners because "Biggie got the fuckin' dollars" (1996). I want to emphasize that female sexual pleasure is not reduced nor made secondary in this interaction, it is *heightened* by it. The market value of this dialectic is directly proportional to an intensification of female sexual pleasure. The direct confrontation with the Other about one's sexual demands helps to make my point on the track, "We Don't Need It." After Lil' Cease, in front of a group of friends, wonders aloud with whom among a gathering of women he wants to have sex, the dialectic booms in a call and response:

Male voices: "If you ain't suckin' no dick, we don't need it . . ."
Female voices: "If you ain't lickin' no clits, we don't want it . . ."
Male voices: "If you ain't drinkin' no nut . . ."
Female voices: "If you ain't lickin' no butts . . ." (1996).

Most important to understanding the corporate operations of this dialectic is the shared pleasure and delight voiced by the females and males at the conclusion of the track. The role-play is revealed as a parody of real sexual frustrations experienced by both sexes. This kind of sexual tournament is by no means new to hip-hop, but its status as an aesthetic convention is noteworthy. This particular dialectic is not only situated across gangsta/bitch borders, but finds capacitance in scenes where men orbit and relish the spectacular female presence: "Who got the illest pussy on the planet?/ sugar walls comin' down/ niggas can't stand it, the ill na na . . . blood hounds tryin' ta hunt down a brown fox/ the ill na na . . ." ("Ill Na Na," 1996). This male chorus promotes Foxy Brown's sex appeal in ways reflective of Lil' Kim's promotion on "Take It!" Female sexuality confronts abusive and inadequate masculinity. But females also scheme for material possessions within a context where economic holdings are themselves sexualized. And so we see a mutual promotion and mass marketing of a sexual materialistic transaction that makes all parties "cream." Lil' Kim sums up my point concisely: "I stay draped in diamonds and pearls. Beside every man there's a bad girl"("No Time," 1996).

It is but a short distance from the brokerage of this sexual dialectic to my contention that "cream" provokes an anti-erotic aesthetic. I believe that Lil' Kim and Foxy Brown (and the other emcees that are sure to follow) reconstitute a strong sense of female sexual pleasure and are able to utilize it for agency in a male dominated rap industry. This central self-awareness sparks an erotic charge that engages patriarchal notions of capital gain, but becomes bound to a commercial exchange relation dedicated to making "cream." However, this sense of self is also perpetuated by a white supremacist patriarchal culture that limits female subjectivity by shackling self-esteem to one's physical appearance. Advancing a point that Toni Morrison makes in her brilliant novel, *The Bluest Eye*, Denard (1988) made this observation: "A physical standard of beauty . . . commercializes the virtue of all women and 'is one of the dumbest, most pernicious and destructive ideas of the Western world, and we [Black women] should have nothing to do with it'" (p. 172). As a result, erotic power is reduced to the presence of bodily stimulation; the erotic is reconstituted as material. Pressures to materialize it in the form of capital erode the spirituality of eroticism—a joyfully speculative and meditative activity. "The principal horror of any system that defines the good in terms of profit rather than in terms of human need, or that defines human need to the exclusion of the psychic and emotional components of that need—the principal horror of such a system is that it robs our work of its erotic value, its erotic power and life appeal and fulfillment"(Lorde, 1984, p. 55). The fabulous commercial success of the sexual dialectic described here virtually guarantees that its features will become stock aesthetic devices in rap music. Indeed, this aesthetic is palpable in the performances of new artists like Eve and Sole. The prominence of such a device threatens to rob rap reproductive forces of their erotic vale. Thus, the obsession with making "cream" sponsors an anti-erotic aesthetic.

I have considered the reclamation of female sexual pleasure in terms of its erotic potential and its entrapment within a dialectic devoted to making "cream." If female eroticism, nurturing an expansive subjectivity, is to enable African American women to "increase their range of possibilities" (Morgan, 1997, p. 134), then it must generate a whole new set of norms, premises, and practices geared toward reconstituting the performance of masculinity as well. Collins (1990) rightly deduced that within a pornographic frame, men are reduced to the size and availability of their penises even as they objectify women. hooks (1990) painted a bleaker picture when she argues that "masculinity as it is conceived within patriarchy is life threatening to men" (p. 77). And therefore, in the last section of this chapter, I perform a textual analysis of a selected rap song in hopes of developing "reading strategies that allow us to make visible the distorting and productive effects these sexualities produce in *relation to more visible sexualities*" (Hammonds, 1994, p. 138, italics added).

"LET'S TALK ABOUT SEX":
THE APPEAL OF THE HIP-HOP EROTIC

Our exploration begins and ends with the sexual hip-hop styling of SNP for three related reasons. First, they are easily the most prominent female rap artists ever. At the risk of suggesting that their popularity make them the most important subjects, consider the argument that their prominence has allowed their subjectivity because they have increasingly wrested creative control of their projects (1994). Their successive offerings, *Hot, Cool, and Vicious, A Salt with a Deadly Pepa, Blacks' Magic,* and *Very Necessary* have not only outsold every female rap contemporary, but have surpassed male artists like KRS-One and Public Enemy (L. Jones, 1994). And so, the arguments they have presented concerning black female subjectivity and agency have been widely seen and heard. Second, SNP have consistently centered their search for a female voice in hip-hop while, finally, maintaining a critical dialogue with their male audiences. And it is this third point that is of particular importance for SNP's sexual verve is also geared toward understanding the role that sexual pleasure plays in the reproduction of community. And so, let us explore the sexual play constituting SNP's appeal.

(Ohhh, how you doin' baby? No, not you. You, the bowlegged one. Yeah, what's your name? Damn, baby. That sounds sexy!)

Here I go/ here I go/ here I go again/ girls what's my weakness?/ men! [a chorus of women]/ ok then, chillin', chillin', minding my business/ yo Salt, I looked around and I couldn't believe this/ I swear, I stared/ my niece my witness/ the brother had it goin' on somethin' kind of, uh, wicked, wicked/ had to kick it/ I'm not shy so I asked for the digits/ a hoe?/ no that don't make me/ see what I want, slip slide to it swiftly/ felt it in my hips/ so I dipped back into my bag of tricks/ then I flipped for a tip/ made me wanna do tricks on him/ lick him, like a lollipop should be licked/ came to my senses and I chilled for a bit/ don't know how you do the voodoo that you do so well/ it's a spell, hell/ makes me wanna shoop, shoop, shoop. . . . ("Shoop," 1993)

In the introduction of the track, "Shoop," Pepa's rap establishes at least one crucial dynamic for the rest of the narrative. By instigating the terms of the courtship ritual and controlling its direction, Pepa appropriates the role of sexual objectifier. She not only sets the intense sexual tone, but by choosing her suitor ("no, not you . . . the bowlegged one . . .") we understand that she has the authority to displace unwanted men. Yet, this authority is immediately troubled by the bold proclamation, "girls, what's my weakness? Men!" This line of the song packs a potent significance for my reading because it will eventually allow us to see more than a reflective appropriation. I argue that it calls into question the strategy of appropriation itself. But for the moment, let's continue to map out the resistive energy that objectifies the male.

After identifying the object of her sexual interest, Pepa constrains him with her gaze. Moreover, her gazing is reinforced by her niece-as-witness to the female appropriation of the objectifying lens. Pepa "freely" admits that she's gotta have it ("had to kick it") but strongly denies that her actions make her a hoe. Her sexual energy is fired as she conceives of a strategy for acquiring what she's gotta have, but is prematurely stemmed by a realization that she ought to come to her "senses and chill for a bit. . . ." She willfully puts her lust in check while mulling over the character of her desire. It is clear she wants to "shoop," but she is somewhat concerned about the "spell" her object casts over her.

> Ya packed and ya stacked/ especially in the back, brother/ make me wanna thank ya mother for a butt like that/ [faint male voice: "thanks mom"]/ can I get some fries with that shake, shake booby/ if looks could kill you would be an uzi, or a shotgun/ bang!/ what's up with that thang?/ I wanna know how does it hang?/ straight up, wait up, hold up Mr. Lover/ like Prince said you a sexy motha . . . / well, uh, I like 'em real wild/ b-boy style by the mile/ smooth black skin with a smile/ bright as the sun/ I wanna have some fun/ come and give me some of that yum, yum/ chocolate chip, honey dip/ can I get a scoop?/ baby take a ride in my coup/ ya make me wanna shoop . . .

In this verse, Salt rolls out a wide array of narrative conventions for the sexual objectification of an Other. Notice how her voyeurism finds its focus on the male butt. As an appropriated gaze, this movement reproduces the male emphasis on the Black woman's buttocks and its ability to invoke sexual response. At this point, let's note some similarities and dissimilarities in the ways a sexual object may be gazed on. It is certainly undeniable that the male is objectified throughout this verse. However, Salt sees fit to give him pet names like "booby" and "Mr. Lover" instead of "bitch," "skeeze," or "hoe." This rhetorical strategy is also present on such tracks like, "No One Does It Better," and "Whatta Man," where SNP make a point of separating the objects of their particular sexual desire from the generalization that "most men are hoes." These artists "give props to those who deserve it and believe [us] y'all, he's worth it." However, this strategy still resembles the logic voiced by Ice Cube explaining some misogynist lyrics in male verse (hooks, 1994). On the other hand, although many men reduce female sexual being by locating it in specific features like breasts and butts, SNP allow the male sexual being to expand so as to include smooth skin and bright smiles. Moreover, I detect a fascinating rhetorical maneuver contained within the line, "if looks could kill you would be an Uzi or a shotgun. . . ." Traditionally, the male gaze having the power to restrain and distort has been understood in terms of a symbolic violence perpetrated on women. When men do the looking, they represent this threat in the form of shotguns or Uzi's—the phallus as lethal weapon. But, here the violent gaze is offset by Salt's appropriation. The qualifying phrase, "*if* looks could kill," tells us that her act of gazing does not represent the same kind of threat; the look is not killing here. And, when it *is* destructive, it is the *male* who uses it as such. Thus, Salt seems to unload the gaze's deadly potential. This is not to suggest that NP are docile in the text, only that these artists do not wish to harm the objects of their desire as men often do. But since this is a voyeuristic tour that begins on the butt and includes a pop cultural reference for sexual service ("can I get fries with that shake"), the gaze does retain some brutal force.

I argue that SNP's erotic appeal approaches the sensibility and power that Lorde described and operates on two intersecting planes: as a form of social agency and as a form of pleasure. The erotic appeal operates as social action by promoting both symbolic and pragmatic changes in a carnal aesthetic and culture industry. The erotic appeal also invites multiple audiences into its experiential perimeter. If we accept the invitation offered by the erotic appeal, we are enticed to assent to SNP's arguments about gender politics. But for clarity of analysis, let's quickly return to Pepa's initial verse. Recall that I mentioned that the call-and-response, "girls what's my weakness? Men!," troubles the practice of sexual objectification. This line is multilayered. On the surface SNP assert that men are the source of female weakness. But, because men and women have changed places in this drama, we can read it as a reminder that women have traditionally been treated as the source of male weakness. That is, women have been objectified, controlled, and put on pedestals precisely because they have been constructed within a male consciousness as the embodiment of eroticism. But because we know that men fear this knowledge, eroticism can be viewed as a kind of sexualized *power over men*. Rose (1994) put the point bluntly: Men have denied consistently that they are in fact slavish "to the pussy" (p. 172). In terms of this appropriation, then, the "weakness" signifies a power the objectified has over the objectifier. But despite the revelation of erotic potential, it remains imprisoned within the (male) sexual object because we are still faced with a reified dialectic of fear and desire. And so perhaps SNP accuse the *practice* of sexual objectification highlighted in this narrative of being the source of "weakness," *not* sexual objects.

In order to understand how SNP work to dissolve the dialectic, I want to examine briefly the role that the metaphor of "voodoo" and "spell" play in SNP's erotic appeal. In *Conjuring: Black Women, Fiction and Literary Tradition*, Pryse (1985) added some needed historical context to references in womanist writing to folk magic. Arguing that in the face of a muting force, Black women who speak their subjectivity in writing and folktelling have performed what has come to be thought of as a kind of magic. Constitutive of dramatic Black female resistance, the act of mending cultural continuity in art is the act of conjuring "the power to reassert the self and one's heritage in the face of overwhelming injustice" (pp. 15-16). Conjuring, therefore, resists sexism and locates the activity of resistance within the concept of both material and symbolic mothering (Pryse, 1985). As such, conjuring represents the power of Black women to conceive, deliver, and nurture subjective voices. In SNP's tale, however, the male sexual object casts the spell forcing Pepa—the gazer—to rethink the nature of her desire. This symbolic action reinforces the interpretation that SNP contend that the sexual abuse of another should not be part of a strategy for constituting one's own empowered self. Furthermore, if conjuring is a kind of "mothering," then the sexual allure the male has in the text is feminized, transgressing the limits of an overdetermined street-coded "masculinity." Seen critically, the "voodoo that you do so well" is the erotic power that *any* sexual object possesses to creatively transform the terms of their oppression. This power is linked to a "mother's" responsibility to her offspring and to the historical role Black women have always played in community building. SNP suggestively gender-bend this role by allowing the male object to work black magic while simultaneously delivering his voice through their own act of mothering. And so, SNP create a performative sphere in which objects are animated into subjects while locating the source of such transformative energy within a buried eroticism.

Well let me bring it back to the subject / Pep's on the set / make ya get hot, make ya work up a sweat / when ya said skip to ma loo, my darling / not falling in love, but I'm fallin' for ya [faint male voice: "su-per sperm"]/ *uhmmmm, when I getcha' / bet ya bottom dollar you work best under pressure /* [fuller male voice: "yo, Sandy, I wanna like taste ya"]/ *get, getcha' lips wet 'cause it's time to have Pep . . .*

On ya mark, get set go / lemme go, lemme shoot to the next man in the
three piece suit / I spend all my dough-ray-me cutie / shoop,
shoobadooby, like scooby-dooby-doo / I love you in your big jeans / ya
give me nice dreams / ya make me wanna scream ooh, ooh, ooh / I like
what ya do, when ya do what ya do / ya make me wanna shoop . . .

Up to this point I have discussed the appeal of the hip-hop
erotic in terms of its rhetorical action. But these latest verses bring
forth its voyeuristic pleasure principle and bring us closer to
critiquing its potential for reconstituting the erotic power of a hip-hop
aestheticism. Bringing the drama back to the "subject" centers Pepa
as both sexual *subject and object*. Her action ("make ya get hot, make
ya work up a sweat") is performed for her subjectivity and for our
pleasure as voyeurs of her play. Indeed, in the video for this song Salt,
Pepa, and Spindarella—their long time DJ—show off their taut bodies
for the camera and for themselves. In a *Vibe* interview, Salt speaks to
this dimension: "'We're more powerful, with more control . . . [other
women] aren't in control-they're being controlled. They're trying to get
in front of the camera, trying to be the sexiest one in the video . . .'"
(France, 1994, p. 53). SNP argue that they don't have to try to be
anything for anybody since "there's nothing wrong with feeling good
about yourself and being sexy. . . ." And so it would seem that their
"unadulterated raciness" (L. Jones, 1994, p. 20) is a part of an attempt
to "'build up women's self esteem. That's something we've always
taken pride in. We're feminists to a certain degree'" (France, 1994, p.
52). It is important to understand that voyeuristic pleasure invites
female and male participants into SNP's performative space. The
metabolism of this single text displays a kind of dialogue between
sexual gazers, deconstructing the strict polarity of an anti-erotic,
gangsta/bitch aesthetic. As a voyeuristic audience, we see women
seeing men and *we bear witness to the joy of being seen.*
The fullness of an erotic aesthetic can be measured by the
sounding of centering. For the dialectic of fear and desire to be
successfully deconstructed, marginal beings must be allowed to
articulate their pleasure for themselves. At the start of this
narrative, the male is completely nameless and voiceless. Later, Salt
calls him "booby" and "Mr. Lover," and we faintly hear him thank his
mom (the erotic conjuring power) for his great butt. When Pepa
willingly performs her sexuality for a voyeuristic audience, we hear
the male object refer to Pepa by her real name, "Sandy," and voice his
desire to "taste" her. In other words, a reified object gradually
burgeons into a subjective voice.

Oh my goodness/ girl look at him/ he's the cutest brother in here,
and he's comin' this way, oooh . . .

[Male Rap] *'S,' 'N' to 'P' wanna get wit' me?* [SNP: uh, huh]/ *cool, but*
I'm Wink G/ hit skins, but never quick a lick/ I hit the skins for the
hell of it/ for the yell I get/ um, um, um, for the smell of it/ you want
my bod, here's the hot rod/ 12 inches to a yard [Salt: damn]/ *have ya*
soundin' like a retard [Pepa lets out a comically exaggerated moan]/
I'm the lover, 6-2, wanna hit you/ [Salt: so what you wanna do?]/
what you wanna do?/ [Salt: I wanna shoop] . . .

At this point, the male is granted his voice and not only
names his desire, but names himself. As a subject in this
performative space, he is partly responsible for its empowering
constitution—its ability to allow for sexual subjectivity. I believe
there is serious tension in the braggadocio associated with penis size
and his lust. But notice how it resonates with SNP's text. Part of
what SNP desire is MC Lyte's "Ruffneck"—a "real wild, b-boy style
by the mile." They do not want to castrate their black men by
appropriating his phallus as "gangsta bitches" often symbolize. They
relish, appreciate, and in fact need his ability to "fuck" the system for
the Black community's sake. SNP bolster this assertion by
encouraging and endorsing his rap. Importantly, Sonja Peterson-
Lewis has clarified that the central animus regarding sexual
objectification in hip-hop is the portrayal of sex as a violent weapon
(Lusane, 1994, p. 62). But this phallic-centered verse is playful, not
brutal. The phallus does not represent a weapon, but a toy. Wink G
uses it as a sign of SNP's pleasure, not of pain.

CONCLUSIONS

Our exploration into eroticism, sexual pleasure and female voices in
hip-hop began by questioning the relationships among artistic
production, subjectivity, and a patriarchal market complex. I argued
that the Black female image was subtly mediated along these
interstices and sought to critique and appreciate these mediations by
drawing on a historical, cultural problematic related to the distortion
of erotic power. Lorde's poetic treatment was valuable in that she
specifically calls for a deep, joyful understanding of eroticism as a
source of information and knowledge about one's humanity and
needs. Erotic power allows us to recognize that which must be spoken
within us—particularly if there have been no words for the speaking.
The metaphor she invokes, associating silence with cancer, places us

at grave risk if we allow violence, abuse, or shame to quiet us. Eroticism gives rise to our resistance to those muting forces—both within the self and outside the body-conspiring to consume us.

I also argued that female artists in rap music have featured their struggles against varied forms of silence, misogyny, and neglect, in their rap strategies. These battles have provoked forms of counterhegemonic appropriation that I demonstrated as having limited value toward the full recuperation of the erotic. Although a centralized female sexual subjectivity is apparent in some of the appropriations, I contend that the "masculine" theme being appropriated is ultimately validated as virtuous. Moreover, by entering into a synecdochic relation with the cultural economy of the rap industry, some rap artists' erotic potential gets dampened by the operations of making "cream."

The appeal of the hip-hop erotic, as I have discussed it, is constitutive of a kind of invitation into a performative space where sexual oppression is deconstructed. It is also where women and men look to one another for not only the reconstitution of their identities as men and women, but also for the redefinition of the nature of their relationships. It is a place where women celebrate their sexuality and present it as a basis for constructive dialogue about sex. I argue that SNP articulate a hip-hop erotic appeal that has given them a peculiarly significant voice. SNP have challenged men on the mic and have helped to sustain dialogue about issues relating to safe sex and parental responsibility (Dunn, 1994). The anticipation of a sexually rewarding experience seduces us into a play that empowers our subjectivities. The hip-hop erotic demands that an anti-erotic aesthetic undergo a bit of gender bending through both symbolic and pragmatic means. In this reclamation of eroticism, role reversal, collapse, and change trouble the dialectic of fear and desire. And, this process must be continued in order for the performance of sexual subjectivity to generate creative options for social identity. To this end, an erotic orientation toward oneself and others provokes a mode of rhetorical reflexivity requiring that we reconstitute our sources in language and action over and over again. What this also means is that Black women and men must engage in a critical dialogue concerning what the Black community needs for soulful living. And so, the sexual energy aroused by Salt's query "so what you wanna do?" does not conclude with the male response, but is maintained by *his respect and care of her desire*—"what you wanna do?"

The point at which the erotic impulse is perhaps dangerously troubled, however, is in its apparent restriction of sexual pleasure to heterosexuality ("Girls what's my weakness? Men!"). Lorde's prescription for the erotic clearly includes all kinds of joyful being and makes plain the fact that African American heterosexuals oppress African American homosexuals even as we celebrate our shared liberation. Within a heterosexual script, therefore, the erotic has limited appeal. However, in terms of its potential for brokering progressive Black female subjectivity and power, the erotic appeal displays a provocative sensual assertion in need of further examination.

REFERENCES

Bartky, S. (1993). Foucault, femininity, and the modernization of patriarchal power. In M. Pearsall (Ed.), *Women and values: Readings in recent feminist philosophy* (pp. 151-164). Belmont, CA: Wadsworth.

Boss. (1993). *Born Gangstaz.* New York: Def Jam Records.

Burke, K. (1969). *Grammar of motives.* Berkeley: University of California Press.

B.W.P. (1991). *Two-minute brother.* New York: Freekworld Music.

Carby, H. (1992). Policing the black woman's body in the urban context. *Critical Inquiry,* 738-755.

Christian, B. (1985). *Black feminist criticism.* New York: Pergamon Press.

Coker, C. (1994). Ghetto Girlz. *The Source, 58,* 42.

Collins, P. H. (1990). *Black feminist thought: Knowledge, consciousness, and the politics of empowerment.* Boston: Unwin Hyman.

Conscious Daughters. (1993). *Ear to the street.* Los Angeles: Scarface Records.

Davis, A. (1990). *Women, culture, and politics.* New York: Vintage Books.

Denard, C. (1988). The convergence of feminism and ethnicity in the fiction of Toni Morrison. In N. H. McKay (Ed.), *Critical essays on Toni Morrison* (pp. 40-47). Boston: G.K. Hall.

Dunn, J. (1994, June 30). The spice of life. *Rolling Stone,* 21-24.

Eure, J., & Spady, J. (1991). *Nation conscious rap.* New York: PC International Press.

Foxy Brown. (1996). *Ill Na Na.* New York: Def Jam Records.

France, K. (1994). The Golden Girls. *Vibe, 2,* 50-53.

Garner, T. (1983). Playing the dozens: Folklore as strategies for living. *Quarterly Journal of Speech,* 47-57.

Giddings, P. (1984). *When and where I enter.* New York: Bantam Books.

Gonzales, M. (1997). Mack divas. *The Source, 89,* 61-63.

Hammonds, E. (1994). Black (w)holes and the geometry of black female sexuality. *Differences: A Journal of Feminist Cultural Studies,* 126-145.

Hoagland, S. L. (1993). Femininity, resistance, and sabotage. In M. Pearsall (Ed.), *Women and values: Readings in recent feminist philosophy* (pp. 90-139). Belmont, CA: Wadsworth.

Holland, S. P. (1988). "Which me will survive": Audre Lorde and the development of a black feminist ideology. *Critical Matrix,* 1-30.

hooks, b. (1990). *Yearning: Race, gender, and cultural politics.* Boston: South End Press.

hooks, b. (1992). *Black looks: Race and representation.* Boston: South End Press.

hooks, b. (1994, February). Sexism and misogyny: Who takes the rap? *Z Magazine,* p. 27.

hooks, b. (1995). *Art on my mind: Visual politics.* New York: The New Press.

Hunt, D. (1994, May 28). *Los Angeles Times,* p. 1.

Jones, A. N. (1994). Are girls turning meaner? *Utne Reader,* 54-55.

Jones, L. M. (1994, June). Salt 'N' Pepa: Very necessarily hot and controversial. *Rap Sheet,* 20-21.

Kaplan, E.A. (1993). Is the gaze male? In M. Pearsall (Ed.), *Women and values: Readings in recent feminist philosophy* (pp. 257-267). Bellmont, CA: Wadsworth.

Kuenz, J. (1993). The bluest eye: Notes on history, community, and black female subjectivity. *African American Review, 27,* 417-430.

Latifah, Q. (1989). *Come into my house.* New York: Tommy Boy Music.

Latifah, Q. (1993). *Black reign.* Los Angeles: Motown Records.

Lil' Kim. (1996). *Hard core.* New York: Big Beat Records.

Lorde, A. (1984). *Sister outsider.* Freedom, CA: The Crossing Press.

Lusane, C. (1994, Winter). Rap, race, and politics. *Alternative Press,* 58-62.

Mayo, K. (1993). Microphone check. *The Source, 47,* 48.

McDowell, D.E. (1988). "That nameless . . . shameful impulse": Sexuality in Nella Larson's Quicksand and Passing. In J. Weixlman & H. Baker, Jr. (Eds.), *Black feminist criticism and critical theory* (pp. 139-167). Greenwood, FL: Penkeville.

MC Lyte. (1993). *Ain't no other.* New York: First Priority Music.

MC Lyte. (1996). *bad as I wanna b.* New York: Electra Entertainment.

Morgan, J. (1997, March). The bad girls of hip-hop. *Essence,* 78-80.

Mulvey, L. (1984). Visual pleasure and the narrative cinema. In B. Wallis (Ed.), *Art after modernism* (pp. 361-374). New York: The New Museum of Contemporary Art.

Olson, L. (1997). On the margins of rhetoric: Audre Lorde transforming silence into language and action. *Quarterly Journal of Speech, 83,* 49-70.

Ortner, S.B., & Whitehead, H. (1981). *Sexual meanings: The cultural construction of gender and sexuality.* Cambridge: Cambridge University Press.

Power 30. (1997). *The Source,* 82-84.

Printz, J. K. (1992). Marketable bodies, possessive peacocks, and text as excess. *Callaloo,* 1065-1081.

Pryse, M. (1985). Zora Neale Hurston, Alice Walker, and the "ancient power" of black women. In M. Pryse & H. J. Spillers (Eds.), *Conjuring: Black women, fiction, and literary tradition* (pp. 1-24). Bloomington: Indiana University Press.

Rose, T. (1994). *Black noise: Rap music and black culture in contemporary America.* Hanover, MA: Wesleyan University Press.

Salt 'N' Pepa. (1993). *Very Necessary.* New York: Next Plateau Records.

Shante, R. (1992). Brothers ain't shit. In L. Stanley (Ed.), *Rap: The lyrics* (p. 284). New York: Penguine Books.

Shugart, H. (1997). Counterhegemonic acts: Appropriation as a feminist rhetorical strategy. *Quarterly Journal of Speech, 83,* 210-229.

Top R&B Albums. (1997, May 17). *Billboard,* 34-35.

Watts, E. K. (1997). An exploration of spectacular consumption: Gangsta rap as cultural commodity. *Communication Studies, 48,* 42-58.

Wu-Tang Clan. (1993). *Enter the Wu-tang (36 chambers).* New York: RCA Records.

TEN

Sweet Honey In The Rock: Building Communities Through Resistant Voices

Jessica L. Davis
University of Pennsylvania

THEORIZING AFROWOMANIST VOICES

Throughout the history of the African presence in America, song and dance have informed the collective consciousness of the Black community in vital and enduring ways. Music has long permeated the daily life of most African-Americans; it has played a central role in the normal socialization process; and during moments characterized by intense movements for social change, it has helped to shape the necessary political consciousness. Any attempt, therefore, to understand in depth the evolution of woman's consciousness with the Black community requires a serious examination of the music which has influenced them—particularly that which they themselves have created. . . . For Black women in particular, music has simultaneously expressed and shaped our collective consciousness.
      —Davis (1990, p. 3)

For Black women, the concept of community has been transformed within the complexity of current media environments, marked by diversification, pluralization, commercialization, commodification, internationalization, decentralization, and globalization. In light of these changes, a new approach is needed (Ang, 1996) to explore the spaces where communities of Black women co-exist as both performers and audiences. Media studies and communications research have not sufficiently addressed the social interactions, the cultural expression, and the consciousness-raising of Black women. We may find evidence of these communicative experiences in ritualized acts of musical concert attendance. The spaces in which music is performed live, and the processes through which it is received by Black women audiences, are necessarily political. This chapter explores the music, lyrics, and performances of Sweet Honey In The Rock, framing them as a discourse of Black women in Diaspora. Sweet Honey's politically charged music engenders the crossing of geographic, racial, and ideological boundaries in order to strengthen identity, build coalitions, and experience the pleasure of movement to sounds and lyrics born through struggle.

Sweet Honey In The Rock is an a cappella singing group, made up of African American women, created in 1973 in Washington, DC. "Sweet Honey In The Rock is a woman born of a struggling union of Black woman singers; she began her journey some twenty years ago" (Reagon & Sweet Honey In The Rock, 1993, p. 13). The metaphor that characterizes the group as "a woman" personifies Sweet Honey as the progeny of a womanist union (see Collins, 1989; Houston & Davis, Introduction, this volume). Sweet Honey was conceived by the members of the Bernice Johnson Reagon Vocal Workshop of the DC Black Repertory Company and has grown to embrace the many women who have given her voice over the years. Sweet Honey speaks to multiple audiences in the United States and internationally, with voices that address partnership, coalition, and the interrelationship of struggles among women, African Americans, Africans, men, children, people of color, and ethnic and ideological minorities. It is this speech, by a collection of African American rhetors, that serves to localize broad social and political movements into the everyday experiences of Black women in particular, and women in general. Sweet Honey's message resonates with many audiences, brought together in a kaleidoscope of colors, representing diverse experiences from all corners of the African Diaspora. The African American women music-makers, who have lifted Sweet Honey In The Rock over the past 25 years, sing and speak words inspired from wide-ranging cultural, social, and political backgrounds.

I employ the metaphor of Sweet Honey as a woman, representing a collectivity of women and women's voices from the African Diaspora, by articulating the interests and situating the struggles of African American women within a global movement of oppressed peoples. This chapter explores the multiplicity of social processes embedded in the ways in which Sweet Honey In The Rock communicates to her audience through the texts of popular music. It explores the unique processes of traditional communication practices that take place in her public sphere, as her audiences respond and participate in the ritualized process of musiking. Sweet Honey offers her music as a form of resistance, opening spaces for cultural expression, racial and gender identity development, and political activism. She is the inheritor of a long legacy of women of the African Diaspora who have made their voices heard through music, forming communities and asserting agency through the interpretation, expression, and production of cultural texts. She uses her musical repertoire to reunite the experiences of women who have been separated by forced and voluntary migrations into a Diaspora that crosses national, ideological, and language borders, spanning the distance of oceans and continents. Sweet Honey inscribes political meanings on messages delivered to her audiences in the "safe places" of musical lyrics and performance. My focus on Sweet Honey In The Rock is intended to illuminate communication practices shared by African American women, as they sustain a legacy of music, sound, and rhythm.

Music, in all shapes and forms, has historically been a medium through which African American women have communicated with one another and shared their voices with others. It has been the mode on which communities are configured as Black women identify with one another through common experiences, spoken through musical texts. It is a key site where womanist theory is born and reconfigured (Collins, chap. 11, this volume). The musical rhetoric of Sweet Honey In The Rock, as an African American communication practice, can be understood through womanism as a progressive analytical frame that challenges traditional scholarly approaches. This critical standpoint opens a space for "nontraditional" theorizing, revealing positions of power in a broader cultural, spiritual, and political context to which the Eurocentric and phallocentric bedrock of academic norms remain closed. Womanist theory provides the cornerstone of this framework within which to launch an integrated approach to the study of Sweet Honey In The Rock as she re-constructs language into hybrid communication forms that challenge the reification of boundaries within communication research paradigms.

Critical feminist scholarship, as one component of this womanist theoretical frame, offers valuable methods to locate hidden speech and alternative meanings in mediated texts. In her work,

Janice Radway (cited in Wallace, 1992) recognized the diversity of these voices:

> I would also suggest that we have to enlarge our notion of voice. In fact, there are people "out there" who have voices. They speak in languages and practices that we don't ordinarily try to hear. The problem is our ability to hear different speech. The issue is that they're already speaking—with actions, with fury, with anger, and we don't know how to hear them yet. The problem is really with our listening practices. (p. 668)

There is a sense that there are voices "out there" that must be listened to (Ferguson, Gever, Minh-ha, & West, 1990), however, it is this voice of the Other, on the outside, that does not appear in print. The rhetoric of African American women is often ignored in the discursive sites of conferences, journals, and universities. It is vital to locate the spaces and the media through which the languages of Black women make themselves heard. This is not to argue that there is some illusive, authentic voice "out there," but that there is a multiplicity of sounds that can be heard if our listening practices are honed. These sounds may vary according to the environment and may be invoked differently by every woman. With a fluid understanding of consciousness, sensitive to the various factors that influence her daily life, such as race, gender, class, and age, an African American woman may employ the most appropriate voice that enables her to negotiate each of these forces. It is not clear whether the voice that she uses to survive when faced with sexism, for example, is the same voice that she uses to confront classism. This journey into the world of Sweet Honey In The Rock offers many areas to be further explored, through a diversity of methods, in order to produce a comprehensive analysis of the voices of Black women as musical performers, political activists, cultural workers, and audiences, in constant negotiation with the forces that impact their lives.

To guide this journey into the rhetoric of Sweet Honey, I employ Boyce Davies' (1994) construct of "migratory subjectivity" to distinguish Black women's speech through song. I identify Sweet Honey In The Rock as a migratory subject, contesting boundaries as she sings her political repertoire. Like her music, "Black women/'s writing cannot be located and framed in terms of one specific place, but exist/s in myriad places and times, constantly eluding the terms of the discussion" (Boyce Davies, 1994, p. 36). These uncharted spaces are characterized by the intersection of culture and community, visual and auditory communication, gender and racial identity, and the influence of music as oratory and expression. The standpoint assumed by Sweet Honey In The Rock is concerned with politics and praxis. Sweet Honey expresses this position by singing in the tradition of African peoples and the hybrid musical forms that have evolved throughout the African Diaspora, performed as rituals of survival and resistance. Her music is marked by fundamental qualities such as improvisation, adaptation, and call-and-response, characteristics of an African inheritance, transformed through generations of migrations.

Sweet Honey In The Rock and her audiences exist in Diaspora, speaking a multitude of languages and having a diversity of historical experiences. "The concept of diaspora, sometimes defined as *galut*—exile or bondage—and as *golah*—a relatively stable community in exile—derives from the historic experience of the Jewish People" (Skinner, 1993, p. 11). In contrast to Jews, who have established Hebrew as a common language that is spoken in their public sphere, serving to unify and create a transnational basis for identification (Band, 1995), the people of the African Diaspora have no such common lexical mode. Spencer (1995) offered African rhythms—multimetricity, cross-rhythms, asymmetrical patterning, and call-and-response, through its dispersal in the Diaspora—as the common voice of Black folk. For the musical texts to have meaning, the audience must develop Diaspora literacy (Clark, 1990). Small (1987) offered music as the common tongue that binds women, men, and children of African descent, thus providing a source for unbordered identification. Music becomes an articulation of the lived experiences of Black people, reflecting individual and group identities in the public space of the African Diaspora.

The last decade has been marked with an increase in scholarly writing about Black identity, aesthetics, and the Black experience. The progressive scholarship of authors such as hooks, Boyce Davies, Lorde, Gilroy, Hall, and others have been on the vanguard of contesting the notion of a Black essence. The scholars acknowledge the complexity of Blackness, countering constructions of Black identity in opposition to a White essence. They also deconstruct a singular Feminist identity by offering the specificity of women's experiences at the crossroads of racial, gender, class, and sexual oppression. It is this intersection of Blackness, femaleness, and otherness, which a womanist theory works to explain.

A critical African American feminist theory, as advanced by hooks (1992), opposes the notion of a Black female essence that, although it can function to affirm common experiences, characterizes community as a monolith that leaves little room for difference and diversity.

> Collectively, we were working to problematize our notions of black
> female subjectivity. None of us assumed a fixed essential identity. It
> was so evident that we did not all share a common understanding of
> being black and female, even though some of our experiences were
> similar. (hooks, 1992, p. 46)

hooks articulated the struggle for subjectivity and survival in
Diaspora, cautioning against the assumption that "strength in unity
can only exist if difference is suppressed and shared experience is
highlighted" (p. 51). Sweet Honey In The Rock focuses on the
diversity of womanhood, embracing multiculturalism and existence
through multiple subjectivities. Her rhetoric underscores personal
and collective freedom and extant individuality, with space for
particularity within unity.

Sweet Honey In The Rock works in community, confirming the
value of coalition politics (Reagon & Sweet Honey In The Rock, 1983),
building bridges among those individuals and groups with shared
struggles. Sweet Honey's message of collective political activism
underscores the commonalties in resistance movements by oppressed
peoples. "[Her] work has always stood for the belief that none of us are
free until all of us are free!" (Norris, cited in Reagon, 1993, p. 300).
Sweet Honey In The Rock encourages her audiences to challenge
signifiers such as "Black" and "woman," as terms "subject to re-
interpretation and deconstruction as they themselves become totalizing
and oppressive discourses" (Boyce Davies, 1995a, p. 2). In so doing, she
offers insights that galvanize a collective consciousness, by enlarging
the circle signified by terms such as *us* and *we*. Her music embraces
multiple communities, where the migratory capacity of each of these
constructed identities is brought forth. In this way, she disrupts a
monolithic understanding of blackness and womanhood to include any
person who chooses to self-identify as such, or who has common causes.
This empowering process involves coming to voice for women, "shifting
privatized discourses to the public arena" (Boyce Davies, 1995b, p. 4).
The public space of Sweet Honey concerts facilitates this process.

For Black women, the process of making ourselves heard and
our politics known, in historically barred sites of public speech,
involves a series of boundary crossings.

> For the women who tell their stories orally and want them told to a
> world community, boundaries of orality and writing, of geography
> and space, engender fundamental crossings and re-crossings. For
> the readers as well, a variety of languages, creoles, cultural
> nuances, history have to be learned before texts can have meaning.
> (Boyce Davies, 1994, p. 20)

In this sense, Boyce Davies asserted that crossing boundaries includes "listening to the 'polyrythms', the polyvocality of Black women's creative and critical speech" (p. 23). Communication then is based on diasporic and multicultural literacy, new understandings of the fundamentals in speaking, listening, and articulation, taking into account the specificity of African American women's language. Boyce Davies offered a framework to explore communication across boundaries, recognizing the tension that exists in the sites where identity, community, difference, and coming to voice converge.

The locations of these intersections can be theorized within the cultural and political work in which Black women are involved on an everyday basis. Convergence may occur, for example, in places of employment where Black women talk as they work together, thus triggering in-group identification strengthened through the use of shared figures of speech. If these conditions are substandard, and the women discuss strategies for its improvement (or their escape), a political and economic dimension is added. These sites are often ignored in academic inquiry. Christian (1987) contended that this disregard is a result of the misfit of African American communication and learning within the Eurocentric canonical requirements for "authentic" theory.

> For people of color have always theorized—but in forms quite different from the Western form of abstract logic. And I am inclined to say that our theorizing (and I intentionally use the verb rather than the noun) is often in narrative forms, in the stories we create, in riddles and proverbs, in the play with language, since dynamic rather than fixed ideas seem more to our liking. (p. 52)

Thus, the locations in which Black women congregate, where stories are told, and where music is played or created, are sites where womanist theory may be explored. Theorizing, teaching, and learning take place during Sweet Honey performances and in the public spaces created by her music.

There is a highly instructive nature in the music of Sweet Honey In the Rock, marked by African-centered belief systems, and formed through collective experiences. Her music plays a vital role in "critical pedagogy," the sharing of information and knowledge by Black women with Black women, crucial for the development of radical Black female subjectivity (hooks, 1992). Sweet Honey In The Rock offers an illuminating narrative that bears "witness to the difficulty of developing radical Black female subjectivity even as [she] attest[s] to the joy and triumph of living with a decolonized mind and participating in an ongoing resistance struggle" (hooks, 1992, p. 56).

hooks identified Sweet Honey with women such as Angela Davis, Ella Baker, Alice Walker, Audre Lorde, and Fannie Lou Hamer, providing historical insight in the framing of Black feminisms, migratory Black female subjectivity, and womanism, spanning generations. These women rhetors and theorists are distinguished by their exceptionalism and by their everydayness.

The theories of radical Black feminists are passed down from one generation to the next through the inheritance of dynamic political activism against the forces of racism, sexism, classism, homophopia and the other forces at work in shaping the multiple consciousness of Black women. By multiple consciousness, I mean that there is a constant awareness of the interrelationship of these factors as they influence the life choices of Black women—even as struggles against one "ism" may take precedence over another at various points in time and across the life span. By being engaged in battle against these "isms," the lived experiences of Black women often come in contact with one another. This kind of convergence was particularly evident during the Civil Rights Movement. For example, Reagon, Sweet Honey's founder, was directly affected by Ella Baker in her work with the Student Nonviolent Coordinating Committee (SNCC). Reagon considers Miss Baker her political mother. With an ideological commitment to community, Sweet Honey teaches the messages of the Civil Rights Movement to her audiences.

> So when I began to work with Sweet Honey, I insisted that this community of music also be a community of support, we would not be isolated, but would be a community organization serving and representing our community as a voice, and seeking support from those we served. I also tried to keep before the women singing in Sweet Honey that we were servants and only as strong as our producers, our audience, and our community. We had to return to them a portion of what we received on entry level as a group and personally as individuals. (Reagon & Sweet Honey In The Rock, 1993, p. 20)

Reagon wrote the lyrics and music to *Ella's Song* in dedication to her foremother. It is a textual tribute that honors the work and vision of this leader from whom Reagon inherited the politics and the vision that serve as the foundation of the Sweet Honey experience. The rhetoric of freedom, struggle and resistance, which this song exemplifies, are central to the music of Sweet Honey In The Rock.

We who believe in Freedom cannot rest
We who believe in Freedom cannot rest until it comes

Until the killing of Black men,
Black mother's sons,
Is as important as the killing of White men,
White mother's sons

That which touches me most
Is that I had the chance to work with people
Passing on to others,
That which was passed on to me . . .

Not needing to clutch for power,
Not needing the light just to shine on me
I need to be in the number,
As we stand against tyranny

Struggling myself don't mean a whole lot,
I've come to realize
That teaching other to stand up and fight
Is the only way my struggle survives

I'm a woman who speaks in a voice
And I must be heard
At times I can be quite difficult,
I'll bow to no man's word.
(Reagon, 1981, track 11)

Through critical pedagogy, Sweet Honey reproduces these lessons through her music, paying homage to the generations of women who have come before and instructing the generations who follow her. For some, Sweet Honey may represent the work of a higher power, where the theories articulated through music are conditioned by the ancestral mothers in whose footsteps she follows. "I walk Sweet Honey In the Rock as a path, a way, a discipline; I do not create the path, which has been carved out by the living and the dying of those who walked it before me with their lives, but I make my own tracks in a mountainous road" (Reagon & Sweet Honey In The Rock, 1993, p. 20). This perspective is emblematic of the African-centered spirituality that informs the worldview of Sweet Honey, with a belief system that includes veneration of ancestors. The path of struggle, which the discourse of Sweet Honey In The Rock articulates, is emblematic of the rhetoric of a diverse and dynamic Black feminist movement.

The focus on the music and musiking of Sweet Honey, as nontraditional sites of theory, is informed by African American feminism, which has a long historical memory and a separate discourse from that of the mainstream White feminist movement. Peterson (1996) traced the specificity of discourse in the Black women's movement, which since its inception, has been based on different ideologies, objectives, and experiences than those from the standpoints of White women. Peterson argued that "black women, traditionally ignored by history books, also constructed a 'woman's rights' discourse that both preexisted that of White women and relied on different rhetorical arguments" (p. 1). There is also a distinction made between Western notions of feminism and Third World womanism, where the latter is a unified movement of women of color throughout the world who are identifying their own issues, and not necessarily in reaction to other groups (Ogundipe-Leslie, 1995). This cross-cultural unification in identity, in opposition to the common hegemonic force of (usually) Western, White, male, heterosexual dominance, has allowed the subaltern to be heard in certain public spaces, like the music and the concerts of Sweet Honey In The Rock. The struggles of women of color challenge the "metanarratives of feminism" (Boyce Davies, 1994), which have historically been antagonistic or unresponsive to the multiple jeopardy of Black women (King, 1988).

> Although the woman's movement motivated hundreds of women to write on the woman question, it failed to generate in depth critical analyses of the black female experience. Most feminists assumed that problems black women faced were caused by racism—not sexism. (hooks, 1981, p. 12)

This movement toward an expression of a Black feminist ideology is evident in the experiences of Sweet Honey In The Rock and her situation within the larger women's movement. Reagon recalls the experience of being contacted by a "woman's consciousness-raising group in Atlanta," whose membership was women mostly from White middle class backgrounds. She, like many others, could not relate to the type of liberation that they espoused. "In 1970, their search was not mine" (Reagon and Sweet Honey In The Rock, 1993, p. 28). Largely a result racism and cultural differences, conflicts arose out of the motivation of these audiences to rename Sweet Honey as a radical "feminists."

> I think the desire to name us was not malicious but came from a position of cultural privilege. When we insisted on our name, Sweet Honey In The Rock, an ensemble of Black women singers, we were asked what was wrong with being called feminist. I would answer,

"What is wrong with being a Black radical woman and calling your
organization an ensemble of Black women singers?" I explained that
our radicallness was rooted in *our* history and models, and that the
words and phrases we used were used by *our* mothers and our
mothers' mothers, and we wanted to always name *that* connection.
(Reagon & Sweet Honey In The Rock, 1993, p. 33)

Over the years, Sweet Honey In The Rock has worked within and
without the women's movement to find common ground, linking the
plight of women with differing backgrounds, in order to develop
theory and action for a women's movement relevant to the lives and
the experiences of Black and Third-World women. This process, in
which Black women come to voice, provides a flagship for the
development and maintenance of Black female subjectivity,
celebrating the multiple dimensions of identities that are uniquely
female at the same time that they are uniquely Black.

The discourse of Sweet Honey In The Rock, like the work of
Collins (1986, 1989) contributes to the development of Black feminist
standpoint theory. Collins (1991) argued that "while domination may
be inevitable as a social fact, it is unlikely to be hegemonic as an
ideology within that social space where Black women speak freely"
(p. 95). The social spaces of Sweet Honey concerts have become
locations, like churches, extended families, and African American
community organizations, where safe discourse can potentially occur.
Collins asserted that there exist three primary places where Black
women's consciousness have been nurtured and where African
American women have spoken freely to articulate a self-defined and
unique standpoint. One location involves Black women's
relationships with one another. In the performances of Sweet Honey,
we are offered visual cues that signal the connection among the
women on stage, where their modes of dress are always coordinated,
either in the same materials with different styles or in
complementary styles in different colors. The performance space is
carved out through the semi-circle in which chairs are placed on the
stage, thus symbolically forming a protected area, within which one
is sheltered/defended/comforted by a circle of many—a circle of
women with the audience forming the other half. With Sweet Honey,
we see women's relationships as an exchange of leadership roles as
she begins a song with the voice that is gradually joined by a chorus
of many.

Within Collins' notion of "safe spaces," a second location where
Black women have found voice is in African American music as art.
Sweet Honey In The Rock opens a space for women to express
themselves as artists. Her success, enabled by the support of her

audience, also provides the institutional structure that permits women, through workshops and community performances, to be exposed to a capella singing as an art form and to find their voices as artists. The third location of free speech for Black women is in their voices as writers. The women who contribute to Sweet Honey write original lyrics and music to accompany them. She has also called on poets such as Sonia Sanchez to offer writings and voice for songs such as *Stay on the Battlefield*. Collectively, Sweet Honey authored the 1993 book, *We Who Believe in Freedom: Sweet Honey in the Rock . . . Still on the Journey,* offering another vehicle for African American women to write in safe spaces, edited by African American women. All of these places and "safe spaces" contribute in the definition of Black female political standpoints. The interrelationship of these spaces is evident in the lyrics, performances, and products of Sweet Honey In The Rock. As she gives birth to music, rhetorical texts, and art, Sweet Honey provides the theoretical guide to articulate the unique experiences of Black women, within an interlocking grid of multiple forces of oppression.

The voice of Sweet Honey In The Rock, and the words she has whispered and shouted for 25 years are the fabric, the map that these Black women and their millions of audience members, have used to discover their voices, expressing joy, pain, and a range of emotions. Sweet Honey In The Rock and her audiences, in their relationships with one another, have created resistant spaces to safely raise and nurture political consciousness. This coming to voice is accomplished through music and movement, in community. "I saw Sweet Honey concerts open up a space in this racist culture" (Reagon & Sweet Honey in The Rock, 1993, p. 199). Through her musiking, on her own terms, Sweet Honey In The Rock has developed a radical Black feminist perspective (Wallace, 1992). It is a standpoint shared by women of color who search for a means to express multiple subject positions with others who identify in a similar vein. Sweet Honey's music brings coalition-building theory into practice.

> To sing in a group which has come from many places within Africa America, to an audience from a wide spiritual background, and then to talk about finding contemporary solace in an old song like "Jesus Is My Only Friend" stretches many boundaries. The range and the tolerance of our audiences give me hope that there can be a world that accepts many cultures and belief systems. There is a way to practice through our living, being of oneself and among others at the same time. It happens in every Sweet Honey concert. In our performances we touch so much of the common human experience, we are given the room we need to be also different sometimes, even as we are embraced because we are the same. (Reagon & Sweet Honey In The Rock, 1993, p. 36)

The social processes that take place in Sweet Honey's live concerts provide a rhetorical articulation of common experiences. Through discourse focused on audiences of Black women, as interpretive communities of significant political beings, individuals find voice and speak freely in the safe spaces of Sweet Honey performances. The process of coming to voice, which Black and Third-World womanist writers articulate (hooks, 1989; Spivak, 1988), is accomplished, in its most literal sense, through the music of Sweet Honey for her audiences. The musical texts of this community of women, interwoven with theory and political activism, are communicated to her audiences through a multiplicity of spaces and through a variety of media. The voices of Sweet Honey In The Rock, heard through song, performed live and preserved in recordings, spoken through autobiographical and scholarly writings, and expressed through her position as a cultural worker, should be further considered through an integrative research paradigm. Too often, differences in textual, artistic, and musical expression, through various media channels, tend to act as boundaries that prevent transdisciplinary examination. By redefining our paradigms, womanist communication research may enable this boundary crossing.

MIGRATIONS THROUGH MUSIC

Relatively little attention has been given to the importance of music in feminist theory and research as well in the debates over modernity and the discourse of postmodernity (Gilroy, 1993). This void may result from the reactionary standpoint of some feminist scholars, interrogating "traditional" areas of communication research with a woman's perspective, without challenging the existence of these classificatory schemes or methods. It may also be that music is on the margins of "hard" communication sciences whose research traditions offer legitimacy in the academy. By offering a greater breadth in areas of "serious" inquiry and by testing fundamental theoretical assumptions, womanist theory helps us critically examine Black women's music as communication behavior. It also encourages us to explore the function of music as an oral medium of communication for people of the African Diaspora, with historically limited access to lexical modes of communication.

> The power and the significance of music within the black Atlantic have grown in inverse proportion to the limited expressive power of language. . . . Music becomes vital at the point at which linguistic

and semantic indeterminacy / polyphony arise amidst the protracted
battle between masters, mistresses, and slaves. (Gilroy, 1993, p. 74)

Music has historically informed a sense of place and identity,
through the cultural construction of recognizable boundaries. It does
so through various practices, styles, rhythm, instruments, and
conventions that enable us to distinguish, identify with, and
categorize music. However, these classificatory schemes may be
reductive in that they often do not acknowledge the range that exists
in a particular song and certainly across a musical repertoire. Yet
these boundaries are slippery. Listeners and audiences gravitate to
the sounds and lyrics that are pleasing, evoke an emotional response,
or meet a cognitive and/or spiritual need.

Stokes (1994) emphasized the role of agency in this process
where "music does not then simply provide a marker in a
prestructured social space, but the means by which this space can be
transformed" (p. 5). Although some artists use music to separate,
drawing boundaries between the Self and the Other, Sweet Honey In
The Rock uses her music to cross boundaries and transform space
into communal areas of multicultural political resistance. Her music
and her audiences exist in a dialogic relationship. Sweet Honey opens
a dialogue with her concert-goers by teaching the words of songs, by
explaining the history behind lyrics, and by asking for the
participation of every audience member in setting rhythms through
words, the sound of hand claps, and call-and-response. The voices in
Sweet Honey In The Rock live concerts are a collective effort of the
interaction between the audience and the performer and the
audience members-as-performers. This practice is a legacy of the
historical role played by music in resistance, identity development,
cultural expression and preservation. It also offers a vehicle for the
rhetorical involvement of Africans, African Americans, and people of
the African Diaspora in politically oriented messaging.

There are many ways in which Sweet Honey uses music, as a
critical art form, to articulate the experiences of Black women and to
create awareness of shared struggles for the uplift and preservation
of the community as a whole.

Art is a special form of social consciousness that can potentially
awaken an urge in those affected by it to transform their oppressive
environments. . . . Progressive art can assist people to learn not only
more about the objective forces at work in the society in which they
live, but also about the intensely social character of their interior
lives. Ultimately, it can propel people toward social emancipation.
(Davis, 1989, pp. 199-200)

Angela Davis echoes the importance of art and music for Black women as locations for coming to voice in accord with the standpoint theory of Collins, as mentioned earlier. The informational and transformative power of music makes it a fundamental and immutable medium of expression, consciousness-raising and resistance for Africans and their descendants. These qualities are evident in the lyrics of traditional African American spirituals, which form the basis for the repertoire of Sweet Honey In The Rock. Spirituals like *No More Auction Block,* are born through oppression and struggle.

No more auction block for me
No more, no more,
No more auction block for me
Many thousand gone

And oh, the one thing that we did wrong
No more, no more
Stayed in the wilderness a day too long
No more, no more

And oh, the one thing that we did right,
Oh yes, Oh yes, my Lord
Was the day that we began to fight,
Oh yes, Oh yes, my Lord . . .
(arranged by Reagon, 1991, track 2)

These spirituals are songs of freedom, sacred music adapted from hundreds of traditional African languages to the languages of the Diaspora, in distant lands where women, men, and children were taken as slaves.

These sacred spirituals attest to the power of a higher force, a Supreme Being that regulates physical existence. It is this belief in God(s), invoked within song texts and performance spaces, that mark the roots of Sweet Honey In The Rock theory. Much of the music is firmly grounded in the Christian religion and in the tradition of the Black church. It is significant that most of the women who give voice to Sweet Honey have grown up in the Black church tradition. Boyce Davies locates the church community as a space where Black women can be assured of some hearing. "In churches, black women's testimonies are affirmed, supported" (Boyce Davies, 1995b, p. 4). Sweet Honey In The Rock brings this reassurance to the public locations where her audiences interact. With this confidence and courage, made possible through spirituality, belief in God and ancestry, and the experience of consciousness, Sweet Honey is able to cross boundaries into public places that have historically threated to the existence of Black women. Sweet Honey In The Rock functions, in her concerts, to re-create the safe places necessary for her audiences of women to come to voice and assert their identities.

> By going inside ourselves and singing specifically out of our lives, our community, and our world, we try to help those listening, in the sound of our singing, to create a celebration based on what they can embrace that is real to them at that time. And again, it is in church (where I first heard songs started by song leaders calling the congregation to help "raise" the song into its own life) that I learned how to create that space. Our audiences are often urged to help up out with the singing, to embrace all that makes up who they are. With those experiences and with that load, they can lift and celebrate being alive at this time with this opportunity to choose, to be clear, and to be heard. (Reagon & Sweet Honey In The Rock, 1993, p. 37)

Although guided by sacred Christian music, Sweet Honey makes space for a pluralistic conception of God, invoked by the name of Allah, and worshiped in the name of ancestors. The spiritual orientation of Sweet Honey is tied into an African worldview, in accord with the traditional conditions of certain African philosophies. Her music speaks of a belief in the human mind and body as spiritual entities, and the continuity of life before and after death. It is a reflection of an African epistemology where particular belief systems counter the Western epistemology of rationalism and empiricism (Gyekye, 1995). The song *Breaths,* a poem by Birago Diop with music by Ysaye Barnwell, demonstrates this epistemological and ontological positioning.

> In the African world view, the invisible world of spirit, man, and the visible world of nature exist along a continuum and form an organic reality. The same is true of the relationship between the past, present and future. In Birago Diop's poem Breaths we are reminded of this continuum.

> *Those who have died have never never left*
> *The dead are not under the earth*
> *They are in the rustling trees*
> *They are in the groaning woods*
> *They are in the crying grass*
> *They are in the moaning rocks*
> *The dead are not under the earth*
>
> *Those who have died have never never left*
> *The dead have a pact with the living*

They are in the woman's breast
They are in the wailing child
They are with us in the home
They are with us in the crowd
The dead have a pact with the living.
(Barnwell, 1980, track 1)

Thus, in her music, Sweet Honey In The Rock asserts a distinct philosophy and a pluralistic ontology, informed by an Africanist world view. She affirms these beliefs in her idea of a performative space, opening the stage to be populated by the spirits of her ancestors. The legacies of women like Harriet Tubman, singing fighters, guide Sweet Honey's performance. "Her songs were instruments of her struggle to destroy and undermine slavery, to free as many of her people as she could. Her stage for her songs was anywhere she was" (Reagon & Sweet Honey In The Rock, 1993, p. 22). Resistance, activism, and worship are at the root of the theories and the practices of Sweet Honey In The Rock, and exist in every space where the spirit of struggle and survival is invoked, across boundaries, through song.

The musical orientation of Sweet Honey In The Rock builds bridges of celebration and reconnection between women in Africa and the Diaspora. Her theoretical focus on the common triumphs of womanhood, across age, class, and sexual orientation, stands in contrast to the work of other scholars who situate the foundation of these diasporic linkages solely on common suffering. Steady (1993), for example, argued that many forms of resistance are common to Black women and in time of crisis, were often the only thing which ensured the survival of communities in Diaspora.

To some extent it can be claimed that the very existence of the African diaspora is due to the strength, resilience, and hard work of the black woman. It is also through her struggle against the myriad forces of oppression that she has been able to generate, preserve, and advance the well-being and development of her people. (Steady, 1993, p. 167)

This standpoint reifies the idea that the Black woman is uniquely qualified, as a result of her struggle, to elevate her people and assert herself. This is a problematic argument that, though it gives a woman credit for her strength and courage in survival, denies her a self-conscious role in the assertion of her identity. It is a standpoint that denies her a position as an autonomous subject asserting agency in and of itself, and not as a reaction to the effects of oppression. Womanist theory, in contrast, is based on self-actualization, agency, and subjectivity. It is this theoretical standpoint that is expressed through the music of Sweet Honey.

Sweet Honey In The Rock offers her repertoire to audiences as "Music of the spirit and music of practical transformation, music that was history and music that was the voice of struggle" (Attlee, 1993, p. 9). It is music that has been sung by generations of Black women, men, and children, for their very survival. The multiple functions of sacred music offer a historical record of the many facets of African American women's experiences, making heard silenced voices. The music of Sweet Honey, in its wide range of genre, are freedom songs. Sweet Honey has effectuated emancipation among her members and among her audiences at many levels, both individual and collective, as evidenced by the following passages. Reagon (1993) described her experience in the group in the following manner:

> There have been times when things happened in my world that I felt strongly about and I had no song that would speak for me. These women/singers/composers give me a range I could never have alone. (Reagon & Sweet Honey In The Rock, 1993, p. 40)

By working collectively to create language and sounds to express emotions and thoughts, Sweet Honey provides opportunities for Black women to identify with one another's experiences and provides the vehicle through which women may empathize with these articulated truths. Ivy Young (cited in Reagon & Sweet Honey In The Rock, 1993), a participant in weekly Sweet Honey In The Rock vocal workshops, discussed the special experience of being part of this community of women.

> We will laugh together, and cry together, and share moments of pain and power. We will stretch ourselves and challenge each other. We will argue and forgive, trust and grow. We will bring to the circle tales of the day and weariness from that day. We will sing songs Sweet Honey brings us, breathe deeply and release the burdens of that day. Sweet Honey created a space where we could be and become. I will be forever indebted, forever grateful. (p. 130)

Virginia Giordano (cited in Reagon & Sweet Honey In The Rock, 1993), a producer for Sweet Honey In The Rock concerts, characterized the relationship between the women and their audience.

> For those who take part, the annual concert is a ritual of tremendous power. Sweet Honey understands the ritual use of music and its healing power. They play their audience like their

instrument. They engage the audience emotionally in their own healing. (p. 241)

Sweet Honey In The Rock invites her audience into community to sing, shout, feel, dance, laugh, cry, and interact with one another. The expression of this emotional range brings a distinct pleasure to the women who have been touched by the simultaneous exceptionalism and familiarity of this group.

As artists and cultural workers, Sweet Honey teaches, nurtures, and sets an example for multiple communities of singers, performers, and political actors. In her choice of performance pieces, Sweet Honey acknowledges that only rarely are the songs planned before the women reach the stage. The decision is made at that time, according to the audience environment, the physical space, and the voice that each women has on the particular occasion. During the concert, the house lights are dimmed, but never turned off. In this way, Sweet Honey is able to "get closer to" her audience, and audience members are able to more easily interact with one another. It is a musical performance which partakes in the nature of ritual, the acting-out of desired relationships and thus identity (Small, 1987). The concerts and the music of Sweet Honey In The Rock are rituals of resistance and community-building, characterized as "conversations with the audience" (Reagon & Sweet Honey In The Rock, 1993, p. 46). Sweet Honey conceptualizes her audience at the center of every performance and the focus of her work. Of the audience Reagon wrote:

I wrote a poem that bowed in salute to this community that has made it possible for these singing women to be so many places with so many songs and in such good company:

We come to you
You in every color of the rainbow
With your freedom and struggle stances
In every position of the moon and sun

We come to you
Offering our songs and the sounds of our Mothers'
Mothers
In libation
To everyone of us

There really is a community
We have seen and felt and been held by you
These ten years

There is this community we belong to without
geographical boundaries
D.C., Atlanta, Berea, Chicago, East St. Louis, L.A., Toronto, Chiba,
the Bay Area,
Newark, Seattle, Chapel Hill, Boston, Frankfurt, London, Richmond,
Little Rock,
N.Y.C., Denver, Albuquerque, Nashville, Brixton, New Orleans,
Vancouver, Portland,
Berlin, Albany, Durham, Tokyo, St. Louis, Detroit, St. Paul, Dallas,
Peoria, Jamaica . . .
There really is a community
Lovers
Searchers
Movers into life
Fighters and builders
of a place where
Military machines, hatred of women, abuse of children,
homophobia, societal male suicide, racial bigotry,
starvation, work that kills and cripples, social orders
driven by greed, the U.S.A. invading whoever....this
week. Where the dying and acting out of fear, anger,
and terror
Will find no feeding ground.
I wanna be there!
(Reagon & Sweet Honey In The Rock, 1993, pp. 68-69)

The audiences of Sweet Honey In The Rock are unique in their diversity and their dedication. Sweet Honey's audience-community is rhetorically and symbolically created in her live performances. The traditional boundary of the stage, constructed between performer and audience, is one that she invites members to cross by asking for participation in musicking. Sweet Honey is the inheritor of a legacy of sacred music and freedom songs, performed through call-and-response, "breathing life" through collective involvement. She sings in the tradition of the African American church, in congregational style. Through her concerts, Sweet Honey provides knowledge to communities outside of traditional communication and information flows (Armstrong, cited in Reagon & Sweet Honey In The Rock, 1993). She brings her messages of freedom, equality, and social justice into everyday contexts. For example, a song might begin with a reference to the events of the day or the telling of a story about the experience of another Black woman. These teachings may be followed by such comments like, "we all know how it is when . . ." thus triggering a sense of group identification. With music, the political activism of Sweet Honey In The Rock slips through the radar of the forces which attempt to silence, constrain, and limit the speech of women of color. Sweet Honey has extended the function of her music with the ability to use it to build bridges between communities of women, social struggles, and political movements.

From her inception, Sweet Honey In The Rock has dealt with political issues through song. Over the past 25 years, her music has shaped and been shaped by a multitude of struggles including civil rights in the United States, the end of apartheid in South Africa, international human rights, worker's rights, and the protection of children. Sweet Honey In The Rock has found unique ways to link and locate common spaces between these struggles, forging conversations and coalitions among the labor movement, the women's movement, and the peace movement. As Black women in a Diasporic community, she makes connections between the local and the global. Sweet Honey In The Rock is one of few politically committed groups engaging in the progressive cultural development of the song movement (Davis, 1989, p. 214). Social movements and political organizations are rarely able to achieve the goal of coalition politics that Sweet Honey advocates. She is successful in this purpose and engages the notion of collective action and consciousness in her musical repertoire, her audience involvement, and the ways in which she expertly locates herself as both a part of and apart from the commercial climate of the music industry. Sweet Honey negotiates this position by working with progressive and women-led publishing and promotional companies, thus maintaining loyalty to struggle and resistance—key tenets of womanist theory.

Sweet Honey In The Rock resists definition, as she transcends the categories of the commercial music industry, straddling boundaries of place, people, and language. Her members are women who have brought their individual gifts to raise a textured, harmonious, and unified activist voice. An example of this resistant work ethic is Amy Horowitz (cited in Reagon & Sweet Honey In The Rock, 1993), who characterized her experience with Sweet Honey as "living in coalition":

> I live on the borderland. My identities crisscross ethnic and cultural boundaries. My passport is stamped with internal landscapes that struggle to coexist. I refuse to establish a hierarchy of importance out of the plurality that is me. (p. 187)

It is this ability to cross borders, accepting the complexity and multidimensionality of others, that distinguishes Sweet Honey and the women who are part of her community. Through her music, Sweet Honey embraces difference, as she transcends it. Her repertoire is radical and profoundly spiritual, drawing on musical genres as wide ranging as her audiences. Of her music, Reagon states, "We do every form that is created by our people from Caribbean, jazz, blues, and gospel, any of the forms we need to tell the story" (cited in Jones, 1993, p. B1). In every way, her music and the community she creates are fundamentally anti-essentialist, embracing contradiction and complexity, honoring difference. Communication research would be improved by emphasizing the cultural products by groups such as Sweet Honey In The Rock, whose music cannot be categorized in unitary musical genres and whose Black womanist message challenges totalizing discourses. She opens a space for her audience to struggle with the unifying categories that suppress difference within communities of Black women.

The literature on the role of audience has done little to explore the musical rhetoric in communities of Black women. Feminist scholars have made it clear that there is a gendered gaze, a standpoint that will differentiate the ways in which women receive media messages (Pribram, 1988). The construct of a Black female gaze is one theorized by hooks (1992) and Roach and Felix (1988), asserting that there is both a female interpretation of communicated messages, and a Black female mode of audience reception. There must be substantive scholarship that explores looking and listening to the music and the media created by Black women, principally for other Black women.

> *The message: To all of us who, by standards of those who set standards—flunk—maybe we don't look right, or love right, or we don't have a home, or a job, or maybe pregnant at 14, or HIV positive, or just the wrong person, in the wrong place, at the wrong time—it is You—Me, Us, who are the voice/s to be heard, it is We who must sing!* (Reagon, in her intro. to *Sing Oh Barren One*, 1987, track 5)

In her concerts, Sweet Honey In The Rock creates sites of resistance. In her music, she offers the means to exercise agency. In her audiences, she works to build communities that transcend boundaries of race, class, gender, and ideological orientation. In her voice, Sweet Honey unifies the polyvocality of Black women as performers and audiences. In her message, she carries forth the political struggles of the marginalized, maligned, poor, weak, hungry, and voiceless. Sweet Honey In The Rock carries on a legacy of women who, in their silence and their shouts, give voice to the survival of a community.

REFERENCES

Ang, I. (1996). *Living room wars: Rethinking media audiences for A postmodern world.* New York & London: Routledge.

Attlee, J. (1993). Sweet Spirits on the Rocks: James Attlee meets the formidable sounding force of a great gospel group. *Weekly Journal, 78,* 9.

Band, A. (1995, March). *Diaspora and diglossia.* Paper presented at the Annenberg Scholars Conference on Public Space, University of Pennsylvania, Philadelphia.

Barnwell, Y. M. (1980). Breaths [recorded by Sweet Honey In The Rock]. On *Good News* [CD]. Chicago: Flying Fish Records. (1981).

Boyce Davies, C. (1994). *Black women, writing and identity: Migrations of the subject.* New York & London: Routledge.

Boyce Davies, C. (1995a). Black women writing worlds: Textual production, dominance, and the critical voice. In C. Boyce Davies & M. Ogundipe-Leslie (Eds.), *Moving beyond boundaries—Vol. 2: Black women's diaspora* (pp. 1-15). New York: New York University Press.

Boyce Davies, C. (1995b). Hearing black women's voices: Transgressing imposed boundaries. In C. Boyce Davies & M. Ogundipe-Leslie (Eds.), *Moving beyond boundaries—Vol. 1: International dimensions of black women's writing* (pp. 3-14). New York: New York University Press.

Christian, B. (1987). The race for theory. *Cultural Critique, 6,* 51-63.

Clark, V. (1990). Developing diaspora literacy: Allusion in Maryse Condé's Heremakhonon. In C. Boyce Davies & S. Fido (Eds.), *Out of the Kumbla: Caribbean women and literature* (pp. 303-319). Trenton: Africa World Press.

Collins, P. H. (1991). *Black feminist thought: Knowledge, consciousness, and the politics of empowerment.* New York & London: Routledge.

Collins, P. H. (1989). The social construction of black feminist thought. *Signs: Journal of Women in Culture and Society, 14*(4), 745-773.

Collins, P. H. (1986). Learning from the outsider within: The sociological significance of black feminist thought. *Social Problems, 33*(6), 514-532.

Davis, A. (1990). Black women and music: A historical legacy of struggle. In J. Braxton & A. N. McLaughlin (Eds.), *Wild women in the whirlwind: Afra-American culture and the contemporary literary renaissance* (pp. 3-21). New Brunswick, NJ: Rutgers University Press.

Davis, A. (1989). *Women, culture, & politics*. New York: Random House.

Ferguson, R., Gever, M., Minh-ha, T., & West C. (Eds.). (1990). *Out there: Marginalization and contemporary cultures*. New York: New Museum of Contemporary Art; Cambridge & London: MIT Press.

Gilroy, P. (1993). *The black atlantic: Modernity and double consciousness*. Cambridge, MA: Harvard University Press.

Gyekye, K. (1995). An essay on African philosophical thought—The Akan conceptual scheme. In A. Mosley (Ed.), *African philosophy: Selected readings* (pp. 339-349). Englewood Cliffs, NJ: Prentice-Hall.

hooks, b. (1981). *Ain't I a woman: Black women and feminism*. Boston: South End Press.

hooks, b. (1989). *Talking back. Thinking feminist. Thinking black.* Boston: South End Press.

hooks, b. (1992). *Black looks: Race and representation*. Boston: South End Press.

Jones, P. (1993). Sweet Honey In The Rock: Building on a foundation "In This Land." *Indianapolis Recorder, 3,* B1.

King, D. (1988). Multiple jeopardy, multiple consciousness: The context of a black feminist ideology. *Signs: Journal of Women in Culture and Society, 14*(1), 42-72.

Ogundipe-Leslie, M. (1995). Women in Africa and her diaspora: From marginality to empowerment. In C. Boyce Davies & M Ogundipe-Leslie (Eds.), *Moving beyond boundaries—Vol. 1: International dimensions of black women's writing* (pp. 15-17). New York: New York University Press.

Peterson, C. (1996, April). *The rhetoric of black and white women's rights discourse and activism, 1830-1860*. Paper presented at the University of Pennsylvania, Philadelphia.

Pribram, E. D. (Ed.). (1988). *Female spectators: Looking at film and television*. London & New York: Verso.

Reagon, B. J. (1981). Ella's song [recorded by Sweet Honey In The Rock]. On *We all . . . everyone of us* [CD]. Chicago: Flying Fish Records. (1983).

Reagon, B. J. (1983). Coalition politics: Turning the century. In B Smith (Ed.), *Home girls: A black feminist anthology* (pp. 356-368). New York: Kitchen Table, Women of Color Press.

Reagon, B. J. (1987). Sing oh barren one [recorded by Sweet Honey In The Rock]. On *Sacred Ground* [CD]. Redway, CA: Earthbeat! (1995).

Reagon, B. J. (1991). No more aution block [recorded by Sweet Honey In The Rock]. On *Sacred Ground* [CD]. Redway, CA: Earthbeat! (1995).

Reagon, B. J., & Sweet Honey In The Rock. (1993). *We who believe in freedom: Sweet Honey in the Rock . . . still on the journey.* New York: Anchor Books Doubleday.

Roach, J., & Felix, P. (1988). Black looks. In L. Gamman & M. Marshment (Eds.), *The female gaze: Women as viewers of popular culture* (pp. 130-142). London: The Women's Press.

Skinner, E. (1993). The dialectic between diasporas and homelands. In J. Harris (Ed.), *Global dimensions of the African diaspora* (pp. 11-40). Washington, DC: Howard University Press.

Small, C. (1987). *Music of the common tongue: Survival and celebration in Afro-American music.* London: John Calder & New York: Riverrun Press.

Spencer, J. M. (1995). *The rhythms of black folk: Race, religion, and Pan-Africanism.* Trenton, NJ: Africa World Press.

Spivak, G. C. (1988). Can the Subaltern speak? In C. Nelson & L. Grossberg (Eds.), *Marxism and the interpretation of culture* (pp. 271-313). Urbana & Chicago: University of Illinois Press.

Steady, F. C. (1993). Women of Africa and the African diaspora: Linkages and influences. In J. Harris (Ed.), *Global dimensions of the African diaspora* (pp. 167-187). Washington, DC: Howard University Press.

Stokes, M. (Ed.). (1994). *Ethnicity, identity and music: The musical construction of place.* Oxford & Providence: Berg.

Wallace, M. (1992). Negative images: Towards a black feminist cultural criticism. In L. Grossberg, C. Nelson, & P. Treichler (Eds.), *Cultural studies* (pp. 654-671). New York & London: Routledge.

ELEVEN

Epilogue

Patricia Hill Collins
University of Cincinnati

Black women's studies has grown remarkably since Toni Cade Bambara, Angela Davis, Audre Lorde, and other prominent African American feminist thinkers published their ideas in the 1970s and early 1980s. Since that time, scholars and activists have generated a seeming explosion of knowledge about African American women's intellectual and activist traditions as well as those of women of African descent in the African diaspora (Collins, 2000). As is the case for any emerging area of inquiry, some themes have received the lion's share of attention, whereas others remain lesser known. These patterns of emphasis, exclusion, and in some cases, controversy signal the overall health of the field. They also point to its continued vitality in trying to make a difference in Black women's lives.

Through its eclectic collection of chapters, *Centering Ourselves* makes an important contribution to Black women's studies. Because the chapters in this long overdue volume explore the virtually untapped area of Black women and communication, they provide a new angle of vision on how African American women empower ourselves, often in difficult or stressful situations. Empowerment, in turn, pivots on questions of culture and community, two important areas of inquiry that are not only subjects of scholarly debate, but that have palpable impact on Black women's everyday lives. The chapters in *Centering Ourselves* examine how African American women construct cultural realities that enable them to craft community. Such communities simultaneously sustain African American women in everyday life and help Black women resist domination. In this sense, the contributions provide a new path through longstanding controversies concerning culture, community, and the connections among them. They also provide a new angle of vision on the significance of culture and community for Black women's empowerment.

Centering Ourselves makes important contributions to our understanding of how African American women use discourse for empowerment. African American discursive styles remain controversial within U.S. scholarship and popular opinion. On the one hand, mainstream scholarship often views all elements of African and African-derived cultures as deviant, backward, and somehow lesser. U.S. racism seemingly requires deeply entrenched beliefs concerning the assumed cultural deviancy of African Americans. Within this perspective, Black women as bad mothers become central characters in passing on the allegedly flawed values of Black culture to their unlucky offspring. On the other hand, influenced by paradigms of Black cultural nationalism, a good deal of Black studies scholarship opposes this depiction, claiming a positive and often heroic status for African-derived cultural values and behaviors. Within this portrayal, Black women become important culture-bearers, passive conduits of a timeless, unchanging packet of cultural ideas and traits thought to protect Black people from the damages done by racism (Collins, 1998).

African American women have long encountered the dilemma of negotiating these two depictions. Within both portrayals, real African American women disappear and are replaced by frozen images of Black women as cardboard, stereotyped figures. Either we are blamed for much of what is wrong with Black America, or we are held up as its salvation. African American women as agents of knowledge remain missing from both portrayals. Portrayals of the complex ways in which women of African descent actively construct meaning in everyday life and use elements of dynamic, changing, syncretic African-influenced cultures to do it are more often the exception than the rule.

The chapters in *Centering Ourselves* focus on this active meaning-making process. They allow us to reclaim an important insight of Black cultural nationalism, namely, that we are empowered by the process as well as the ideas that enable us to construct alternative realities through which to define our lives. The authors in this collection ground this insight not in abstract theories, but in empirical studies of how African American women operate as agents of knowledge in constructing meaning in our everyday lives, making it clear that communication is at the center of constructing culture.

Questions of community constitute another important area of inquiry with great implications for Black women's empowerment. Here the controversies encompass how Black community structures such as families and churches as well as schools, industries, and other social institutions alternately affirm or victimize African American women. Within dominant scholarship, if Black women are mentioned at all, studies of jobs, schooling, housing, health care, and other public policy initiatives that affect Black women's neighborhoods and communities rarely portray Black women as social actors. African American women routinely appear as nameless, passive objects serving as topics of discussion for others. In a dominant discourse whose "welfare queens" substitute for sustained and sensitive attention to the realities of poor Black women's lives, we are left with portraits of Black communities as stagnant social structures, and with depictions of Black women as equally static within them.

One important contribution of Black women's studies has been its insistence on resisting this objectification and portraying women of African descent as social actors who participate in building and running Black communities. In this context, *Centering Ourselves* builds on this new tradition and offers important new insights concerning the complexities of Black women's actions in constructing community. For one, eschewing the tendency to ignore or trivialize the significance that differences in power have in framing the communication patterns among individuals necessary for constructing communities, *Centering Ourselves* confronts issues of power head-on. Because Black women are both Black and female–two identity categories that are routinely viewed as lesser–excising these criteria from analyses of Black women's communication patterns seems especially shortsighted. Rejecting this approach, the chapters in this volume offer a preliminary analysis of the range of sophisticated strategies that African American women use in coping with, and often confronting those power differentials. For another, just as African American women as individuals must respond to the vast differences in power created by intersecting oppressions, communities as collective entities are also situated within these same complex and changing power relationships. Thus, an especially intriguing insight provided in this volume lies in how African American women construct Black women's communities in settings characterized by considerable differences in power. In essence, Black women deploy different communication styles in response to the varying political demands of the communities in which they find themselves. By providing alternative explanations as well as alternative realities to the ones held out to us, such communities aim to protect Black women from the damage done by oppressions of race, gender, and class among others.

Moving beyond culture and community as discrete areas of inquiry, *Centering Ourselves* also demonstrates how culture and community are linked, with studies of communication providing an important framework for examining the connections between these two important areas. Overall, the individual essays provide important pieces of a much larger mosaic. For example, Eric K. Watts' (chap. 9) examination of the female voice in hip hop offers a deeply textured analysis of the contested nature of communication by hip hop artists. Moving beyond a simple content analysis, Watts explores various features of the construction of voice, from the political economy of hip hop itself, to the lives of the artists, to the meaning of the lyrics. In contrast, Marsha Houston's (chap. 4) exploration of Black women's use of "triumph stories" in everyday conversations offers a complementary exploration of how the struggle for voice occurs in a very different context. Houston reveals how sharing individual triumph narratives serves an important purpose in collective empowerment.

Sometimes muted, often boldly stated, always negotiated, a thread joining these disparate essays is how Black women deploy sophisticated communication strategies in service of our own empowerment. *Centering Ourselves* makes important contributions, yet it can only scratch the surface of exploring how African American women create cultural realities that alternately construct new forms of community and resist structures of domination. My hope is that others will see the vision in these essays and use it to guide their work.

REFERENCES

Collins, P. H. (1998). *Fighting words: Black women and the search for justice.* Minneapolis: University of Minnesota Press.

Collins, P. H. (2000). *Black feminist thought: Knowledge, consciousness, and the politics of empowerment* (rev. ed.). New York: Routledge.

Author Index

245

Subject Index